MW01173515

African Personality and Spirituality

African Personality and Spirituality

The Role of Abosom and Human Essence

Anthony Ephirim-Donkor

LEXINGTON BOOKS
Lanham • Boulder • New York • London

Published by Lexington Books
An imprint of The Rowman & Littlefield Publishing Group, Inc.
4501 Forbes Boulevard, Suite 200, Lanham, Maryland 20706
www.rowman.com

Unit A, Whitacre Mews, 26-34 Stannary Street, London SE11 4AB, United Kingdom

British Library Cataloguing in Publication Information Available

Library of Congress Cataloging-in-Publication Data

Ephirim-Donkor, Anthony, author.
African personality and spirituality : the role of abosom and human essence / Anthony Ephirim-Donkor.
pages cm
Includes bibliographical references and index.
ISBN 978-1-4985-2122-2 (cloth : alk. paper) — ISBN 978-1-4985-2124-6 (pbk. : alk. paper) — ISBN 978-1-4985-2123-9 (electronic) 1. Akan (African people)—Religion. 2. Africa, Sub-Saharan—Religion. 3. Africa, Sub-Saharan—Religious life and customs. 4. Religion and ethics. I. Title.
BL2480.A4E639 2015
299.683385—dc23

2015033400

∞™ The paper used in this publication meets the minimum requirements of American National Standard for Information Sciences—Permanence of Paper for Printed Library Materials, ANSI/NISO Z39.48-1992.

Printed in the United States of America

Contents

Guide to Pronunciation

Ā, ā: pronounced as an "A, a" in SP*A*CE.
Ɔ, ɔ: pronounced as an "O" in *O*RGAN.
Ɛ, ɛ: pronounced as an "E" in *E*ARLY.

Preface

I have always been fascinated with what the Akan refer to as Abosom (primeval Gods and Goddesses) for reasons that are an enigma to me. Yet growing up in Ghana as a Christian, I heard the Abosom being bashed repeatedly by priests. Nowadays, and with the proliferation of churches and self-trained pastors—particularly the so-called men of God—the bashing of the Abosom has become the obsession of many Christian clerics. Yet some, if not many, of the clerics consult with traditional clergy (Akɔmfo, Asɔfo, Abosomfo) for spiritual power. Specifically, they seek out their traditional counterparts for what the Akan refer to as *Āduro* (juju or gri-gri) to enable them to grow their churches. Occasionally, disputes between these Christian clergy and their traditional counterparts (the Akɔmfo) for nonpayment of fees due the Akɔmfo for preparing magical portions for Christian pastors would spill over into the public arena and be picked up by newspapers and radio stations. The fact is that Christian pastors seek the intervention of Abosom (Gods and Goddesses) and their Akɔmfo (diviners) because they believe in the power of the Abosom to help them raise lots of money, among other things.

Unfortunately, some of those entrusted with propitiating the Abosom and the Nananom Nsamanfo (Ancestors) seasonally, periodically, and annually—traditional rulers like myself—become very defensive when told that they are not Christian because they worship the Abosom and Ancestors. Some of us—traditional rulers—feel ashamed of the very institution and ancestors' stools that we swear to protect, defend, and preserve for posterity because it is fashionable to appear Christian. Perhaps, we fail to realize that we are "seated" on ancestors' stools that are as numinous as other religious symbols around the world. Traditional rulers and Ghanaians in general ought to be as proud of their ancestors and Abosom as any other people around the world, in addition to their Islamic and Christian faiths.

As such, this book is as much about the Abosom—as the Akan refer to them—as it is about human beings, because human beings are Abosom in corporeal form.

This study stems from my own fascination and curiosity with these primeval Abosom since childhood. As an adult, I have spent many years of research in the fields of African religion and spirituality, studying developmental psychological theories as pioneered by Erik Erikson and James Fowler. However, my concern here is not so much who the human being is, as to what constitutes a human being. To discover the essences of a person, the focus falls on the Abosom as key to unlocking the mystery of human nature. As such, chapter 1 introduces my reader to the Akan (and Africans in general) and their preoccupation with life's end and expectations. Thus, the chapter defines Akan spirituality, primacy of the spiritual relative to the corporeal world (Wiadzie), their eschatological concerns, and belief in the Ancestors (Nananom Nsamanfo) in their heavenly abode at the Samanadzie, the abode of resurrected abstract or spiritual personalities, the Nsamanfo.

Chapter 2, titled "The Nature of the Spirit" or *Sunsum* (pronounced *soon-soom*) delves into the nature of the Abosom by examining their essences as spirits (*Āsunsum*) of God. Human beings descended from God via the Abosom, as the Akan believe; this being the case, human beings share the same essences as the Abosom. Thus, the chapter takes a critical look at four essences that make up the nature of the Abosom as basis for human nature.

Chapter 3 explores the mystery of becoming a human being, and so the chapter is titled "The Spirit Incarnate." There is a firm belief that all human beings are children of God, although they are willed by the Abosom into the corporeal Wiadzie (world) as human beings. In this vein, the chapter focuses on how intangible agencies like the Abosom are capable of manifesting themselves physically in the flesh.

Having established the transforming nature of the Abosom into human beings, other Abosom retain the right to "call" into the clerical vocation as well as manifest themselves on those that they choose to fall in love. For this reason, chapter 4 focuses on the phenomenon of divination and mediumistic experiences when Abosom alight on their human subjects in order to bring them under their dictates and psychological control.

The final chapter examines the ethical and moral imperative of *Ɔbra bɔ* (ethical existence and generativity) as a teleological quest as basis for spirituality (immortality). Potentially, the ethical path leads to the discovery of a person's existential career blueprint (*Nkrabea*), the discovery of which leads to a fulfilled and meaningful living. Thus chapter 5, titled "The Ethical Pathway," offers an in-depth discussion on the meaning of life, a person's ultimate goals and objectives, ethical and moral choices made as an adult, and above all, an explanation as to why human beings were created, in accordance with Akan metaphysical thought.

Africanists and those interested in black spirituality and religious hermeneutics, cultural anthropologists, scholars of religion and theology, and counselors and developmental psychologists should find this book informative, educational, and inspiring and insightful.

Finally, I am extremely grateful to all the Akɔmfo that I have worked with and continue to work with in pursuance of understanding the Abosom. I am also thankful to the countless elders that I engaged in attempting to seek clarification on issues pertaining to this book. Of course, I will be remiss if I do not thank the Abosom who availed themselves to me and continue to do so during divinations and in other ways.

Chapter One

Akan Eschatology

African spirituality, as postulated in the mid-1990s[1] makes three fundamental claims as seen from the perspective of the Akan, a people found in the countries of Ghana and the Ivory Coast.[2] African spirituality, first, maintains that an individual originates in a spirit realm as a deity (Ɔbosom) and journeys to the corporeal world, the *Wiadzie*, pre-endowed ethically. Therefore, the stage is set during adulthood for a person to become ethically and morally concerned with existential and spiritual issues and their repercussions, the basis of which determines whether or not one attains ancestorhood upon death after first achieving eldership existentially.

The basis of the ethical imperative is anchored on the Akan conception of *Ɔbra*, which J. B. Danquah defines as "ethical existence."[3] However, as we will see in subsequent chapters, there is more to Danquah's "*obara,*" because, more than ethical living or existence, ethical existence encompasses "generativity"[4] and hence *Ɔbra bɔ*. The reason for the ethical imperative has to do with the lingering mandate to realize one's existential career or professional blueprint (the *Nkrabea*). Existentially, then, the ultimate goal of an individual is to aspire to the highest socio-ethical, political or spiritual office, the attainment of which leads to the conferral of the honorific title of elder (*Nana*) upon an altruistic person by society. In other words, eldership is a prerequisite to the attainment of an Nkrabea (existential career blueprint). The actuation of this ethical imperative (Ɔbra bɔ) existentially is engendered by the need to acquire a name worthy of evocation after realizing an Nkrabea.

Second, upon the demise of an elder (Nana), a spiritual or an abstract personality emanates from a deceased person called *Ɔsaman* (also *Saman*). The Ɔsaman, which R. S. Rattray describes as ". . . a ghost, an apparition, a spectre,"[5] is the same deceased person wholly except that it exists in an intangible form, indeed an imprint of the dead person. Most importantly, this posthumous personality, the Ɔsaman, returns to a realm reserved solely for resurrected spiritual personalities, *Nsamanfo* (plural of an Ɔsaman), where an account is rendered as to whether or not one lived a worthy life on earth. Having been found worthy, an Ɔsaman is apotheosized, joining the collective body of apotheosized agencies referred to as Nananom Nsamanfo (Ancestors) that directly influences the affairs of their posterity on earth. Thus, the ancestral Nananom Nsamanfo are worshipped by the living in return for humanity's well-being, healthy living, and protection from all harmful agencies.

Finally, there is a definite spiritual realm for all those found to be worthy after death, the Nananom Nsamanfo, that the Akan refer to as the *Samanadzie* (also *Nsamankyir/Asamando*). As the abode of the Nananom Nsamanfo, the Samanadzie is headed by the primordial woman and mother of all living beings, the NaSaman, in accordance with Akan cosmogony which speaks of the primacy of the mother. The Samanadzie, moreover, is apart and different from the abode of the Abosom, primeval nature gods and goddesses of incomparable power and intelligence thought to have been *There* in the very beginning with God. As God's "children," the Abosom are in charge of the universe at the behest of God. Furthermore, the Samanadzie is different from the realm of Āsunsum (spirits), some of whom await reincarnation into the corporeal Wiadzie (world) because they died prematurely and therefore were unable to realize their Nkrabea (existential career or professional blueprints). But most saliently, the Abosom—who are incapable of death—do not enter the realm of the Samanadzie because the Samanadzie is reserved for only those who have tasted death and been resurrected as Nananom Nsamanfo or just Nsamanfo (spiritual or abstract personalities). One attribute that the Akan are adamant about when speaking of the Samanadzie is that the Samanadzie is dark (Samanadzie *yɛ sum*), making inhabitants there agencies of light. Meaning, residents there—as well as all spiritual beings—do not require the sunlight to enable them to see, an indication that they are truly beings of light. In fact, the sun's light is only meant for living things, as an instrument of blinding living beings from seeing spiritual agencies starting at the very moment of parturition. Actually, spiritual beings, though still seen during the day, avoid the sunlight as much as possible because they do not want to be discovered easily.

By spiritual or spirituality we mean a world, place (the Samanadzie), and an existence as an Ɔsaman (abstract, spiritual personality) beyond the corporeal, because for Africans the spiritual realm is a "real" place where life, as we know it, originates. Existentially, the concern here is eschatological as all things spiritual are manifested tangibly as real in the corporeal, although they are teleological in scope. This, then, is where I begin because this is what the project is about—the way that Africans, the Akan, perceive their corporeal environment and influences, meaning of existence, and ultimate end of existence.

The supernatural is thought of as spiritual; that is, everything beyond the realm of human reasoning, rationality, and tangibility borders on the spiritual requiring extra sensory explanation. To explain the unexplainable requires equally irrational methodologies which penetrate the supernatural in order to make some sense, meaning, valuing, and interpreting of irrational thoughts. Thus the arbiters of African axiology are the elders because of their awareness of the spiritual all around them, influencing daily activities and directing or misdirecting actions. Even so, some elders[6] are more aware than others of the influences that affect humanity and as a result harness the influences positively—or even negatively—while most people are blind to spiritual agencies that we share the environment with every day.

Naïvely, non-Africans refer to realms that they are blinded to as *space* because they think it is empty.[7] For the Akan and other African groups, it is the awareness of "others" that cause people to blame their misfortunes on spiritual forces believed to inhabit every inch of the so-called space watching every endeavor of human beings. This is known because the unseen, the spiritual, will, from time to time, materialize just enough to remind people that they are still around, like when people claim to see the dead momentarily. Therefore, spirituality is understood as a here-and-now phenomenon because people seek treatments for what they believe to be spiritual causalities of their illnesses. For Africans, spirituality is concerned with the awareness of and the way people deal with unseen spiritual agencies on a daily basis. And while this study may not necessarily address spiritual epistemology, it will, however, address the eschatological as well as soteriological concerns that people face within the context of Ɔbra bɔ (ethical existence and generativity).

Eschatology is concerned with the end, but it is the present that informs the end, just as the spiritual, unseen informs and manifests itself in the present, the mundane Wiadzie (world). And so it is when people fail to address their present predicaments, which they believe are informed by the spiritual that caused them to be concerned about the end. Even so, there is a distinction between the spiritual and corporeal realms, as evidenced by the way Africans categorize illnesses as having spiritual or earthly origins. Additionally, the strong desire to discover an Nkrabea (existential career or professional blueprint) or inability to achieve life's full meaning for not discovering and living an ideal life is the basis for soteriology in the context of *Bɛbra* (reincarnation). That is, everyone has the chance to be born again and again to live a meaningful life as long as one lives a good life but dies before he or she has the chance to live a full life. So we see how the spiritual impacts on the corporeal and human life, the body especially.

The dynamic between the spiritual and physical, especially when it comes to diseases, is a fascinating phenomenon. However, the diagnostic methods and approaches used by practitioners of traditional health or healing to determine which disease is spiritual or physical in origin may be guided by greed.[8] In a study to examine the cultural hermeneutics of healing, first, the study looked at the underlying psychological and religious factors for seeking spiritual healing, and second, why traditional healing and healthcare practices were aimed at placating the spiritual in order to maintain a healthy personality and well-being. What was disturbing was that often the methodology used by spiritual practitioners in determining the basis for spiritual causality of illnesses was complex, as many sick people wasted away under the guise of having a spiritual disease when a simple visit to a hospital would have addressed many of the illnesses misdiagnosed as spiritual.[9] In 2014, for example, an intervention was needed to have a sick man moved to a government hospital in Simpa (Winneba) for hernia surgery to be performed after a stranger offered to pay his bills. His family and wife had taken him to a spiritualist saying that he has bewitched by a co-worker when he only needed a hernia repair.

The line between the spiritual and the mundane when it comes to illnesses is blurry when the sick are at the mercy of traditional practitioners. If an illness is deemed to have a spiritual causative and diagnosed as such, then healing could take place by first placating the spiritual causative agency. Once placated, then healing or curing would manifest itself corporeally in a matter of days. Well, this makes perfect sense since the spiritual takes precedence over the material. Normally, this way of offering holistic health would be idealistic if it were not for greed. Motivated by greed, many healers attempt to heal every patient that walks into their churches, shrines and temples, sending the patients home only when it is too late in most cases. Still, the spiritual disposition of Akan is such that it is impossible to dissuade families from taking patients to healers who are thought to have communicative capabilities with causative agencies. How then is the spiritual identifiable?

Some children "see" events, things in their dreams, some of which are ominous and sometimes scary. Different people deal with their dreams and revelations in their own unique ways as they attempt to forestall their fulfillments or even hasten their fulfillment. For some, one way is to repeat the dreams or revelations to oneself or, if one were of the clerical profession, to announce the dreams or revelations to his or her congregants. Others, if they are married, may ask their spouses to hear and listens to their scary pronouncements. Unfortunately or fortunately, inspired dreams or revelations ultimately come true, some very painfully.[10] Perplexed, sometimes some people find themselves asking the perennial question: Why me! This is because sometimes events may have absolutely nothing to do with anyone personally. However, one thing that revelations have in common is that most deal with future occurrences bordering on what may be termed as religious or the supernatural. On a personal level, the existential focus for me has always been on spiritual things, or rather on a "world" and sights that are beyond the corporeal. Therefore, choosing to attend seminary and becoming a clergyman came as no surprise to friends, some of whom simply referred to me as *Nyamensɛm* (the theologian), because I was always speaking about God.

Raised a Roman Catholic and as an altar boy, my ordination into the clerical profession in the United States was the fulfillment of my childhood desire of becoming a priest, although my ordination was void of the ritual and sacramental aspects of my Roman Catholic upbringings. It would be years later after I became a traditional ruler that I would discover what my Nkrabea (existential career blueprint) was all about during a divination rite when my "spiritual father" (*Āgya-bosom*) revealed to me what my Nkrabea was. Suddenly, everything made sense to me because everything fitted together, to the extent that my ordination was the fulfillment of my Nkrabea as a theologian, though just the beginning of my service to God. However, the ritual differences and solemnity between my ordination into the Western clerical profession and king-making rites as an Akan traditional ruler were as night and day. The rites I had to undergo as king were wholly profound and life altering. The training and ordination rites that the traditional clergy, especially diviners (the *Akɔmfo*), undergo have a lot in common with those of traditional kings,[11] although those of the Akɔmfo (diviners) are more austere than those of kings and queen mothers.

While graduate seminary may have influenced my doctoral dissertation[12] years later, the choice of my doctoral dissertation was purely coincidental, although it seemed to have followed my life's trajectory as well. It affirmed my deeply held belief that life—or rather existence—is an ethical endeavor, a journey at the end of which is something very rewarding—a longing to return to where one might have originated. Moreover, the basis for a spiritual journey is a deeply held desire; that is, there are certain inherent spiritual attributes that, if nurtured, could lead to a life of immortality as an ancestor. However, while all spiritual beings are immortal and exist eternally, it is the transformation of a spiritual personality, an Ɔsaman, into an ancestral god or goddess that makes life worth living. The human being, then, is more than just flesh and blood, the basis of our physicality; in fact, a human being is a spiritual being wholly. Thus, the goal here is to discover the innate essentials not readily apparent but which exercise so much psychological and emotional control in the life of a person. The spiritual quest, personal or collective, is to discover and identify those inherent attributes, their precise roles and capabilities in existence, develop and refine their potentialities, and utilize and maximize their effectiveness individually and collectively.

NANA

The most endearing and ultimate socio-political and spiritual name, term or title among the Akan is *Nana*, conferred meritoriously for living an altruistic life after a successful integration of Ɔbra bɔ (ethical existence and generativity). But though the highest existential title aspired, Nana may be one of the most common names that one might hear because it commands respect, as the person using it, if not a child, may have some standing in community. Above all, the term or title *Nana* is a spiritual title universally shared by the Akan, as both Akan and non-Akan scholars agree. In the 1880s, for example, Ellis wrote that: "The word *Nana*, literally 'grandfather,' is a title of respect, and is one used in addressing the King of Ashanti."[13] Decades later, Rattray would confirm Ellis' observation by saying that: "*Nana* is the Ashanti word for grandparent, and is also used as a term of respect in referring to dead ancestors," in addition to it being used for a grandchild, although in some cases used to affectionately address an "infant not as 'grandchild' but as 'grandparent' or ancestor,"[14] because a grandchild happened to be named after its grandparent. A grandchild bears the same name—Nana—as his or grandparent because he or she just arrived from the ancestral or spiritual world. Intellectually both grandparents and grandbabies share the same fluid minds. Thus Jesus was right in saying that unless one (a grandparent) becomes like a little child physically and intellectually, one cannot enter into the kingdom of God. In other words, unless a grandparent becomes very old and loses his or her mind like a child, one cannot enter into heaven. Longevity then is an ideal, a requisite to becoming a deity. As such, Nana is used in reference to the Abosom (Gods and Goddesses) and God, hence God is Nana Nyame or Nana Nyankopon. Therefore, more than any singular Akan term or title, *Nana* is one of those unique genderless titles shared by humans, together with kings and queen mothers, ancestors (Nananom Nsamanfo), and the Abosom and God.

Developmentally, after successfully transitioning and integrating the stages of life intellectually, physio-biologically, and emotionally, to the extent of having mastered the art of living, a community nominates, elects—and in cases where an individual is slated for the kingship—installs a person as an elder (Nana). This is after a person has exhibited grace and humility, courageousness in the face of adversities, lived altruistically, demonstrated intelligence and wisdom during group discussions, especially in public discourses, and shown qualities and attributes worthy of emulation. These qualities are deemed comparable to those of the ancestors and God and therefore anyone demonstrating them is worthy of emulation by society, some of whom may respond by naming their children for living elders. The attainment of eldership (Nana) means that one has aspired to the highest existential and spiritual estate tantamount to a life of perfection and immortality, because one has acquired on earth a title comparable to those of ancestors, the Abosom and, indeed, God, making senior elders infallible. The anticipation and reward of ancestorhood (Nana Saman) after death is a reward worth having, because a senior Nana would be transformed into an ancestral Ɔbosom (God or Goddess) and remembered forever, *Afibɔɔr*. Ancestorhood then is having earned the right to be worshipped as an Ɔbosom (God or Goddess), and hence the worship of ancestors among the Akan and other African groups. Ancestor worship then is the religion that professes and guarantees eternal living for adherents, because the elders, especially kings and queen mothers, do not die but move on to a spiritual world designed solely for resurrected posthumous personalities, Nsamanfo (plural of Ɔsaman) called the Samanadzie. Indeed, if the Akan and other African groups worship their kings—who do not die—then ancestor worship is the religion of royals, because only kings and queen mothers guarantee eternal life for their peoples. The belief in the eternity of kings and queen mothers and therefore of ancestor worship is such that the Akan would use euphemisms like "Nana has gone" or "travel to the Village" or "A great tree has fallen" when announcing the death of a king or queen mother. This is how Rattray puts it:

> No one in Ashanti would ever dare to use the equivalent of our phrase "the king is dead." Neither a king nor any one of any importance ever "dies." "A mighty tree has been uprooted"; "He is absent elsewhere"; "He has departed, or gone out"; all these are circumlocutions by which such an event is described. "Death" and a great man's name may never be coupled. In olden times any one saying . . . "Grandfather so and so is dead" would have been killed if speaking of the king. Even in using these euphemistic expressions the voice is dropped almost to a whisper.[15]

The truism that ancestor worship is the religion of kings and queen mothers and that kings and queen mothers ensure eternal life for the peoples that they rule over and all those who believe in them is enshrined in the deeply held belief that the kingship is divine (*Ahendzie fir sor*), originating with God and therefore the eternal existence of the kingship.

The notion in the eternity of ancestor worship and the kingship is African, old and ancient. It is well established that the ancient Egyptians, for example, also shared the same beliefs as contemporary Africans like the Akan. The nature and role of the kingship in ancient Egypt is provided by John Baines who quoted a text from the Middle Kingdom as saying that the king is ". . . on earth 'for ever and ever, judging humanity and propitiating the gods, and setting order in place of disorder. He gives offerings to the gods and mortuary offerings to the spirits (the blessed dead).'"[16] Baines goes on to explain that ". . . the king 'took on for humanity the task of dealing both with the gods and with the negative forces that surrounded the ordered world.'"[17] It is abundantly clear that Akan beliefs are consistent with those of the ancient Egyptians and other African groups.

But, does the lack of ancestral remembrance by a community also mean that the ancestors are "dead"? Absolutely not! As a person who teaches African religion (ancestor worship), sometimes my students argue that if the names of the ancestors are forgotten, then the ancestors and ancestor worship are rendered impertinent since the ancestors are nonexistent. This notion is, however, wrong because it fails to take into account how spiritual beings operate and the praxis of what ancestor worship is all about.

First, ancestor worship is tenable and viable precisely because living beings are bio-genetically linked to their ancestors making it impossible for the living to dissociate themselves from their ancestors. What this means is that the ancestors continue to live in and through their living descendants, sympathetically partaking of meals, wines, sacrifices of all kinds and the sharing of gifts and activities that the living undertake. In other words, we are our ancestors today, just as our ancestors were us yesterday.

Second, when we talk of the ancestors, we have in mind a collective body, unit, and matrix of gargantuan group. Even on earth, while the pursuance of eldership is an individual endeavor, the very moment that one attains eldership and becomes a Nana, he or she becomes a part of the collective; hence elders—or as the Akan refer to them, Nananom Mpānyinfo—are a body of esteemed elders. As such, they act as a collective unit in all matters of community and state; meaning, without a quorum they do not proceed deliberatively. Similarly, while an African community may forget about its ancestors to the extent that a community may not offer their ancestors sacrifices any more, it does not mean that the ancestors are forgotten in the larger context, because those ancestors join a self-sustaining phylogenetic spirit. Subsequently, they act together as a collective body, meaning when another community is remembering its ancestors, then all other phylogenetic spirits participate because they are all one. Thus, in the same way that the head of the Greek deities, Zeus, led the Greek deities to Africa in order to partake of offerings and sacrifices offered by Africans (according to Homer), the ancestors, as apotheosized beings, travel to communities other than their own to partake of ambrosias offered by those communities.

And finally, the ancestors could not be dead and forgotten because they are alive and well, hence they are dead-but-alive (dead-alive). Africans do not worship the dead, because the dead are buried in the ground, generally speaking. Rather, what people worship are the resurrected personalities of the dead, the *Nsamanfo* (also *Asaman*). Just before death, the Ɔsaman (posthumous spiritual or abstract personality) emerges from the physical personality making it possible for a death to occur. The dead body (*fuun*) is interred, while the spiritual or abstract personality, the Ɔsaman, journeys to a world designed entirely for all spiritual personalities in the Samanadzie. It is they, the Nananom Nsamanfo (Ancestors), who are worshipped by Africans when propitiatory sacrifices of animals, liquors, meat, money, etc., are offered them, because Africans know them to be alive and well—not as dead bodies buried in the ground.

NOTION OF ETERNITY

African religion—ancestor worship—is divine in that it originates with God, through the primeval Abosom (Gods and Goddesses), who in turn taught it to humanity. In other words, the notion of kingship will always survive on earth because it is ordained by God as the only religion dedicated to the worship of kings and queen mothers, who, as divine beings, never die, as the gods and goddesses that they are. Therefore, religions that do not have royal origins could not ensure or guarantee eternal life, because to worship kings on earth is tantamount to living forever in heaven before one's king who, even on earth, lived forever, as Rattray points out among the Akan. In fact, the Akan believe that kings and queen mothers are living ancestors (Nananom Ahenfo); meaning, they are ancestors (Nananom Nsamanfo) in human form, watching and ruling their peoples on earth and in heaven, forever, as Baines clearly states was the practice in ancient Egypt.

To expatiate on the concept of eternity, everlasting in the context of time, we must begin with what the Akan refer to as *Afibɔɔr* because there is a relationship between Afibɔɔr (forever, infinity) and immortality of the apotheosized ancestors, the Nananom Nsamanfo. The reference to Afibɔɔr has to do with linear time, stretching indefinitely into an unknown future, as opposed to an annual or seasonally cyclical time called *Afinhyia,* which rounds itself up at the end of every season. But while Afibɔɔr is conceptually abstract, *Nfi pitsepitsee* has to do with indefinite but concrete time in terms of eons; meaning, countless number of years. And so Afinhyia is seasonally and ritually regenerative, meaning it is tied to life and death and rebirth within the context of planting and harvesting and replanting. However, Afibɔɔr has to do with perpetuity—with no beginning or an end. While Afibɔɔr is defined in the context of eternity, ironically, it is Afinhyia that is ritually tied to life as rounding itself up at, ideally, old age, and the resultant death and rites of remembrances enacted to propitiate the ancestors. That is, it takes an Afinhyia to bring into focus Afibɔɔr when prayers and libations and other sacrifices are offered to the ancestors. Immortality for the ancestors is achieved through birth, ethical existence, and death on earth when the cyclical nature of corporeal existence catapults a senior elder into an eternal bliss. Thus Afibɔɔr existence, within the context of immortality, is contingent on the maximum cumulative cycles of chronological age accompanied by altruistic endeavors that are verified and confirmed by society. Thereupon society confers commensurate stage titles on an individual until one aspired to the highest existential stage estate. The reward, upon death, is when a senior Nana (elder) becomes a deified spirit, with the capacity to will agencies into the mundane, a capability that other non-ancestral spirits lack.

Next, spirituality as a teleological quest implies an eschatological—not apocalyptic—aspiration. The reference to apocalypticism only suggests that the Akan do not conceive of a sudden and violent end to the world. That is, they do not live their lives in fear of and in anticipation of a messianic hero at an abruptly violent end-time. This is not to say that people do not think of or even live in fear of the end sometimes, especially when life or living becomes unbearable; rather they live in anticipation of a spiritual world where dead and resurrected relatives (Nsamanfo) await them, in the same way that we are born into the hands of parents and relatives in the corporeal. So, there is a nostalgic embrace of spirituality due to the finite nature of corporeal existence: a sense of loss and therefore the innate desire, wish, yearning, to return to an ideal estate characterized by eternity and absence of pain and suffering. Indeed, spirituality supposes an ideal epoch that the living acknowledge intrinsically, thus spirituality is an intrinsic quality. Spirituality then is a quest to be achieved existentially, as a developmentally intrinsic phenomenon, leading to outward expressions of beneficence acknowledged by a community of faith. In other words, spirituality is within, although its rippling effects are without, requiring witnesses to a life lived and authenticated by a community of faith because life cannot be lived in isolation. Spirituality then is the innate desire, yearning for immortality.

Human beings are naturally spiritual in that they aspire to that which they have lost, as Abosom that they once were and which they would want to regain ultimately. The transformation from spiritual to human beings is not the result of *sin*, as Christian scriptures teaches, but rather individual decisions made by Abosom to transit from one mode of existence to another, an existence of eternity to one of finitude. Being transient beings in the corporeal suggests, first, that corporeal existence is only temporary, and second, the real destination for human beings is other than the corporeal. Does the final destination require corporeal form of existence? The answer is, of course, yes, due to the impermanence of the mundane as a result of death. Indeed, God created death for corporeal existence as part of Nkrabea (existential career blueprint), and yet death ended up killing God, the Akan would say. Of course, God does not die, so what do the Akan mean? Simply, the life that God created in the mundane is also ended by death, another creation of God. The fact is that corporeal existence has its limitations and drawbacks and the moment an Ɔbosom becomes a human being is to inherit everything mundane. The only way out of corporeal existence is death, which serves as a catalyst for a new spiritual "personality," which is the Ɔsaman.

Even though God created death, which, in turn, killed life (God), as the Akan would reflect, it does so in manner designed for a person to surmount the finite nature of corporeal existence and usher in a new life-form called the Ɔsaman (abstract personality of a deceased person). It would appear then that the purpose of corporeal existence is to create new life-forms (as will be expounded upon in subsequent chapters). Death then only kills the physicality of human beings leaving the ethereal, nonphysical portion of the human being to linger on somewhere else. Still, the capriciousness of corporeal existence and the looming threat of death make life anxiously unnerving because, instinctively, life should not terminate. The intrinsic desire for permanency in the mundane is spurred on by an innate feeling of having missed immortality and therefore the desire to regain that which is lost. This, then, is the basis of spirituality: the propensity to aspire to eternal life. Though an individualistic quest, the path toward eternal life emanates from a long established ethical, socio-religious, and cultural matrix. However, spirituality could not be attained in a vacuum: spirituality must be sanctioned by a community of faith and conform to societal norms and axiology. In other words, one cannot create one's own ethical path alien to one's own socio-cultural and ethico-religious traditions.

Finally, spirituality is a two-prong quest: the first of which is achieved corporeally when the title Nana is conferred on the person who has successfully mastered the art of living; the other—contingent on one's earthly life as to whether or not one lived an ideal life verified by one's community resulting in the conferral of eldership title—heavenly, when a senior Nana is apotheosized as an ancestral Ɔbosom or deity upon death and immortality is achieved. Whereas immortality is a dynamically active state of eternity, eternity encompasses all immortal beings. Moreover, whereas immortality is an aspired, meritoriously achieved state of being, eternity is—and was—the linear state of *Thereness*,[18] forever. Actually, immortality must first be earned on earth as a senior elder, or ideally as a king or queen mother. Apotheosis then must occur on earth, when a community confers on an individual the highest socio-political and religio-spiritual title for living an altruistic life coupled with grace and humility, patience, and peace. The point is that eldership is indispensable to achieving immortality or spirituality.

Attaining eldership (Nana), first, suggests that life exists developmentally. Human beings mature physically, emotionally, and intellectually from one stage—biologically or otherwise—to the next. Usually the transition and integration of stages are vetted by a select group within African communities that one is born into, and who normally prescribe the series of rites delineating the stages of development until one attains the highest socio-political and spiritual estate as a Nana in the Akan context. In urban areas, both rites of transition and verification processes by elders are in oblivion or blatantly ignored due to economic constraints, Western influences, and the sense of shame associated with such rites because they are thought to be antiquated.

And second, concurrent with the notion of stages of development is the idea that life—or existence—is lived teleologically in anticipation of an existential end point in death, after which permanency in a different mode of existence is achieved, albeit ethereally in a world quite different from the corporeal, although the corporeal reflects the idealistic realm of the dead-alive, ancestors. Teleology, though practical in nature because one lives an ethical life clearly toward achieving an Nkrabea, is deeply engrained in the Akan psyche and manifested practically in the form of a complexly meandering ethical path (*Ɔbra bɔ*), traveled individually with skill, creativity, and dexterity. So what appears to be the highest existential stage title upon attaining senior eldership only serves as the prelude to the ultimate spiritual prize upon death—apotheosized ancestor as Nana Saman in an incorporeal world called the Samanadzie. The reason why the process of deification begins on earth is because what is earned on earth, the title of Nana, follows a deceased elder in death, when its spiritual personality joins the esteemed company of ancestors, the Nananom Nsamanfo. It further suggests that one cannot attain *Nanahood* in heaven if one was not already a Nana on earth. Moreover, the attainment of Nana Saman (Ancestor) status is not automatic for every Nana or elder in heaven, because some elders, upon attaining eldership, live less-than-ideal lives making them ineligible for ancestorhood in Samanadzie.

A distinction must also be drawn between junior and senior elders, however. The difference between the two may be likened to ripe and rotten fruits. A ripened fruit, while mature and enticing enough to be edible, may not be old enough for its seed to germinate when planted, meaning it cannot reproduce. A rotten fruit, on the other hand, is so mature and old that its fruit may be beyond edibility. But what it has going for it is its capacity for regeneration; its ability to germinate when planted, grow to maturity and fruition, and reproduce anywhere. Similarly, while junior elders exhibit jurisprudential qualities and attributes, in general, they may lack the judicial temperament of patience and delay—or what the Akan called *Abotari*—that goes with the position of being a Nana. In other words, they are presumptuous because they sometimes have the tendency to act precipitously. Junior elders are not fully mature enough to be granted ancestorhood upon demise, in the same way that ripe fruits are incapable of regeneration. Senior elders, on the other hand, epitomize all the qualities and attributes of ideal leadership, having passed junior eldership stage, and are now in the position to supervise and moderate proceedings led by junior elders. With longevity on their side after living to be very old and seeing their grandchildren and even great-grandchildren in the course of administering justice, they patiently await final transformation into ancestors (Nananom Nsamanfo). Most importantly though, senior elders who are transformed into *Nananom* (Gods and Goddesses) upon death are in the position to marry and produce offspring who, in turn, are willed back into corporeal existence. Saliently only the Abosom replenish the corporeal with their own kind because they have always been *There*. While there are no marriages in the Samanadzie, the Nananom Nsamanfo are capable of willing offspring into the corporeal Wiadzie. Thus the stage is set for reincarnation (*Bɛbra*) to take place in order to allow the Nsamanfo who did not attain senior eldership on earth and died to be reincarnated. Reincarnation must be understood soteriologically in that it ensures salvation for all created order, hence one reincarnates several times in order to make it to the Samanadzie.

The basis of spirituality—actually what undergirds the nostalgic desire for immortality (or spirituality)—are two fundamental beliefs: one celestial—albeit symbolic, and the other, corporeal. First, symbolically, is the Akan attitude toward the moon, the Ɔsrɛn.[19] There is a genuine connection, a filial relationship between the Akan and this celestial symbol, the Ɔsrɛn, going back to the very beginning of human and non-human existence on earth, a period when the earth and moon were in close proximity. In fact, the earth (Asasi) and the moon (Ɔsrɛn) were so close that the earth used to bump into the moon causing the moon to protest. However, a severance occurred between the Ɔsrɛn and the first earthly humans—the Abrewah (Old Woman) and her children—resulting in the onset of death which the Old Woman caused due to her intransigence, and subsequent departure or distancing of the Ɔsrɛn from earth. With the departure of the Ɔsrɛn—husband and father of the Abrewah's children—which ironically ensured the survivability of earth, a strong nostalgic sense of having missed the Ɔsrɛn was felt by the children of the Abrewah, who desired a return to normalcy, to the time of eternity. Perhaps also missing his children—or perhaps hearing the cries of his children—the

Ɔsrɛn returns monthly. Upon spotting the Ɔsrɛn by humanity, his children celebrate because it evokes a sense of originality, a period when existence was eternal, Afibɔɔr, with the moon. The feeling was—and is—mutual, as the Ɔsrɛn (crescent moon) reciprocates by ensuring the survivability of the human race as life-giver when it assumes the ills and misfortunes of humanity upon itself and wipes the slate clean for humans. So whenever the Ɔsrɛn makes its monthly apparition, humanity is renewed, again and again, forever (Afibɔɔr). Therefore, as the soul of the earth and husband of the first human, the Abrewah (Old woman), and emblem of God, the Ɔsrɛn is the symbolic focus of ancestor worship because human beings have missed the eternal epoch now superseded by finitude.

Second, when one has missed something valuable, the tendency is to reach back and grab that which is missed, retrace one's steps to the original point, or turn around and travel to the junction where the missing occurred in order to correct the mistake. This corrective process is what the Akan refer to as *Sankɔfa*, stressing on the moral and ethical imperative to return to the past in order to correct misdeeds. Indeed, it is not an offense or even criminal to have to return and retrieve a forgotten item or to admit culpability for a past misdeed. But where the point of reference is irretrievably lost, then it is still proper to re-create that which one has missed from memory, especially if circumstances have changed to the extent that it is impossible to return to the original destination. History is replete with such phenomena. The most relative recent example is the enslavement of African peoples by Europeans in the New World. In a journey more than geographic, Africans in the New World lost their humanity and all symbolic forms of their religious expressions and yet African religions survived to play critical roles in the spiritual development of descendants of Africans in the New World. Missing their African relatives and homes and unable to return, Africans in the New World created the Africa that they knew from their collective memories in spite of the draconically inhumane treatments they received from their captors and masters. From memory, African slaves and their descendants found hermeneutical ways to contextualize their milieu socially, culturally, and religiously so as to create some semblance of their lost African heritages. The resultant religious traditions created include Candomblé, Santeria, and Voodoo among many others. In studying these religions and actually teaching a course on Candomblé, I sometimes wonder if the devotees of African Diaspora religions in the New World are not the true practitioners of African religions (ancestor worship).

From their mythical collective memories, the Akan created the worship of the Ɔsrɛn (moon) on earth, in the absence of, but in memory of both the Ɔsrɛn and the Abrewah. How did they do it? From observation of the crescent moon, Akan artists created ancestral stools after the Ɔsrɛn (moon),[20] which became the single most sacrosanct symbol there is among the Akan and their kindred peoples. So even though the moon is too distant from his offspring, his offspring seek to bring the moon's likeness closer to home, on earth. In addition to the one numinous ancestors' stool housing the soul of the living and the dead-alive and hence the ancestors' stool, every household too has a replica of the crescent moon. Like the crescent moon, an ancestors' stool takes on the mystique of the crescent moon by being hidden from the people, only making cameo appearances during festivities honoring the ancestors when the stool is propitiated. Though hidden from public view, the Akan firmly believe in its physical or temporal and spiritual existence. They know that the stool is *There*, exists forever, as an Ɔbosom. More than an act of faith, it is kerygmatic in that traditional rulers are emblematic of salvation, when season after season citizens converge around their ancestors' stool in order to reaffirm their faith in the ancestors' stool represented on earth in the person of a living ancestor and occupant of the ancestors' stool, the king or queen mother.

As for the Abrewah, the wife of the Ɔsrɛn, she was the ruler par excellence, as well as the ultimate judge in place of her wandering husband, the Ɔsrɛn. Ensuring legitimacy and the unadulterated chain of succession, only her children occupy the ancestors' stool, the very emblem of her husband, in accordance with Akan tradition. Her children are defined as only those who emerge from her womb and composed of her blood, *Mogya*. This definition of family then is the basis of the Akan system of descent called *Ābusua*—descendants of a single womb. Seven Ābusua in all, the Akan are the first to belong to one of seven Ābusua blood types, originating with the Abrewah and her six daughters. The purity of the Ābusua system is ensured in women in that only women transmit blood, making blood uniquely female. Only women then perpetuate the original woman's (the Abrewah's) bloodline when their children are physically composed of the very blood of the first mother and her daughters.

Expressively, what it means to be an Ābusua is on display during funerals. This is explained thus:

> Sadly, it takes a funeral to observe the ābusua at work, because it takes the death of an ābusua member to bring the larger ābusua together. Thus, the first responsibility of an ābusua is to converge in order to bury their dead in the same way as blood coagulates when exposed. The symbolism of blood coagulation equals the earthly mother gathering her living children together in order to ritually prepare her dead child before sending it to the . . . Spiritual Mother. Before the formal gathering of an ābusua, the head of the ābusua would have acted quickly to first secure the deceased's belongings by sealing or locking up the deceased's personal room. . . .

> Next, the ābusua reconvenes after the burial to share the funeral expenses. Every adult member is obliged to pay towards the cost of the funeral obsequies prior to burial or during the actual funeral rites. . . . Therefore, the re-convergence is to tally the overall expenditure in order to determine the profitability or loss of a funeral, in which case the debt is shared by the ābusua members. . . .
>
> Next, the ābusua set the date for the spiritual funeral obsequies for the deceased. Unlike the previous funeral rites with a corpse laid in state, this time there is no corpse. . . . Before any final funeral obsequies, however, there are periodic rites of remembrance on the eighth, the sixteenth, the fortieth, and the eightieth days after interring the deceased and culminating with the final funeral rites of remembrance . . . on the anniversary. . . .
>
> The anniversary . . . is extremely important in that an ābusua chooses the deceased's successor and divides or distributes the personal belongings of the deceased among its members . . . when . . . prayers and libations are offered.[21]

Though the Akan lost their father, the Ɔsrɛn, and their mother, the Abrewah, they ingeniously created—or re-created—lost paradise on earth. As the emblem of God (Nana Nyame), the Ɔsrɛn also assumes the title *Nana*—with all the praises and exultations—when the crescent moon makes its monthly appearance. Thus, any occupant of an ancestors' stool, the physical emblem of the crescent moon, also assumes the same spiritual and earthly honor accorded the crescent moon as Nana. Meaning, the occupant of an ancestors' stool has, most importantly, surmounted death and lives forever, because the occupant has come in contact with the very emblem of God, the ancestors' stool which God first made himself[22] (and is copied by humans) in the shape of the crescent moon. For this reason, it is a taboo to announce that a king or queen mother is dead, as already noted above by Rattray.

Indeed, the Akan never refer to a deceased king as dead but merely as one who has embarked on a journey. If the kingship is divine because it originates with God and is symbolized by an ancestors' stool, then anyone who is seated on an ancestors' stool is also divine. And if one lives forever, then one is worshipped as an ancestor, hence ancestor worship is not only the worship of kings and queen mothers, it is the only religion instituted by God, who is the ultimate King.

In African thought, philosophically, the notion that kings and queen mothers do not die is meant to underscore the enigmatic nature of death. Paradoxically, it is meant to deny the existential reality and inevitability of death, as happening to a king. In itself, it is an eschatological expression, meant to look beyond physical death as the final existential reality. After all, a king or queen mother is a living ancestor, meaning he or she has transcended death as a human being. Still, the Ābusua performs all funeral and posthumous obsequies associated with a decedent ruler. To perpetuate the myth of a decedent king as having traveled to the village, periodically his personal stool, known as

Kra-gua (Soul stool), receives ablution and propitiation, together with the ancestors' stool as though the king were still alive physically. This, then, is the basis of ancestor religion: ritual preparation of a corpse, burial of the dead with ceremony and pomp, belief in eternal existence of the dead as dead-alive (ancestor), periodic remembrance of the ancestors, and the notion that the ancestors exercise direct influence on the affairs of their descendants existentially. A religion that does not focus on the death of its founder—a king or queen mother—as object of worship, where a people periodically commemorate the life, tragic death, and resurrection of their leader as ancestor, could not be divine. And so, we start with death and the beyond, because death, as far as the Akan are concerned, is the single most important phenomenon that brings together people from all walks of life.

ƆDOMANKOMA OWU (DEATH)

The conundrum about death, in the first place, is why would God create death to destroy God's own creation? Secondly, why did God create death long before the creation of life, as the Akan believe? And thirdly, why would spiritual beings not subjected to death enter the corporeal and subject themselves to death? The simple answer to the last question is that while some Abosom are in the corporeal Wiadzie (world), they do so not as physical beings but rather as spiritual agencies still, although capable of materialization. Subsequently, God is not subject to materialization because God does not reside in the Wiadzie, hence from time immemorial Africans have never had any iconic or symbolic, or even anthropomorphic, representation of God, ever.

Death (Owu) is *Ɔdomankoma*; meaning, it was—and is—everlasting, forever just like God. Death is created by God from the very beginning, for a definite purpose, not against life but rather to complement life in the corporeal, which was created much later. Still, Owu is perceived as a destroyer of families and of life in general; thus Owu is experienced as wrecker of homes when death annihilates entire families and societies. Absolutely, no one, no living thing escapes the grip of death, which makes death a universal phenomenon and an enigma. Death does not discriminate precisely because it originates with God as Ɔdomankoma (eternal, everlasting, and forever), which means it is for all of God's creation, meaning no living being escapes it.

In acknowledgement of Owu's absolutely grip on all living things, the Akan even claim that there is a ladder of death (*Owu atwir*) not ascended by any single person, but by all. The very mentioning of a ladder of death points to a destination with a narrow entrance or passage only accessible by a ladder.

But narrow as it may, the throngs of spiritual beings (Nsamanfo) descending and ascending the ladder of death is voluminous, hence *Owu atwir Ɔbaako nfou* (the ladder of death is not ascended by one person).

Next, the very mentioning of a ladder conjures up an image of two adjoining worlds, or even two separate realms, one below and the other up and accessible only by a ladder. On this ladder are spirits descending into the corporeal Wiadzie (world) and the dead-alive who ascend it in order to enter the world to which they are destined, the Samanadzie. Clearly, the Nsamanfo climb up, suggesting that the realm to which the dead-alive are destined is higher than the one that they left behind on earth, unless they travel elsewhere before climbing the ladder of death. The revealed knowledge is that there are at least two worlds: one clearly for the living in the corporeal Wiadzie, and the other for the Nsamanfo, or dead-alive, which indubitably is higher than where the living currently reside. We know that the Wiadzie is below because God is said to have created all things below (*Ɔdomankoma bɔadzie brɛbrɛ*). But while it may appear as though only the dead are to climb the ladder of death, there is also the belief that there are other spiritual beings descending to be born into the corporeal. It seems—whether spiritual or corporeal beings—that there is a great deal of movement to and from the two worlds.

Finally, on the motif of a journey or destination to somewhere, there is a symbiotic relationship between Ɔbra bɔ (ethical existence and generativity)—as a quest by an adult to discover one's niche in the world—and *Nkrabea* (existential career or professional blueprint), in the same way that there is an embryonic relationship between Nkrabea and Owu (death). After all, Ɔbra bɔ is the process of actuating Nkrabea. So without Ɔbra bɔ there is no realization of Nkrabea, and the more reason why Ɔbra bɔ has a beginning point in adulthood when an adult is personally held responsible for one's actions. When everything else fails in the pursuance of Nkrabea—and in the face of death—only then would the Akan acknowledge that: *Ɔbra twir owu* (ethical existence is unto death). The *Ɔbra twir owu* comment is a statement of last resort, acknowledging the futility of existence and only when death has already occurred—not before, although sometimes out of tiredness or frustration one may make that statement too. This is because society does everything to save a life, but when death finally occurs, then in a sigh of relief one may be heard saying: *Ɔbra twir owu*. That is to say, that death has the ultimate say in ending all things alive.

Along the same lines, it may be said that: *Onyimpa brɛɛ ma owu* (suffering, tiredness is unto death). In general, whether one is tired of living because of harsh economic conditions, or suffering from chronic illnesses for which there seems no relief, the anticipation—and sometimes even the wish—is death. Far from accepting death as an inevitable final existential event, it seems, however, that death has its own unique way of ending all suffering or tiredness; in fact, existence is suffering, because Ɔbra bɔ is not only tiring but also elusive. Indeed, all of life is suffering, because the human being is predestined to suffer and tire due to the very nature of the search for the Nkrabea, as one meanders one's way ethically in search of the one elusive Nkrabea. The way out of suffering is discovering one's Nkrabea, which leads to contentedness (*Ahontɔ*), although Ahontɔ does not necessarily mean free of the pains and hassles of life, whether personal, relational or communal. If anything, Ahontɔ leads to more awareness of social ills and vices, at least complaints increase for the simple reason that the person who has realized his or her Nkrabea through Ɔbra bɔ and achieves Ahontɔ is capable of handling and dealing with life's vicissitudes.

For the Akan, one has Ahontɔ (contentedness) precisely because one has *Atsenayae* (satisfaction, prosperous living or life). One cannot have Ahontɔ without first achieving Atsenayae because upon achieving Atsenayae (satisfactory living) society piles on an Atsenayae person much more of society problems. The danger of achieving Atsenayae, which in turn leads to Ahontɔ (contentedness), is complacency or, more precisely, forgetfulness (*Awerɛfir*). The state of Awerɛfir must not be understood as simply forgetfulness or the omission of something; rather, Awerɛfir (forgetfulness) is a state of being in which the one who has realized his or her Nkrabea and achieved Atsenayae and Ahontɔ deliberately chooses not to help or assist anyone and be bothered with people's problems. Ideally, the attainment of Atsenayae and Ahontɔ lead to *Asomdwe* (peace), although absolute peace is attained in death. However, what achieving Asomdwe means is that, while aware of internal and external problems, by the time those problems get to the person in the state of Asomdwe, the problems and issues have gone through a series of hierarchical steps, requiring only final pronouncement of approval or rejection of what has been adjudicated. In other words, one is at a state where not every petty issue gets to him or her, because Asomdwe means the absence of chaos in one's ears, literally. Contextually, suffering then is the result of misplaced or unfulfilled Nkrabea, the result of which is death. We are not speaking of death in general since everyone is subject to death; rather, we are speaking about premature deaths of those experiencing suffering and tiredness.

The term *Brɛ* (suffering or tiring) could be engendered by economic, physical, emotional, psychological, or spiritual problems that all human beings are destined to experience in their lifetime. Dynamically, suffering could be experienced in many ways—whether privately or overtly. And the only phenomenon capable of ending suffering of any kind is death. In this sense, death becomes a welcoming and liberating event, especially after a painfully prolonged illness. Indeed, there is freedom, ultimate freedom in death, not because one seeks death, but because death seeks to abrogate one's agony. How else would humanity have ended suffering when some people find themselves in perpetual state of suffering? Still, as J. H. Nketia warns, ". . . death is not regarded as a happy or welcome event."[23] But whatever activity human beings engage in from sunrise to sundown in the context of Ɔbra bɔ—though sleep seems to rejuvenate the body to enable human beings to undertake their tasks repeatedly—the lingering presence of death is a constant reminder that at some point in time death ends all suffering. Actually, suffering (or tiredness), like death, does not discriminate among existential beings, and while there may be degrees of suffering, in the final analysis all living things suffer, some sufferings leading to cessation of life in general. Still, regardless of suffering, the "good news" is that suffering, while real, is fleeting, while death is forever, Ɔdomankoma.

So, what should human beings do in light of the lingering presence of death? Should humanity lose sleep over that fact that death is all-present (*Yɛ bowu ntse mɛ yɛnda*)? There is a symbiotic relationship between sleep and death, to the extent that sleeping reminds the living about the lingering effects of death. Since all living things do sleep, it also means that all living things do die. Only spiritual beings are incapable of sleep for the simple reason that they do not die, although they rest. Even so, God could put any spiritual being to sleep, while the deities are also capable of putting any corporeal being to sleep. Death, however, is uniquely God's and the only leverage God has over God's creation, making death God's insurance against all living beings. Subsequently only God knows the exact time and manner of death for any living thing. After all, death (*owu*) is an intrinsic part of Nkrabea, which originates with God as part of the soul (*Ɔkra*), although the contents of Nkrabea belong to the person who first spoke them to God before corporeal existence. The Abosom may prolong the life of anyone they desire to the maximum, but they are incapable of preventing death, because they are—and were—not the authors of death: only God was—and is. The point, however, is that no matter what human beings experience on perpetual basis—for good or ill—existentially it never lasts forever because death, in its own unique time, manner, and place, terminates everything mundane, forever. In fact, there have been moments in human history where death has ended the sufferings of countless numbers of human beings in order for the dignities of those individuals to be preserved. Death, then, is the common denominator; so whether one is poor or rich, death, like sleep, does not discriminate.

Finally, death is extremely strong; its strength unparalleled. After all, death is everlasting (Ɔdomankoma). So, who is capable and mighty enough to fight against that which lasts forever? The might of death is contrasted with life in attempt to understand how incredibly powerfully death is when the Akan often measure the strength and power of death against life by saying: *Adze a owu dze mu no, nkwa ntum ngyina ano* (What death has a hold on, life is incapable of wrestling away). Even life does not stand a chance when death has its grip on anything corporeal; indeed, life cannot wrestle away anything from the grips of death. This goes to show that death is the premier of the two and the very reason why death is Ɔdomankoma (eternal, everlasting, forever). But why will God create death against the very life that God created?

Existentially, there are two *times* that are certain: the time that we are born and the time we die. When it is *time* for a baby to be born, nothing stands in the way of parturition. I recall a doctor telling my wife and me when her water broke at six months that the longer my wife was able to keep our twins in her womb, the chances of our twins surviving increased exponentially, but in the end the doctors had to perform a C-section to save our twins because it was *time* for them to be removed from their mother's womb. While we can generally predict when babies may be born, we are unable to predict the exact time and place, unless doctors intervene. Similarly, when the *time* comes for a person to die, it may happen just as suddenly and at a place destined by God alone. The fact is, that we do not know where and *when* one may fall dead because the *when* (time) is enigmatic to humans. The reason is that these times—when one is born and when one dies—originate with God because they are inextricably tied to Nkrabea (existential career or professional blueprint), making God both the author of life and death. Even when people predict or announce certain events based on past experiences and science, as when one may be born based on when a pregnancy occurred, sometimes people come up short, because time changes or takes turns (*Mbir dzie adandan*) for the simple reason that God's time is not the same as human time. Consequently, human beings cannot know divine time for the simple reason that humans are not the originators of divine time. However, what human beings may do to actuate divine time is to re-create divine time ritually by performing rites on the same days that they were thought to have taken place. This is because sacred time or day does not change, and by re-creating certain events, rituals or rites on those days and times, fusions are created when the sacred and the profane realms merge for ritual efficacy.

Interestingly, society readily accepts the notion that God is the giver of life but not necessarily the author of death. This is attributed to the fear of death, and the notion that death is bad and a good and benevolent God could not be responsible for death. This is a typical human reasoning, but we forget that we are not gods and goddesses, in the same way that the Abosom are not human beings. Actually, there is a curious relationship between the Nkrabea and the ultimate fate of a person with regard to the manner of a death. After all, the Nkrabea originates with God as a part of the Ɔkra (soul) and the Akan attempt to explain the mystery of death and God. The enigma is that Nyame *yɛ ɔdɔ* (God is love) and yet *Ɔdɔ yɛ wu* (love is death); moreover, Nyame *bɔɔ owu, owu na okun* (God created death, and death killed God). R. S. Rattray, the British anthropologist who carried out the most in-depth study of the Asante, the largest of the Akan groups, interpreted the last statement as, "The Creator created Death and so caused his own death." These paradoxical statements go to show the nature of God as giver (love) and taker (death) of life. Yet the tantalizing fact is that God is not subject to death because of the eternity of God as Ɔdomankoma Nyame. But the conundrum deepens in that death is also Ɔdomankoma Owu. Are the two then one and the same? There is yet another justification for the eternity of God in relation to death expressed aphoristically as: Nyame *bowu no na maewu* (When God dies, I will already be dead). What this means is that no one, absolutely none, will be around to witness the improbable demise of God who is everlasting, Ɔdomankoma, and therefore incapable of death.

For the Akan, then, death, like God himself, is a mysterious, inscrutable, and an elusive phenomenon beyond the imagination of humans. What death has a grip on, life is incapable of saving. And while people generally do not welcome death by any means—even though it is the vehicle through which one becomes an ancestor—people still question God vis-à-vis death as they console the bereaved trying to understand death and why death takes people away without mercy. What is being communicated is that, like God, death is inevitable because it is the ultimate existential eternal reality, Ɔdomankoma owu. In fact, only death shares the same title as God, Ɔdomankoma Nyame (Everlasting God).

When God created life in the corporeal, the idea was to allow life to exist like spiritual beings and live forever. After attaining a certain age and status living things would then remain at that stage forever as the Abosom. And initially life existed as such, as corporeal "gods" in the flesh. But the evil deeds of corporeal beings caused God to allow death, which was already in existence, to take its natural course and was God's way of recalling that which God had created, and hence God created death, and death killed God. That is to say, both death and life are uniquely God's—although death existed in the "beginning" with God—and so to allow death to terminate the life that God created is to say that God created death and death killed God. Therein lies the paradox. Death existed long before corporeal existence, and as long as earlier corporeal beings feared God and walked upright with God, death was held back until the very ethical nature of human existence caused death to manifest itself. Specifically, one could not remain a human and attain the same status as an Ɔbosom, because to be human is to die due to Nkrabea which has an in-built nature of one's death. The human being then was created to die, although initially death was deferred as long as necessary until hubris caused God to activate the onset of death.

To admit that *Adze a owu dze mu no, nkwa ntum ngyina ano* (What death has a hold on, life is incapable of wrestling away) is to have exhausted every conceivable means of saving a life, so that when finally death takes its course on life, then one would say that what death has a grip on, life is incapable of snatching away. Still, the manner of death may be explained in the context of an Nkrabea making Nkrabea the bearer of death, while the soul (Ɔkra), in turn, is the bearer of Nkrabea. But the statement attributing all power to death vis-à-vis life is also meant to remind humanity of its finitude, that when the moment of death arrives, living things do not stand any chance. Death, in fact, has the final say in all existential matters. Hence, Owu (death) is Ɔdomankoma (eternal, everlasting), the same term or title as God, Ɔdomankoma Nyame.

Normally just before a person dies water is offered to the dying to facilitate the eventual journey to the ancestral world, but most importantly, it is believed he or she may already be in judgment before the ancestors and so the water is to smooth the dying person's throat as he or she faces the ancestors. This is especially true for those who have been ill for quite some time. During the same time, family members ask the dying questions that they expect him or her to answers regarding where asserts, money, etc., are and who among his or her children or family may receive which property, money, clothing, etc. These dying pronouncements or confessions (*Nsaman si*) are generally respected after death.

When an illness turns grave, an elderly woman seated on a stool would brace the dying from behind in order to perform the last drink ritual. She calls her name to the dying and says to the dying person that if his or her death is due to the dying's own Nkrabea, then she wishes the dying person her sympathy. However, if the death is being caused by another person or persons, then upon his or her death, the dying person should strike the culprit dead within forty days. Normally, the death of such a person is generally regarded as good because it was expected since the dead person may have been ill for quite some time.

The death of a person marks the beginning of the second and final leg of the journey that began with God when, as a spiritual being, an Ɔbosom (God or Goddess), took leave of God to become a corporeal being—with a unique Nkrabea. This means that life has an incorporeal antecedence, existing prior to corporeal existence. So, what happens to the Nkrabea, on the one hand, and the corpse and incorporeal aspects of the now deceased human, on the other?

First, immediately upon death, preparations indicating that a corpse, or rather the Ɔsaman, is about to embark on a journey are begun by an *Ābusua* (matrikin). Existentially, there are two sureties: the day a life comes into existence, and when death terminates life. Africans believe that corporeal existence begins as a journey in the spiritual or incorporeal world, with an Nkrabea (existential career blueprint) to be accomplished in the mundane. Upon arrival, the neonate (Ɔsaman) is welcomed on the eighth day by a supportive Akan family and community, with necessities of the neonate's new environment. These gifts include introduction of the new arrival to water and liquor and money. But above all, the neonate is granted citizenship into its new environment by being offered a name on the eighth day. Some of the gifts—powder, oils, combs, beads, perfumes, sponge, etc.—find their way into a cosmetic tray (*ɛguradzie*) and used on the neonate whenever it is given a bath. All these are done to increase the survivability and well-being of a neonate, considered an Ɔsaman because it just arrived from Samanadzie. Saliently, the neonate is totally dependent on the family for its survival and nurturing. This is truly the ultimate act of faith, in believing and trusting that a totally helpless neonate would have caretakers ready to care and nurture it in an environment totally alien to it. The source of this faith, while time tested, is having prior non-corporeal knowledge about existential conditions, which assures spiritual beings of exactly what occurs existentially. That is, the Abosom know exactly what would happen to them as neonates before they undertake such huge leaps of faith. The welcoming ceremony, most of which is the responsibility of fathers—the spiritual representation of the Abosom on earth—is important if we are to understand what happens to a corpse upon death and the role of family or Ābusua and society.

Similarly, the living have the kerygmatic assurance from the ancestors via elders and traditional rulers that society would take care of them upon death. The dead too have a sending-off gift of ɛguradzie prepared for the Ābusua from which a deceased belonged by family, and in particular children—who purchase a coffin for their decedent parent—and daughters-in-law of the dead person. In the absence of children or daughters-in-law, the Ābusua (matrikin) step in to provide the ɛguradzie. An ɛguradzie (funeral cosmetics) for a deceased person is similar to that of a neonate and also markedly different from the ɛguradzie of a neonate for the simple reason that a deceased person's ɛguradzie is bigger and larger because it contains more items (adult items) than a neonate's. If a deceased person happens to have several daughters-in-law, then each daughter-in-law is required to provide her ɛguradzie in honor of her deceased father or mother-in-law. The items, like those of a neonate, would be used on the dead. Items include pieces of cloth (some of which are torn into pieces and used by the women who bathe the corpse), bottles of liquor (consumed by women who bathe and attend to the corpse), perfumes, sponges, soaps, canned meat, beads, wigs, blankets and bed sheets, towels, shaving blades, trays, buckets, etc. The items are inspected by women from the deceased's Ābusua. When my mother died, for example, my Ābusua demanded that my wife's ɛguradzie (funeral cosmetics) include an ancestral stool, because her mother-in-law (my mother) was the mother of a king (me). The point is, that an Ābusua may demand a lot of things from in-laws, especially if the in-laws are wealthy. Most of the ɛguradzie commodities end up with those who inspect the ɛguradzie and prepare the dead for burial. This is an opportunity for an Ābusua inspectors to extract as many items and money as they can from children and daughters-in-law of the deceased person, in accordance with tradition.

All these are happening when the children are at their lowest ebb emotionally and psychologically; when children are weak and vulnerable after losing their parent. These ɛguradzie inspectors perform their duty with glee and pride; in fact, as a sense of duty in honor of their deceased Ābusua member. One reason is that sometimes children neglect their parents, especially when parents reach old age, and so when a parent dies—in a society where children are supposed to be fiscally responsible for their parents—the ɛguradzie inspectors feel they owe it to their deceased kin to collect from the children (and daughters-in-law) of the deceased what the deceased should have received while still alive. Sometimes, even petulant children whose parents are alive are warned to mend their ways in order to receive favorable treatment from an Ābusua upon the death of their parents. What is fundamentally paramount is the role of the Ābusua relative to a corpse and in particular the group of women selected to oversee the ɛguradzie. A corpse belongs to the Ābusua; that is, to the mother (Ābusua) who bore her child—the dead, which is the very blood of the mother and so must be returned to the mother, the Ābusua, defined as a mother and her child or children. These children are composed of the very blood of their mother, hence they constitute an Ābusua.

The practice of an Ābusua owning a corpse is often misunderstood by foreigners who have Akan spouses and living overseas, as I am sometimes called by Ghanaians and told in my role as a traditional ruler. An Akan wife or husband may want their corpses returned to Ghana to their Ābusua upon their deaths but suddenly upon their deaths their wishes are not respected by their non-Akan spouses—sometimes their Akan spouses too. With economics dictating their decision, their non-Akan spouses suddenly do not see the sense of having to ship a dead body thousands of miles across the oceans to Ghana for burial when they could be buried in, say, the United States, for a fraction of the costs even when the dead had life insurance. I am aware of an elderly woman who is still awaiting the arrival of her son's corpse a decade or so after her son died and was buried by her son's Akan wife in the United States without her approval. The elderly woman has her son's photos all around her bed, weeping over the photos each time she enters her own bedroom. This is the power and nature of the Akan Ābusua system and an Ābusua's love for its dead (*Ābusua dɔ fuun*).

In the past where people took their responsibilities seriously, women, whose duty it is to examine an ɛguradzie (funeral cosmetics) and prepare a corpse for burial, were simply offered money to buy the commodities they needed themselves and prepare their own meals. Nowadays, with the abundance of Western commodities, the ɛguradzie ritual has taken on a life of its own. Daughters-in-law compete against one another for the biggest and largest (in terms of the number of people conveying the items) and most expensive ɛguradzie. These are paraded in trays through town. One such ɛguradzie presentation by a daughter-in-law that I observed in September 2013 even had a brass band following the young women who carried the trays. Yet I never knew the daughter-in-law as ever taking any interest in the care of her mother-in-law when she was alive. Children also make it a point to purchase the most expensive and unique (or odd-looking) coffins. In the end, children are saddled with huge amounts of funeral debts, which they spend years paying off. In consequence, there have debates in recent years concerning the relevancy of ɛguradzie, with some advocating its abolition. Some even go as far as to say that the money used for the ɛguradzie must be paid in advance to in-laws while they are still alive to enable them to appreciate what their in-laws do for them. Yet society maintains that traditions and rituals must not be trifled with, and so it does not make any sense when people suddenly call for abolition of certain cultural practices without examining the ramifications of such abolitions.

What those calling for the abolition of ɛguradzie (funeral cosmetics) rituals fail to realize is that the ɛguradzie rituals are not meant for the living and therefore could not be offered to mothers and fathers-in-law while they are still alive. These are items used on the dead, and someone must provide them, otherwise how do the living take care of the dead? A corpse must be bathed, ritually cleansed, dressed up, and put in state for viewing and so one way or another the ɛguradzie must be provided. Likewise, the ɛguradzie for babies are used in the same manner as those for the dead, because neonates are unable to take care of themselves, meaning their mothers are the ones who must use the items on their babies. Mothers bathe and oil their babies, comb their hair, and dress them with items in their cosmetic trays, the ɛguradzie. A woman in Simpa (Winneba) who claimed to have given her ɛguradzie to her mother-in-law while she was alive was still forced to provide another ɛguradzie because the Ābusua of her mother-in-law claimed not to have any knowledge of her statement of having already provided her mother-in-law's ɛguradzie (funeral cosmetics). The fact is, that—as the Ābusua rightly pointed out to the woman—an ɛguradzie is always put together and presented to the Ābusua of the deceased person who thoroughly inspect the ɛguradzie for accuracy of items requested. After all, a deceased person belongs to his or her Ābusua and therefore anything that anyone might have given to the deceased while he or she was still alive was between the deceased and the giver, and had nothing to do with the Ābusua.

How then are the items applied on the corpse? As described by Nketia:

> When the last breath is drawn, the nails of the deceased are trimmed. The body is thoroughly washed with hot water, sponge, soap and lime, and the hair is done in a way that befits the age and sex of the deceased. (The head may be shaved if the deceased is old, or if younger, plaited in the case of women and trimmed in the case of men, boys and girls.) The toilet of the deceased is never omitted under normal circumstances for two reasons: First the body must be clean so that mourners could sit round it comfortably. Second, it must be clean as the deceased sets out on the inevitable journey.[24]

As already noted, the journey that Nketia is referencing is the journey that the Ɔsaman of the deceased is expected to take to the Samanadzie forty days after the burial. What this means is that the Ɔsaman stays with its corpse until burial, enabling the Ɔsaman to own its body during future visitations to earth.

In the same way that a corpse is taken care of by an Ābusua, immediately upon birth a neonate is also received by midwives and giving a meticulously thorough bath by an experienced mother, ideally a grandmother. The goal is to remove all bodily concomitants on a neonate from the "other world," otherwise a person would emit bad odor in adulthood. Likewise, immediately upon death, a corpse is sat on a chamber pot or turned faced down to enable water and other bodily fluid to drain. Following this the joints of the deceased are massaged with black palm oil or *Nku* (shea butter) and the body preserved with plantain leaves or *Akyeampong* vines, especially in the past. Later a corpse is given a thorough bath by a group of experienced women and all "this worldly" growths and filth on the body eliminated as much as humanly possible. But first, they must shave the dead person's armpits and pubic hairs, in addition to what Nketia has already noted. A corpse must take on the appearance of a clean hairless neonate before undertaking a final journey to whence it came.

In general, bathing of corpses is done by women for both sexes although exceptions are made for the aristocracy and kings in particular.[25] Bathing takes place at night and in time for a corpse to be readied for viewing at dawn. If, for instance, a death is thought to be controversial or suspected to be cursed, then the corpse is considered a taboo. In such a case, no one from the family touches the corpse ritually until purification rites removing the curse are performed for the causative agency. The fear is that without the cleansing rituals, anyone who touches the dead body, together with one's family or even Ābusua, would also be cursed and start to die in successive order. Consequently, the Akan always enquire, spiritually, about the causality of their deaths to ascertain if a death requires cleansing. Cleared, ritual bathing ensues with the bathers (women) helping themselves to the liquor accompanying the ɛguradzie, as some of the women serve as support holding the corpse at different positions to enable others to have access to difficult places of a corpse.

Dressing and adornment of corpses depend on the station of the deceased. Even how a corpse is "laid" in bed has to do with the kind of profession the deceased had. If the dead was a member of the clerical profession, for example, the dead priest, diviner or doctor is not laid down on a bed for viewing; instead the dead clergy is seated on a stool adorned in his or her priestly regalia as though still alive. Royals are adorned in gold or golden regalia and laid in state for viewing.

A very important ritual takes place during viewing of corpses which goes to reinforce not only the belief in an afterlife, but the notion that the Ɔsaman (posthumous abstract personality) is about to undertake a journey and must sever ties with the living, as well as accept messages for ancestral relatives in the spiritual worlds. The ritual is called *Mpaemu* which means to part-company with, as in bidding farewell to or breaking off of a friendship or relationship. If the deceased belongs to a club or an association, professional body, secret or mystical organization, or even if the deceased had a strong friendship with anyone living, then representatives from the organization need to sever ties with their departed comrade, friend, colleague, etc. Sometimes, money or a handkerchief is physically "offered" to a corpse by the living friend telling the corpse that they now live in different worlds; or, a ring will be put on a finger of a corpse and told that the ring represented their parted relationship or friendship.

As for a royalty, there is a ritual performed for a deceased king or queen mother as a member of a traditional council by the paramount king or his representative. Furthermore, the ruler of the town where a royal died would have to perform his or her Mpaemu (severing of ties) ritual for the departed royalty. For example, if the deceased ruler is the queen mother of a king, then in addition to what is done by the paramount king, a local king performs the Mpaemu ritual for his queen mother or head of a royal family (Ābusua-pānyin).

Two years after the death of the queen mother of Gomoa Mprumem, Nana Apaaba III, a royal mpaemu ritual was performed for her on Saturday, September 14, 2013. Accompanied by a select group of elders and standing beside the body of Nana Apaaba as she lay in state, her king, son, and "husband" offered the following prayers and libation holding a bottle of liquor (whiskey):

Nana Adjoa Apaaba, Ɔwom Nana
Sɛ ɔbaa no dɛ, yɛnfa sika, anaa ahonya, anaa dɛ mogya mpo mpir wo nkwa a, ankyɛr wo ābusuafo nna wo amanfo bɛyɛ dodo.
Na amba no dɛm; osan dɛ ɔbra twir owu. Dɛ ma ɛnyiwa nnyim awerɛho no, dɛmara so na sɛ owu dzie adzie mu a, nkwa ntum nngyi.
Nndɛ afa nsaman kwan. Akɔhu Nananom hun ɛnyim. *Akɔ yi, kosew nsamankwan ma yɛn, na ka kasapa so ma yɛn, amaa hɛn a yɛ aka ākyir ye, yɛtum ahwɛ* ākyir *ama hum.*
Ndɛ yɛ nnhwɛhwɛ wo wɔ nyimpa mu bio—yɛ hwehwe wo wɔ abosom mu
Nana, nyi Nyame nkɔ
Nana, Apaaba nana, nyi Nyame nkɔ
Nana, Ɔwom nana, nyi Nyame nkɔ
(Nana Adjoa Apaaba, descendant of Nana Ɔwom
If it had come to a point where money, wealth, or even blood had to be used to save you, then your family and citizens would have done so readily.
But it did not happen that way; because ethical existence is unto death. For in the same way that the eyes do not know sorrow, so too is the reality that when death has its grip on anything, life is incapable of saving.
Today, you have traveled the path of the dead-alive. You have seen the faces of the ancestors. Now, block the path of death for us, and speak well of us to the ancestors, that the living may be better stewards for you.
Today, we do not search for you among human beings; rather, we seek you among deities
So Nana, Godspeed
Descendant of Apaaba, Godspeed
Descendant of Ɔwom, Godspeed.)

Then immediately upon concluding the prayers, the bottle of liquor was turned upside down in order to empty the bottle, but almost immediately an elder snatched away the bottle from the king's hand, in accordance with tradition. Ritually a bottle of liquor must not be emptied and so invariably a linguist (*Ɔkyeame*) keeps a keen eye on the liquor to make sure that some liquor remains (for him) by snatching the bottle away after some amount of liquor has been poured.

At another entrance and prior to the departure of the royals from the hall where the queen mother was lying in state, a purification rite was performed when a sheep was slaughtered and its blood poured on the feet of the royals beginning with the king. Kings and queen mothers are prohibited from going near corpses or anything unclean in order that they may maintain their purity or sacredness at all times. But the fact is, that they do approach the corpses of their dead colleagues in order to perform rites like an mpaemu (severing of ties), and when they do, they undergo blood purification immediately. The lack of blood purification defiles royals and anyone accompanying them; therefore, any royalty and members of the traditional clergy who go near dead bodies must undergo blood purification immediately.

The Akan fear anything associated with the dead, and one of the items that evokes fear is the coffin. It is not so much the coffin itself that evokes fear, as people actually appreciate the estheticism of coffins, rather an empathy is developed with corpses as they are put in coffins. Sealed coffins are thought to be hot (*Adaka mu yɛ hyiw*) and so mourners sympathetically imagine themselves in coffins feeling hot too, especially at the point where a corpse is just about to be put in a coffin. This is where the insane reverence[26] of family members is at the highest. Having observed several people faint, I am not sure if they faint as a result of being overcome by the sight of seeing their loved ones for the last time, or the fact that corpses are put in coffins. Either way, it does not matter, because death is the ultimate existential loss, hence it is forever.

Physically, corpses are buried at an *Ɛsiāye* (cemetery). However, the name Ɛsiāye is very revealing of how the Akan view their burial sites and posthumous beliefs. The Akan view the Ɛsiāye as a complete world unto itself, reflecting their fears and perceptions of the world of the dead. The Ɛsiāye (cemetery) is the first world that the dead go and reside permanently until such time as the "body" is needed again by its owner. And unlike, say, the United States, where cemeteries are well kept, visited periodically, and mostly found in cities and towns, an Akan Ɛsiāye is usually a forest, thicket, and a place which evokes fear as well as awe. For this reason the living are not supposed to enter an Ɛsiāye world until and when a dead person is to be buried. And in the same way that a corpse does not reside among the living, at an Ɛsiāye a living person must not enter or visit the physical world of the dead until a dead body must be disposed of. The reason for this is explained in the name Ɛsiāye itself, which means "a place where something is hidden." But the question is: For whom is a corpse being hidden or kept and for how long?

Albeit a physical place, an Ɛsiāye (cemetery) serves as the entrance to an otherwise spiritual abode of the dead. The Ɛsiāye therefore is where the physical and spiritual bodies of what was a living person converge, because the Akan are firm in their belief in a physical being—*Onyimpa*—and a spiritual being—Ɔsaman. As the holding place of a corpse, an Ɛsiãye is where an Ɔsaman visits in order for it to put on, quite literally, its physical body in order for it to enter the realm of the living. What this suggests is that a corpse is kept at an Ɛsiãye for the owner of the "body" that died until such time as it is needed again by its owner, the Ɔsaman. For this reason, when elders invoke the ancestors, they offer prayers and libations focusing on the ground where droplets of liquor are poured, because the dead are buried in the ground. Subsequently, the ancestors emerge from their graves, after putting on their earthly apparels and visit with their earthly counterparts to discuss matters affecting their descendants. The elders are absolutely convinced that whenever they converge to deliberate and adjudicate on matters affecting their peoples, the ancestors are always there not only to attest to the veracity of their deliberations, but to offer them the mandate they need as custodians of the traditions that the ancestors bequeathed to them. Clearly, there is an absolute belief in the resurrection of spiritual personalities, the Nsamanfo, who are the same as the persons who died except in abstract forms.

In terms of the duration of a corpse at an Ɛsiãye (cemetery), it is forever. After all, this is about death and death is an eternal, timeless phenomenon. Where a corpse is finally laid to rest is where the Ɔsaman (or posthumous spiritual or abstract person) would visit first upon invocation. Therefore, it does not matter how many times a corpse is moved: the spiritual personality would always follow for the simple reason that the corpse (body) belongs to it. If, for instance, a death was violent and sudden, and occurred especially away from home in what the Akan called *Ɔtɔfo*,[27] then the Ɔsaman stayed with the corpse until claimed for burial, although the Ɔsaman would make periodic visits to the original spot where the person died. It does not, however, mean that the Ɔsaman always stays with its corpse, but it always "puts" on its "physical body" before entering the world of living beings, attired in clothes that it used to wear in order to make itself recognizable to living beings.

THE SAMANADZIE

The Samanadzie is the ultimate destination of the Ɔsaman, after the Ɔsaman ascends a ladder, as already discussed. Indeed, the Samanadzie is a specially created world for a unique life-form called Ɔsaman, formed as a result of collaboration between God and the Abosom. Thus an Ɔsaman is an imprint of the original Ɔbosom which became a human. With regard to the ultimate world of an Ɔsaman, the Samanadzie, it is designed only for those who suffer physical death but are spiritually resurrected by God to occupy a world that is different from the corporeal but similar to the world of the Abosom in that existence there is eternal. Furthermore, because the Samanadzie is solely for posthumous abstract personalities, the Nsamanfo, it follows that the Abosom are incapable of entering the Samanadzie because they do not suffer death. Existentially then, the belief in the Samanadzie also makes it a religious, philosophical, and a teleological concept because it is the spiritual destination of every Akan, whether one believes in it or not. More than a teleological destination, it is the ultimate abode of every living thing, making the belief in the Samanadzie a soteriological destination in that every Akan ends up there, in the vastness of the universe.

The reason why the Samanadzie is a world specially created for the Nsamanfo is supported by the claim that the residents of the Samanadzie are only interested in augmenting their numbers (*Nsamanfo pɛ hɔndodoo*). It strongly suggests that there is a divine plan for the universe, to populate the entire universe, seen and unseen. Furthermore, there is a sense, indeed a strongly held belief, that the original population of the Samanadzie was small and therefore the need to create more of their kind. Obviously there is strength in numbers. Nowadays, there is the sense that God, according to the Abosom, has stopped creating new life-forms, as there are too many Nsamanfo of every kind at the Samanadzie already. Those being born nowadays are actually those who have been born before but did not achieve their Nkrabea the first or second times around and need to return to accomplish their Nkrabea. In other words, corporeal beings are now being recycled or, put it spiritual terms, reincarnated. If the singular goal of the Nsamanfo is to augment their kind, then, as Bob Marley, the reggae superstar and legend from Jamaica sang so perfectly, there is "One Love" at the Samanadzie. Meaning, there is no divisiveness of any kind, no fighting or wars of supremacy, no hatred of one another at the Samanadzie; rather, there is cohesiveness of purpose, and an objective and collective sense of affirmation and solidarity.

And finally, the notion that the Nsamanfo are only interested in the augmentation of their kind, lends credence to a journey motif, which points to a destination other than the corporeal world for all living things (*Onyimpa wɔ bɛbe kɔ*). The human being is pre-potentiated, destined to travel, to be an adventurer, not to stay at one place in this world, but to move on to somewhere else, the Samanadzie. In itself, it is an ethical conundrum (Ɔbra bɔ), of not knowing exactly where the journey would take an individual, although physically the journey ends in death, while teleologically Samanadzie is the ultimate destination. Thus across Africa and the African Diaspora, there is a deeply held notion of a journey: an intrinsic desire to travel or fly to another place, a spiritual world, a world that is different from the mundane because there is no suffering of any kind, which, as we have seen, is attained only through death. In this context, the human being is destined an adventurer, undertaking journeys to places and exploring new opportunities ethically until one reaches the Samanadzie, ultimately.

The Samanadzie, then, is a definite ideal world upon which the corporeal world is modeled. This being the case, was the Samanadzie in existence prior to the creation of the corporeal world? Secondly, was the Samanadzie void of any kind of existence and hence the need to create Nsamanfo? And thirdly, how could the corporeal world be modeled after a Samanadzie world that was empty of non-beings—assuming it was indeed void of existence of every kind?

What is known about the Samanadzie could not have been known without prior knowledge of some sort of life at the Samanadzie. There was definitely some form of spiritual existence at the Samanadzie but certainly not composed of the Nsamanfo that now exist there. Obviously the life-form that existed at the Samanadzie was not ideal, prompting a new kind of existence in the form of the Nsamanfo, as created by God (and the Abosom). By ideal, I mean pre-corporeal existence where life could not be lived to its fullest extent and hence the need to create more life-forms on earth capable of undertaking Ɔbra bɔ and achieving Nkrabea before sending them to the Samanadzie. This explains the retention of some memory of how life was at the Samanadzie and the fear of returning to the Samanadzie by the Akan (*Samanadzie wɔnnkɔ*). To realize one's Nkrabea is to accomplish one's full potential and live to be old as a corporeal being. This realization is essential if human beings are to live as the Abosom that they were.

There are two very important statements supporting life-forms and conditions in the Samanadzie which only could have been known by prior inhabitants or creators of that environment who entered corporeal existence—the Abosom. The first is that *Samanadzie yɛ sum* (the Samanadzie is dark). The darkness may be attributed to the fact that the Samanadzie is located far from the sun, or at a location shielded from the influence of the sun; or, the kind of darkness Samanadzie has is such that the sun has no effect on it. Darkness, in fact, is the first son of God.[28] Darkness only refers to originality; God first created darkness because God himself dwells in darkness and hence the illusiveness and enigmatic nature of God. It further explains the relationship between darkness and sleep, on the one hand, and between sleep and death, on the other. So, the Samanadzie, in a way, is a return to originality, to God.

Secondly, if the Samanadzie is dark and synonymous with a return to originality, darkness, then why are people fearful of the Samanadzie? The Akan have a genuine fear of darkness probably because darkness on earth is associated with wickedness.[29] Another reason is that human beings are blinded by the sunlight, to the extent that human beings are incapable of seeing in the dark and therefore our fear of the dark. Since we are incapable of seeing in the dark we are afraid of darkness because of what might be hidden in the dark. One does not go to dark places because of what might happen to such an individual, and since the Samanadzie is said to be dark, it follows that darkness is synonymous with the Samanadzie and in consequence makes the Samanadzie a dreaded place, which humans must do everything humanly possible to avoid (*Samanadzie wɔnnkɔ*). Obviously then the Samanadzie is not an ideal place to visit by an agency who originated in Samanadzie as a dark place. However, an Ɔsaman is a unique being perfectly fitted for the Samanadzie, something that the pre-Ɔsaman would not be aware of since it had not entered the Samanadzie as an Ɔsaman. The reality is that no one has ever returned from the Samanadzie as a physical being to inform the living about conditions there. In the end, the fear of darkness and the Samanadzie have less to do with the avoidance of death and Samanadzie and everything to do with the love for living in the temporal. After all, life on earth—with all its relational bonding and attachments—is all that is known, realistically, as no human has directly experienced a futuristic Samanadzie. Ultimately, alleged fear of Samanadzie has less to do with darkness than the fear of the unknown and anxieties of leaving loved ones behind. The good news, or rather the assurance after death, is that the Nsamanfo (posthumous, abstract personalities) and spiritual agencies, as beings of light, do not need the sun's light to enable them to see because they have transcended corporeality; meaning, they do not live under the sun anymore and therefore are not subject to the blinding and other effects of the sun. Subsequently, the Akan refer to corporeality as the *Wiadzie* (under the sun). In the dream world, for instance, we observe ourselves as normal beings engaging others in a "world" that is similar to, if not the same as, our physical world but without the sun's light. The point is that this happens when we are asleep, with our eyes closed—in darkness. So, death is to live beyond the sun as a spiritual agency of light and hence the Samanadzie. Yes, the Samanadzie is dark, but it is only dark to those blinded by the sun living under the sun.

Like the gateway to the corporeal world that has only one entrance through a woman's birth canal, the Samanadzie too has only a single gateway to it through a male. And like parturition, entrance to the Samanadzie is guarded by a ferryman whose duty is to regulate entrants to and from the Samanadzie. Furthermore, just as parturition is first facilitated by the breaking of an expectant mother's water, a river also runs between the temporal and Samanadzie worlds, crossed with the aid of a ferryman, after which a ladder is climbed, then a hill[30] (although Rattray thinks it is the Ɔkra [soul] that does the climbing) into the Samanadzie. In other words, entry into the Samanadzie is exactly the reverse of gestation and parturition to the corporeal world, the Wiadzie.

The evidence for the two worlds and symbolism of a ladder and gateways are borne out by the Akan creation story, which in the beginning speaks of two worlds coexisting harmoniously although punctuated by periodic bumping of the worlds due to their close proximity. The resultant separation of the worlds and humanity's attempt to build a tower of mortars (ladder) to link the two worlds again represent the ladder that is climbed to the other world and the restoration of paradise. Clearly, for the Akan, earth (Asasi) was—and is—female and emblematic of the Old Woman and her children who first occupied it. As for the moon (Ɔsrɛn), it was—and is—regarded as male and progenitor of humanity and worshipped as the emblem of God. Thus the moon is the Nana, symbolically, while God is the ultimate spiritual Nana. But if there is any more evidence of the symbolisms of the two worlds, then the human body is proof.

There is yet another world associated with the dead. As we will see in chapter 3, the human being is composed of many agencies, including a shadow, image, or double called the *Sunsum* (pronounced *soon-soom*). Although human beings recognize their shadows as mimicking everything that they do, meaning shadows are an integral part of the personality, the shadow's true nature and identity is revealed as none other than ourselves during dreams when we see ourselves engaged in activities with other shadows (Āsunsum). Upon death, however, the Sunsum separates from the Ɔsaman creating two identical but separate spiritual personalities. The Ɔsaman being the same individual who lived as a human being except that it no longer needs the Sunsum to make it viably active now that it has achieved spiritual status, an abstract body. No longer needing the Sunsum, the original Ɔbosom, the Ɔsaman departs the temporal world to join other Nsamanfo at a world created uniquely for them, the Samanadzie. The Sunsum too, having accomplished its mission of making a human being viably active in a corporeal milieu, returns to the phylogenetic world of Abosom to await another possible reincarnation (*Bɛbra*).

NOTES

1. See Ephirim-Donkor, Anthony. *African Personality and Spirituality: The Akanfo Quest for Perfection and Immortality*. (Ann Arbor, Michigan: UMI Dissertation Services, 1994).

2. The Akan are bound together by a common cultural heritage, belief in a monotheistic God (Nana Nyame), and speak related languages. Under the umbrella name Akan are the Asante, the Fante, the Akuapim, the Akyem, the Akwamu, the Khwahu, the Nzema, the Ahanta, the Wassa, the Bono, and the Safwi, as the major groups.

3. Danquah, J. B. *The Akan Doctrine of God* (London: Frank Cass & Co., Ltd., 1968), p. 162.

4. Erik Erikson uses "generativity" to mean procreativity, productivity, and creativity to describe the "maturity" stage of his psychosocial stages of the life cycle. Erikson's use of generativity best captures the functionality of the *bɔ* accompaniment of *Ɔbra*. For details, please see Erikson, Erik. *A way of Looking at Things: Selected Papers from 1930–1980*. Ed. Stephen Schlein (New York: W. W. Norton & Company, 1987), p. 607.

5. Rattray, R. S. *Religion & Art in Ashanti*. (Oxford: At The Clarendon Press, 1927), p. 152.

6. Gbadegesin, Segun. "Eniyan: The Yoruba concept of a person." In P. H. Coetzee and A. P. J. Roux, eds., *The African Philosophy Reader, second edition* (New York: Routledge: Taylor &Francis Group, 2003), p. 179.

7. Ibid.

8. I first presented a paper on this study to the African Health Consultation of the General Board of Global Ministries (United Methodist Church) at the Carter Center on February 8, 1996. Again in the same year and as an advisor to the Emory University Task Force on Health Development for Africa, an Emory University and World Health Organization Collaborative Initiative, I presented a paper on the same issue. The goal of the presentations—in my role as both a scholar and traditional ruler in Ghana—was to offer an African traditional hermeneutic to African well-being within the context of a holistic healthcare system. The study, which originally formed a part of my doctoral research, focused on the Guan-speaking people of Simpa (Winneba), the Āwutu-ābe (Effutu), and the Fante (Akan) community of Gomoa Mprumem, in Ghana.

9. Ephirim-Donkor, Anthony. *African Spirituality: On Becoming Ancestors*. (Trenton, NJ: Africa World Press, 1997), pp. 51–52.

10. Ibid. pp. 58–59.

11. For a complete discussion of clerical vocation, see Ephirim-Donkor, Anthony. "Akom: The Ultimate Mediumship Experience Among the Akan," *Journal of the American Academy of Religion* 76, 1, 2008.

12. Ephirim-Donkor, Anthony. *African Personality and Spirituality: the Akanfo Quest for Perfection and Immortality*. (Ann Arbor, Michigan: U.M.I Dissertation Services, 1994).

13. Ellis, A. B. *The Tshi-speaking Peoples of the Gold Coast of West Africa: their religion, manners, customs, laws, language, etc.* (Anthropological Publications, Oosterhout N.B.: The Netherlands, [1887] 1970), p. 24.

14. Rattray's footnote in *Religion and Art in Ashanti*, (Oxford, Oxford University Press, 1927), p. 321.

15. Ibid. p. 108.

16. See Baines, John. 1991. "Society, Morality, and Religious Practice." In *Religion in Ancient Egypt: Gods, Myths, and Personal Practice*. (Ed. by Byron E. Shafer. Ithaca: Cornell University Press), pp. 123–203.

17. Ibid, p. 124.

18. For an in-depth discussion of the concept of *Thereness*, see Ephirim-Donkor, Anthony. *African Religion Defined, a Systematic Study of ancestor Worship among*

the Akan, Second Edition, (Lanham, MD: University Press of America, 2013), pp. 4–21.

19. Ephirim-Donkor, Anthony. *African Spirituality: On Becoming Ancestors.* (Trenton, NJ.: Africa World Press, Inc. 1997), p. 32.

20. For detailed discussion of the ancestors' stool and its creation, see Ephirim-Donkor, Anthony. *African Religion Defined, a Systematic Study of ancestor Worship among the Akan, Second Edition,* (Lanham, MD: University Press of America, 2013), pp. 169–192.

21. Ephirim-Donkor, Anthony. *African Spirituality: On Becoming Ancestors, Revised Edition.* (Lanham, MD: University Press of America, 2011), pp. 16–17.

22. Rattray, R. S. Capt. *Akan-Ashanti Folk-Tales.* (Oxford: At The Clarendon Press, 1930), p. 73.

23. Nketia, J. H. *Funeral Dirges of the Akan People.* (Achimota, 1955), p. 6.

24. Ibid. p. 7.

25. It is clear from Rattray that for Ashanti royalty, as well as Akan royalty in general, their corpses are handled by special men. For more, please read Rattray's *Religion and Art in Ashanti*, (Oxford, Oxford University Press, 1927), pp. 103–121.

26. Ephirim-Donkor, Anthony. *African Spirituality: On Becoming Ancestors, Revised Edition.* (Lanham, MD: University Press of America, 2011), pp. 146–156.

27. For more discussion on this phenomenon, please see Ephirim-Donkor, Anthony. *African Spirituality: On Becoming Ancestors, Revised Edition.* (Lanham, MD: University Press of America, 2011), pp. 157–158.

28. Rattray, op. cit. pp. 73–75.

29. Ibid.

30. Ibid. p. 154.

Chapter Two

The Nature of the Spirit

A student interested in African religion walked into the department of Africana Studies one day and asked if she could sign up to do an independent study. When asked to identify the area that she was interested in pursuing, her response was that she would like to explore the notion of African spirituality and holistic health. Directed to me, I explained to her that "African spirituality" was too broad an area to be pursued. Subsequently, she narrowed her focus on healing,[1] although her interest later expanded to include herbal treatment and holistic health.[2]

When it comes to health concerns, the role of the spiritual as a causative agency seems to have a firm grip on the Ghanaian psyche. Many families, including mine, have lost relatives due to pronouncements by spiritual healers that illnesses were spiritual in origin and would therefore not require hospital care, which some families viewed as Western and therefore incapable of offering spiritual healing.[3] Unfortunately, the lack of hospital care has resulted in unnecessary deaths. The nonsensical nature of some of the deaths, including of a sister of mine, caused me to research the phenomenon; that is, the notion that the spiritual is the source of most, if not all, illnesses. Like the student who wanted to pursue an independent study on healing, I also wanted to know why belief in spirits and the notion that spirits must be consulted in everything that Africans do persist. How was it possible that belief in spirits affected human behavior wholly? What discussants repeatedly stressed during meetings with elders in the 1980s and early 1990s was the fact that spiritual agencies influence human affairs at every turn, that spirits are everywhere making them aware of all human actions. In light of that, my focus shifted singularly to the spiritual, because if one can identify a source of an ailment as spiritual then perhaps one can explain why people do the things that they do. Similarly, the focus of this chapter is on the nature and essence of spirits and how spirits exercise such profound effect on the psyche of people, the Akan, to cause people to do their will.

The fact is that in Africa all speculations begin with the spiritual, and so I begin this study with the spiritual as well. The Akan word for spirit is *Sunsum* (pronounced *soon-soom*); meaning, a shadow, image or double. It also includes anything intangible or unseen. However, the fact that something is not seen does not mean that it does not exist, because the Akan believe that spirits exist in some form or kind and have independent existence, making them spirits. In the dream world, for example, Rattray asserts that the Sunsum leaves the body, while the Ɔkra (soul) does not.[4] Therefore the Sunsum is seen as self, image or double. Moreover, spirits influence human activity and nature. In this context, a shadow is Sunsum because, while it is observable as a shade in the form of a physical object, it is beyond the control of a tangible object. So, a Sunsum (spirit) is a phenomenon that is "seen" as a shadow and also in dreams, yet unseen as independent, non-human agency of some sort. Rattray goes on to explain the Sunsum as: ". . . a man's sunsum that may wander about in sleep. 'It may encounter other sunsum and get knocked about, when you feel unwell, or killed, when you will sicken and die.' Perhaps the sunsum is the more volatile part of the whole 'kra." The specific role of the Sunsum relative to a person is that the "sunsum is what protects you."[5] Akan scholars like Danquah, Gyekye, and Konadu, etc., have generally followed Rattray in defining Sunsum as spirit.

From the realm of dreams, the Sunsum is thought to be an active agent capable of influencing objectivity having an independent existence. Thus the corporeal and incorporeal domains are full of Āsunsum (plural of Sunsum) of all kinds and influences. This chapter, however, is about the nature of the most powerful of these innumerable Āsunsum (spirits) traversing and influencing the known and unknown universes, the Abosom (Gods and Goddesses). Of all the spirits, the single most supremely powerful, incomparable Sunsum of all Āsunsum is God, whom the Akan call Nyame (Nana Nyame). Nana Nyame (God) is not an Ɔbosom, however. And so by spirit, the Akan refer specifically to the Abosom as the primeval offspring of God and administrators of the known and unknown worlds at the behest of God.[6] The terms "*Bossum*" and "*Fetiche*" were used interchangeably by William Bosman in the early 1700s when he studied the peoples of West Africa to mean idols or objects worshipped by the Akan. He goes on to write that "they have such Multitudes of Images of their Idol-Gods, which they take to be subordinate Deities to the Supreme God, without considering what sort of Trifles they are, and only believe there are Mediators betwixt God and Men, which they take to be their Idols."[7] Clearly, Bosman is confused, as he could not make sense of how an image or "Bossum" could serve as a mediator between God and human beings. Fixated on a physical object, Bosman failed to realize that among Africans, the so-called idols are only objects of manifestation for some Abosom, who are spiritual agencies. So while Bosman could not conceptualize anything but a physical object, the Africans that he encountered were focused on otherworldly spiritual beings. As such, when an Ɔbosom is invoked, for instance, the object, idol or "fetiche" is where an Ɔbosom comes to reside. Thus, the idols only serve as symbols of hierophany for the Abosom and not objects of worship in themselves. As such, every Ɔbosom that is worshipped among the Akan, for example, has its own symbol or stool[8] propitiated during festivities honoring the ancestors and Abosom.

On Monday, June 24, 2013, a *New York Times* reporter contacted me about an article that he was writing about Nana Kwaku Bonsam, a famous Ghanaian tradition priest, saying: "I'm writing a story for the *NY Times* about a fetish priest in Ghana who is currently living in the Bronx, and I thought you might know him and/or have some insight into what he represents to Ghanaians. If so I'd love to hear from you if you're available."[9] We went on to exchange email messages, one of which was about his use of the term *fetish*. In one of the exchanges, I wrote the following to him: "Thanks for your note. I might know the traditional priest that you are profiling, but remember that there are hundreds of traditional priests in Ghana. Also, I would suggest, strongly, that you desist from using the term 'fetish,' as it perpetuates the colonialist-missionary condescension of genuinely, ancient Ghanaian-African clerical order." In yet another email to him, the response was: "What I also know of him is what I have read in newspapers. However, if you have questions about the *akɔm* or mediumistic tradition and wish to seek my input, then please do not hesitate to let me know. About the term 'fetish,' I do not use it in my writings because I, in my own small way, am trying to rid Ghana and Africa of the negative and inferior connotations associated with such terms."

Unfortunately, African journalists are still unable to free themselves from the "mental slavery" associated with colonialism, unaware of the psychological reinforcement of colonial ideas dismissive of ancient African institutions like *akɔm* and the *akɔmfo* (divination and diviners) in general. For example, Western-trained clergy like myself have usurped (or hijacked) the ancient clerical term for an Akan priest, *Ɔsɔfo,* so that nowadays Western-trained clerics are *Asɔfo* (priests), while the more ancient colleagues like Nana Bonsam have become a *fetish priest* when the term *Ɔsɔfo/Sɔfo* was reserved for Akan priests and some members of the *Akɔmfo* long before Europeans came to Africa, as Ellis, for example, noted.[10] In order to distinguish between the two groups of clerics, the least scholars can do is to refer to our ancient priests as "traditional" to differentiate them from Western-trained Ghanaian clerics.

To continue to use the same condescending and demeaning term, *fetish*, is simply borne out of ignorance.

The private emails are meant to stress the need for African intellectuals, academics, and, especially, journalists to serve as corrective agents to all misappropriated African socio-cultural and religious terms by Europeans like Bosman rather than simply regurgitate colonially demeaning references bequeathed to Africans by European colonizers. To his credit, the author of the article about Nana Kwaku Bonsam in general used "traditional priest" in his *New York Times* piece. However, a radio presenter he interviewed in Ghana used "fetish priest" instead, typical of those still trapped in intellectual colonialization.

Indeed, my obsession with the Abosom goes back to my youth for reasons that are innate and hard to explain, not that the Abosom are symbols or idols to be admired but extrinsic spirits. Even so, one must be scared of them. Thank God the Abosom know the limitations of mere humans and so do not take some probing questions of them seriously during divinations. Occasionally during divinations, experience teaches that when the Abosom refuse to answer curious questions, then that is a signal that one has gone go too far. When that happens, the prudent thing to do is quickly apologize, although it makes one feel guilty and sick to the stomach, prompting a researcher to question oneself as to why a particular question may have been asked. But epistemologically, there is always the need to ask certain follow-up questions because a question or an issue, for example, may have been nagging a researcher for a while.

My obsession with spirits in general and the basis of my curiosity formed quite early in childhood, when certain "images and sights" appeared normal, I thought. But soon there was the realization that what appeared normal was actually "abnormal" in the eyes of adults, some of whom accused me of being a witch or strange. For those accused of being strange, the next logical step for them is keeping "things" to themselves, not saying anything or even lying when asked about certain events. Even during adulthood, my anxiety has been when those events still come true; as such, I have been praised as well as admonished by spiritual adepts for telling them what I had "seen" in my naïveté or during moments of levity because I was not supposed to have seen the same "things" that, for example, a diviner sees in her divining pot containing sacred water. One diviner even accused me of being strange when I told her about the number of spiritual agencies appearing in her divination water, not thinking that it was a big deal. Again, I learned to be silent.

The Abosom avail themselves to traditional rulers (kings and queen mothers) because they represent the Abosom and the ancestors (Nananom Nsamanfo) on earth as living ancestors. This relation between traditional rulers and the Abosom and ancestors is sometimes taken for granted by traditional rulers, or they become oblivious of the overwhelmingly powerful and infinite beings that they commune with them. But those who are not remiss in their duties and responsibility to the spiritual forces and activity seek the Abosom are rewarded with the presence and graciousness of the Abosom who reveal themselves to their earthly representatives. For one thing, the Abosom accord traditional rulers the opportunity to interact with them in ways that are profoundly rewarding. One of my surprises came during my first divination rite as king when two Abosom arrived and wondered why it has taken such a long time for me to seek them. While the enquiry confirmed what I already knew insightfully, their presence and enquiry surprised me and made me aware of the sense of expectation. Taking things for granted sometimes, I was now expected to seek after them, or should have sought their "face" earlier. Perhaps in appreciation of the encounter, the Abosom told me to express my gratitude to the "person" who led me to them.

The reference to Abosom (primeval gods and goddesses) or even the Nananom Nsamanfo (Ancestors) in the plural—rather than singular—is because they exist in collective groups (*Abosom Kuu*). As such, they communicate in unison via their leader or head of an Abosom Kuu (collective Gods and Goddesses). Even so, every *Ɔbosom* (singular of Abosom) is fiercely independent of all others as well as unique. Every single one of them is capable of convening a meeting of the Kuu (group) to discuss matters affecting their corporeal subjects or matters affecting them spiritually. Like human communities, the Abosom too are composed of colonies, communities or groups with their own leaders. They are always looking to augment their numbers and therefore welcome new friendships and members. During divinations, for instance, a leading Ɔbosom is usually the first to respond, especially if it pertains to an ancestors' stool and if the seeker is a king or queen mother. The reason is that a leading Ɔbosom is the protector and keeper of the soul of an ancestors' stool of a community, and so it responds to ascertain why an ancestors' stool is being sought. To speak to the leading Ɔbosom is to speak to all of the Abosom because upon returning to its realm, the leading Ɔbosom usually convenes a meeting to discuss what transpired. As for ordinary seekers, it is always the Ɔbosom of a particular diviner who comes through for consultations, unless a seeker has a relationship with another Ɔbosom requiring the Ɔbosom to make an appearance, in addition to the original Ɔbosom of a diviner. That is, a diviner's Ɔbosom would depart from the diviner to seek out the Ɔbosom being called for consultations. Chances are that the Ɔbosom being sought may be around during the divination and responds momentarily.

Like God, the Abosom are spirits, spirits of God; they are unseen primeval forces of incredibly immense might, power, and intelligence, with the capability of materialization and transformation into anything they desire. As gods and goddesses, the Abosom are of the same essence as God, although God is the ultimate combined spirit of all the Abosom, and so to speak of the Abosom is to speak of God because the Abosom are on earth at God's behest. God, however, is not considered an Ɔbosom because he is the creator of all things. As Bosman correctly observed among the peoples of the Gold Coast about God vis-à-vis the Abosom, he writes "that they never make any offering to God, nor call upon him in time of need; but in all their difficulties, they apply themselves to their *fetiche* . . . and pray to him for success in their undertaking."[11]

Traditionally, God has never been worshipped directly by Africans, nor has God had any temples or priests.[12] In the same way that Bosman was told that God is invisible, meaning spirit, and therefore no image—imagined or otherwise—could be made to represent God, the Abosom are worshipped because they are endowed with materialization capabilities to cause human beings to "see" and worship them directly at the behest of God. This does not mean that Africans do not believe in or worship God; on the contrary, Bosman emphatically stated that "almost all the Coast *Negroes* believe in one true God, to whom they attribute the Creation of the World and all things in it." Nowadays the name of God is on the lips of people constantly, although when it comes to religious praxis, people still turn to the Abosom both overtly and covertly for fear of being called hypocrites because many people are now Muslim or Christian.

Another reason why the Abosom are worshipped directly is that the Abosom are capable of materializing before human beings who could therefore make images or icons of them. These images are what non-Africans misconstrue as idols or so-called fetiche. What non-Africans fail to understand is that the so-called idols are symbols—like those of other religions—of hierophany for the Abosom during invocations; that is, they act as a location where the Abosom reside when invoked. So it is not the icons or fetishes that are worshipped but the spirits thought to reside in them during moments of high rituals. Actually, according to E. Bolaji Idowu, the word *fetish* was first used by the Portuguese to mean "charms and sacred emblems of West Africa" and was therefore applied generally "to describe the religion of West Africa."[13] The danger, Idowu warns, is taking "appearance for reality without adequate verification," because European explorers, missionaries, and adventurers like Bosman were going round describing West Africa and "the whole of Africa as a place governed by 'insensible fetish'"[14] without understanding the spiritual hermeneutics from which African worshippers operated.

On the contrary, God does not have any image or icon because God is only one—unlike the Abosom—and he does not reside in the corporeal as the Abosom do for an image or fetish of him to be made. R. S. Rattray, for example, has defined an Akan *Adinkra* symbol for God as "Except God," although the more precise definition is God Alone or Only God to best describe God as the One and Only God. All these mean that God cannot be compared, let alone materialized, for anyone, ever. Meaning, God cannot be divined. This is different from the multitudes and individuality of the Abosom, some of whom reside in the corporeal Wiadzie at the behest of God.

The Abosom arrived on earth in different stages. The first wave of Abosom was sent to the corporeal world by God to govern it, while the second group of Abosom joined their siblings later on earth after they were expelled by God for repeatedly challenging God. When the second wave of Abosom arrived they found a well-governed earth covered entirely with forest, with animals and creatures but no humans. The earth that the Abosom governed was—and is—the outer of inner spiritual worlds. The solid earth is the shell of inner worlds that are not seen or known to humans and are apart from the realm of the Abosom which the earth reflects. The Abosom world has everything existing on earth and more. For example, they do not drink the same water that exists on earth; instead, their water is delivered to them in packages or containers, as pure and pristine a water as one can imagine. Similarly, some Abosom returned to their original abodes after finding corporeal living unsustainable. This is to say that the Abosom travel back and forth between the corporeal and their spiritual original abodes freely.

The reference to spirit or spirits here must be understood collectively as referring to the primeval Abosom, and by extension God because God works through the Abosom. The Abosom are not apotheosized agencies like the Nananom Nsamanfo (Ancestors) or even the *Orisas* of the Yoruba people. Rather, they are creatures of some sort and therefore the fascination of this study. Particularly, it is the essence and nature of the Abosom—and with their own help—that this study tries to gain some understanding. While human beings have features and appearance of the Abosom, the Abosom stress, however, that they are not human beings by any means. If they were, then no human being would be alive today due to humanity's evil deeds, because they abhor evil and injustice. And despite the horrific deeds of humanity which may call for expedited judgment from the point of view of humans, they still are slow to anger and are in no hurry to render judgment.

The Abosom come in all kinds of shapes, heights, colors, sizes, and forms. For example, the goddess Birim, the middle sister of the gods Kɔbena Ayɛnsu and Yaw Dɛnsu, is shaped exactly like the female of the human species, except that she is made entirely of diamonds. As evidence, diamonds are plentiful in the Birim River. On the contrary, her younger brother, Dɛnsu, is wholly different from her, with three heads: one looking forward, the second backwards, and the third, upwards, enabling him to be all-seeing. Their older brother, Ayɛnsu, has never revealed himself, and attempts to photograph him has only yielded a finger of his, although he has a bindi dot on his forehead and some gray in his hair, which he revealed during a divination rite. Yet another deity in the Ivory Coast by the name of Booboo has what may be called human features except that he has a very small head in proportion to his "body," a huge stomach, and ten arms—five on each side of his "body." In the 1880s, Ellis also described an Ɔbosom (deity) that he called "Bobowisi" (blower of smoke or fog) in Simpa (Winneba): "The god himself is described as being about twelve feet in height, black in colour, of human shape, and with hair like that of a mulatto. He is always depicted as bearing a native sword . . . in his right hand, while the left arm is folded behind his back."[15] So, if the Abosom are not human beings, with material substances—although human beings clearly take after some of them, physically—then what are they?

As already stated, the Akan refer to anything immaterial, unseen with the naked eyes, or even observable but elusive because it is without substance, as a shadow or spirit (*Sunsum*). Most importantly, the Sunsum (spirit) is understood to be a living agency of some sort capable of having a reflection or an image. Thus Sunsum means a shadow, double of anything physical or even ethereal, spirit or that which is invisible, an image of a tangible object, and a reflection of an elusively tantalizing agency. So a human being, for instance, though not a Sunsum because he or she is a physical being, has a Sunsum nonetheless, which becomes visible under a light. The resultant apparition is exactly as that which is revealed, a person, although the angle and degree of light may reflect disproportionally on a Sunsum of the person. Similarly, the absence of illumination also conceals a Sunsum even though the Sunsum is still present.

In order to speak about an Ɔbosom (God or Goddess), one does not have to observe a spirit—which is unobservable without revelation—to believe or make empirical analysis of that agency because there are several ways in which an Ɔbosom makes itself known. Further, an entity that is unobservable does not render that agency unrealistic or nonexistent for there are several ways of "seeing" and degrees of revelation. Naturally, a scientist would insist on empirical evidence and yet there is no denying of the many unexplained phenomena that simply defy scientific scrutiny. Reality in the grand African scheme of things is the unobservable, the spiritual, and hence the primal role of the spiritual in African speculative thought. This does not make an African any less scientific; rather, Africans are more aware of realities far beyond the observable, the basis of which are steeped in time-tested traditions. Such awareness is anchored in time, an indefinite time-tested evidence of people believing in the same unchanging phenomena from the very beginning of time, which, in itself, is scientific because the same result is expected each time. Consequently, the Sunsum (Spirit) in all its meanings is a phenomenon that is feared and for that reason alone must remain hidden from physical view. It further means that there are spiritual spheres that are strange, powerful, and far beyond human comprehension.

In this context, a shadow (sunsum) appears black because it must remain mysterious—the real identity hidden from human view. To express the spirit in the context of darkness (*Sum*) is to acknowledge that it is incapable of being known or penetrated and therefore unaffected by the tangibility in the corporeal Wiadzie. Corporeally, darkness must be understood in the context of ontology and transcendence, because God first created darkness. Ontologically, life is black, because out of the blackness of the womb life emerges into new life-forms in the corporeal world. Darkness then has to do with secrecy, where agencies engage in unique acts in private and away from others, especially human beings. For instance, the God of the Yoruba, Olodumare, gave life to the first human, unseen by his assistant, Orisa-nla, after God Olodumare put Orisa-nla to sleep. Unlike the Abosom generally thought of as primeval nature forces, the *Orisas* of the Yoruba are mostly "deified ancestors or personified natural forces,"[16] which, in this context, are like the Nananom Nsamanfo (Ancestors) of the Akan who are worshipped daily, seasonally, situationally and periodically, and annually led by kings and queen mothers who propitiate their ancestors' stools as living ancestors.

Sleep, like death, is a timeless state of darkness and therefore a sleeper is unaware of what transpires in corporeal time until told, although, like sleep where a spirit having an independent existence may roam free as a shadow (Sunsum), an Ɔsaman too departs a corpse just prior to death and roams free as an abstract personality until its departure to the Samanadzie after a culturally defined period. Similarly, in Old Testament scriptures, the Lord God puts Adam into a "deep sleep" before creating "a woman" (Gen. 2:21–22 RSV). Darkness then is the inability to be observed, as well as the inability to observe in darkness like human beings, unless one is a spiritual agency endowed with the capacity to see through darkness. The exception is God, because God cannot be observed by any created being, except one, that is an Ɔbosom. Most importantly, God observes from and in darkness because God is the ultimate Sunsum.

Generally darkness is thought of as absence of light or the sun, but what it also means is the inability to determine exactly what activity goes on in darkness. Actually the sun and its light are blinding to human beings, preventing us from seeing in the dark, like spirits, as we will see later. As human beings, we are always sure of the regenerative potency of darkness, suggesting that darkness is not the absence of inertia. Darkness conceals a lot, so much so that sometimes those who feel left out of major decisions or activities by loved ones may complain that they have been kept in the dark. Contextually, darkness may be understood as deliberately hiding (*suma*) activities away from those who should know but for some reasons were kept uninformed and uninvolved. Conversely, then, the Sunsum is not darkness, because unlike darkness (*sum*), which is the lack of being observed, the Sunsum, could be revealed under the guise of light, structurally, although not in essence. While the shape and form of a Sunsum could be "observed," the true essence and nature of a Sunsum still remains mysterious. If the true essence of a Sunsum is observable, then there would be no darkness or secrecy, sleep and death, or even God, since there will be nothing for the other to observe. All things would be equal, tangibly or even spiritually.

There is no denying that intrinsic darkness, illusiveness, is a strong component of the Sunsum, as the term *Sunsum* itself illustrates. More than a shadow, double, or even a reflection, the Sunsum is a teasingly active agency making it a spirit as it is, because it reveals and conceals simultaneously. For this reason, all ethereal phenomena are subsumed under Sunsum, because, figuratively, anything that people do not understand or observe and yet think to be *real* or *there*[17] is time tested. Conceptually, the utilization of *Thereness* refers to God and the Abosom as agencies existing forever by just being *There*. During my experiences at divinations, when the Abosom are asked about their well-being, they invariably respond: "*I am There*" (*Me wɔhɔ*), as in forever existing, or have always been *There*. *Thereness* also has to do with the "age" of the Abosom measured in terms of weight as to how long an Ɔbosom has been *There*. Paradoxically, as agencies of light, diviners describe the Abosom as being heavy during divinations, as will be explained in the next chapter. The concept of *Thereness* could be something pointed at if observable, or that which remains elusive although known to be *There*, like God. In itself, it is an act of faith; the kerygma of God's *Thereness* although God is elusive and even unknown. The Sunsum then refers to all kinds of non-human beings and forces capable of transforming themselves into objects or forms of varying shapes and degrees in the mundane to influence events and affairs of human beings without revealing their true selves. They do so only in their images, suggesting that a Sunsum, although invisible, may be tangible (weightier) enough to be experienced during spirit alightment when intangible agencies take hold of corporeal beings in order to bring them under their dictates. Some of these dictates may assume the form of procreativity.

As William Bosman utilizes Bosom (Ɔbosom) and fetish to be physical objects interchangeably, so too is the concept of *Thereness*—as that which exists forever—applied symbolically to the ancestors' stool of the Akan and kindred groups. For the Akan, every ancestors' stool of a community is an

Ɔbosom, *There* forever as the very soul of a people. As evidenced, anyone who is "seated" on it three times during a high ceremony of king-making is also transformed as an Ɔbosom because he or she has come into contact with the very sacred symbol of the Abosom. In consequence, the one seated on the ancestors' stool becomes a living ancestor and representative of the Abosom and ancestors corporeally. In response, a king or queen mother propitiates the Abosom and ancestors as their representation on earth. In return, the traditional ruler is worshipped by the people as their way of worshipping their Abosom and ancestors. Even though the seating of a person on an ancestors' stool, or whichever symbol is used by a group, is a one-time historical act, as long as the ruler is living it means the sacred ancestors' stool or comparable sacred object is thought to be occupied (seated upon) by the king or queen mother. But while kings and queen mothers pass on (die) to different modes of existence, the ancestors' stools remain on earth, forever, as the soul of a people. Indeed, for every Akan group, the ancestors' stool is an Ɔbosom par excellence, because it is the one and only singular object housing the souls of all of a community's *dead-alive* (resurrected spirits of the dead as Nsamanfo). Thus, an ancestors' stool is the most sacrosanct and numinous symbol for all the people, which they protect, defend, and preserve for posterity. An Ɔbosom therefore is more than otherworldly primeval gods and goddesses (Abosom), it encompasses sacred objects on earth that also exist in perpetuity as symbols of manifestation for spiritual agencies.

While the conception of the Sunsum and its manifestations are explored in detail in subsequent chapters, it is worth noting that the concept of the Sunsum is a paradox even as it is an enigma. Sunsum is a spirit, shadow or image, making it observable although incapable of being held tangibly. Most importantly, the Sunsum has an independent existence apart from its material object as Rattray has already noted. It is during the independent escapade of a Sunsum that the essence of the Sunsum may be revealed in colors and detail, meaning the Sunsum has an identity other than the physical. Thus, the starting point of finite existence in Africa is always the spiritual, or that which is eternal, and the Akan are not an exception. Indeed, while it may appear that a Sunsum is an imprint of its host, the physical, on the contrary, the corporeal is instead an imprint of the Sunsum because the material is fleeting while the Sunsum is not. This is especially so when during the mystery of creation, God as a spiritual being commands or intellectually acts in a manner that results in the creation of human beings and all thing tangible.[18]

Further exposition on the nature of the spirit is illuminated by Jesus in the Gospel of John 3:5–10 (RSV). Jesus is believed to have told a disciple of his, Nicodemus, that in order to enter the kingdom of God one must be "born of water and the spirit." And, like with Nicodemus, the question is: How is one born of a spirit, an intangible agency not seen with human eyes? Can a spirit give birth to a tangible entity like a human? In explaining his point, Jesus also mentions wind to illustrate exactly what he means, and in doing so he offers insights into the composition of a spirit. Jesus equates spirit to wind when explaining how human beings can discern the movements of the wind as to whether one is born of the spirit or not. So, entrants to the kingdom of God, according to Jesus, are those of water, spirit and wind, or those influenced by the spirit. Similarly, corporeal beings are also capable of transforming themselves into intangible agencies and may remain unseen by corporeal beings.[19]

But the question still remains: How can a spirit (or wind) procreate that which is tangible? Of course, we know that God's words are transformative enough to cause all life-forms to come into existence, but can the Abosom also do the same? We observe the destructive power and effects of the wind all around us, but can it create tangibility? Yes, if the wind is God. While Jesus does not explicitly point out how one is born of the spirit (to the astonishment of Nicodemus), except to suggest that a person born of the spirit is as active as the movement of wind, Jesus was, without question, onto a concept that is prevalent among the Akan and other African groups. Without doubt, the spirit is the progenitor of all there is, existentially, because the movement of the wind reveals tangibility. As evidence, there is a divine pronouncement among the Akan that all are offspring of God, none the child of earth or corporeality.

WATER

When we speak of water (*Nsu*), we are talking about how life depends on it. Akan elders sometimes state during deliberations that water is not a substitute for liquor and vice versa. What is meant is that each has its unique place ritually. While acknowledging that water is unique and different from liquor, what the elders wish to communicate is the fact that one cannot mix two diametrically opposing issues during deliberations. Each issue must be treated as distinctly as possible by allowing it to stand on its own without blurring matters under discussion with unrelated issues so as to confuse people. After all, the process of adjudication and deliberation is to discern truth from falsehood and therefore clarity is of the ultimate concern. The ability to listen intently then is a virtue, because if one does not listen intently one may not hear the nuances of a case.

The same is true when it comes to ritual enactment. Sometimes only water is used depending on the ritual. For example, when a traveler arrives home safely from a trip, the second ritual performed after first giving a traveler a seat to sit on, is to offer the traveler water to drink. Ideally a traveler may first pour some of the water on the floor or ground to the spiritual forces believed to accompany him or her home before drinking the water; or, the traveler will first drink most of the water but leave just enough at the bottom of the cup and then put it on the floor or ground to the ancestral spirits accompanying him or her. Water has always been the element used for this ritual—never liquor. When tired after a long or even a short trip, water is the element used to satiate a thirsty traveler and for one's regeneration. However, whenever elders convene a meeting, liquor takes center stage (but since this segment is on water we need to stick with water for now).

The use of water symbolically or otherwise by elders to affirm orthodoxy of social and cultural traditions is quite interesting. Apart from breast milk that neonates take in immediately upon parturition, the first tangible element that neonates taste is water, followed by liquor. The use of water is not accidental; water is, in fact, one of the four elements in the universe, a fact acknowledged by the ancestors of the Akan and other African peoples and hence the first to be introduced to a neonate because it sustains life. Ideally, this psychosocial ritual occurs on the eighth day of a neonate's existence outside of the womb during the Akan naming rite. For many people in the urban areas nowadays, the eighth day is purely symbolic, because many wait until they have the money to undertake the rite, if at all. One reason for this changing dynamic is that they have turned a simple rite involving a few immediate family members into a huge social church event requiring some considerable financing. Consequently, some babies are actually denied their first psychosocial rite because some parents are not culturally grounded enough to ensure the primacy of tradition over whatever they may have picked up under the influence of their Western-trained clergymen.

What may seem contradictory with regard to not substituting liquor for water is that, at some point during a naming rite, water and liquor are mixed together in order to effect the symbolic result for both parents. The mixture connotes symbolic onset of breast milk, while a father after drinking the mixture proceeds to pour the rest between his legs as a sign of fecundity. This being the case, what is one to make of the prohibition against using one element for the other or even mixing them? The answer is that the desired effect may not be obtained, and in African social context where ritual efficacy is paramount, it is better to use the proper elements than the wrong one in hopes that the right result could be obtained.

A week after a sister-in-law of mine gave birth, my wife called Ghana to check on her sister and baby, and after my sister-in-law complained that her breast milk was not enough for her son and was the reason, she believed, her son was crying constantly, my wife instinctively asked if her sister gave the baby enough water to drink. To her utter surprise her sister told her (my wife) that the nurses told her not to give her son water to drink until about six months later. This infuriated my wife who immediately asked her sister to give the baby bottled water, of which the thirsty baby drank his fill and then stopped crying. Then my wife warned her not to stop giving the baby water, in addition to supplementing her breast milk with baby formulas. At one point I interjected and asked my sister-in-law as to why, if babies are not supposed to drink water, our ancestors offered us water and other elements as neonates immediately upon parturition and on the eighth day? Apparently, recent postpartum instructions to new mothers by nurses is that they should avoid offering water to their neonates for about six months after parturition for fear of giving unclean water to infants. Water is basic to all living things and so it does not make any sense to deny neonates water. I have even observed some birds collect water in their beaks for their chicks, while even the most inhospitable deserts still have water enabling certain organisms to survive. Therefore, instructing new mothers not to give water to their neonates is puzzling, alien, and symptomatic of a copycat society that Ghana has become, absorbing everything foreign at the expense of its own.[20]

Before a naming rite—or rather before water is given on the eighth day to neonates—immediately upon parturition "the infant's throat is moistened with the juice of a lime or sometimes with a little rum, with which the finger is wetted and the back of the throat touched."[21] Then after the umbilical cord is severed "against a piece of wood," "the infant is then washed with water which must not have been boiled." Following this, neonates are given several baths with lukewarm water several times a day. Then on the eighth day, the day set aside traditionally for naming infants, neonates are again given baths at dawn, dressed and readied in attires presented to them by their fathers for the naming rite performed by their patri-folks.

Customarily, as already stated, anyone who arrives from a journey is offered water to drink to quench his or her thirst and those believed to accompany one spiritually. Similarly, as a last sacramental act water must be offered to the dying to facilitate the journey to the world of the dead, the Samanadzie, as addressed in chapter 1. Failure to perform this last rite due to the abruptness of a death means that the journey to the Samanadzie is thought to be arduous for the Ɔsaman (posthumous abstract personality). Thus water is the first and last element tasted by an Akan, making it an indispensable element for survival, either as a human or even posthumous abstract personality undertaking a journey to the world of Nsamanfo. Therefore, it is absurd to place moratorium on the use of water on neonates because of new foreign health theories, which health authorities wholly accept without considering the socio-cultural implications. No wonder some mothers and the sick ignore

Western medicines claiming they are not holistic enough.[22] I recall one grandmother challenging a nurse at a hospital and offering her granddaughter water in the presence of the nurse who asked the nurse if her parents refused her water at birth. When the nurse said no, the grandmother demanded to know why they are teaching new mothers not to offer water to their newborn babies.

To understand the precise nature of the spirit in the context of water, Jesus laid down the criteria for what would be required of entrants to heaven. Jesus was believed to have made it a point for entrants to the kingdom of God to be born of water (John 3:5–6 RSV). Of course, to be born of water may simply mean water baptism, but there could be other meanings as well. From a cross-cultural standpoint, it could also mean the amniotic fluid that fetuses float in. But then all humans are conceived in such fluids, meaning everyone is born of water, which would qualify everyone born a member of the kingdom of God that Jesus referenced. Or, Jesus was simply referring to water baptism as a requirement for membership to his movement and therefore to the kingdom that he described, and by extension for converts to Christianity. This view seems to be the prevailing Christian dogma and which I have heard preached many times as the clergy, including me, attempt to make sense of what Jesus was believed to have meant. In fact, Jesus was unambiguously clear that the spiritual person is the one born of water and spirit, suggesting that water and spirit are one and the same.

Water and spirit have always been paired in many cultures. For instance, in ancient Egyptian cosmogony, the spirit of God (wind) moved on the surface of the primeval mass of water in darkness before the created order materialized. Jesus, as we have seen above, was unto something much deeper than the baptismal water at the heart of Christian conversions or early Jewish baptismal rites. Of course, Jesus' own baptismal rite was said to be quite dramatic, leading to his own awareness of his mission. But, other than this, how exactly is one born of water and spirit?

Interestingly, the Akan too pair water with spirit for the simple reason that spirits walk or travel on water. Furthermore, they equate all bodies of water, rivers, and ocean with spirits and vice versa. By spirits, the Akan have in mind gods and goddesses with unique identities whom they refer to as Abosom (singular Ɔbosom). Yet the Abosom are not apart and separate from any body of water or river—indeed, they are one and the same. Thus to drink water, any water, is to have drunk the Abosom, literally, therefore one cannot divorce oneself of the Abosom or even claim not to worship the Abosom or ancestors who are connected genetically to their posterity. What may appear as a single body of water or river, with a distinct name, for instance, is actually composed of many rivers flowing together as one mighty river making its entry into the sea. Needless to say, that the sea may not be the final destination of rivers flowing into it, so who knows where rivers ultimately end up, if they end up at all in the sea. Or, perhaps, the sea is just an umbrella for a cyclically continuous flow of all rivers joined together. Since rivers do not flow from sea to land but rather land (rocks) into a bowl-like basin below at sea, what are the sources of rivers on land from which rivers emanate perpetually? How do we also explain lakes, ponds, and man-made reservoirs that do not have outlets to sea? Since water or rivers seem to emanate from rocks and since the Akan maintain that rocks preceded the ocean, it means that the ocean could not be the final destination of rivers.

During a casual discussion with a diviner friend of mine one day, suddenly she was alighted upon by the spokes-deity (*Ɔkyeame*) for the deities of the community of Mprumem in order to deliver a message to me. Toward the entrance to the community from the main highway, there is a pond there that was created by Caterpillar machinery that dug up soil to build the road in the late 1950s or early 1960s. Since the area has a lot of clay, the water collected as a result of rain never dries up, even during the dry season. Before Mprumem had pipe-borne water in the 1970s; the pond served as one of the sources of water for the community even when the Brushyɛn River that runs through the town dried up. Caterpillar, the name that the pond is known by, had never had any deity reside in it until the spokes-deity, Ɔbaa Yaa, suddenly alight on the medium. On Ɔbaa Yaa's way home from an errand she saw a different Ɔbosom inhabiting the pond and so she confronted him and gave him the choice of either joining the Mprumem pantheon and in which case she would allow him to inhabit the pond or depart. The new deity, who had been expelled from his pantheon for not conforming to the collective will of his pantheon, refused to join the collective at Mprumem and so Ɔbaa Yaa forced him to vacate the pond, but not until she gave him money for his next journey in search of some form of settlement. This action, she informed me, she took even before she went home to report the matter to the pantheon in Mprumem.

The Abosom are spirits and do reside in rivers and bodies of water for renaissance because one of their essences is water. Rejuvenation and renaissance is not only for themselves but also for procreativity in humans and other temporal creatures. All living things are essentially the Abosom that we drink as water. As such, they are within all living things because water is found in all of creation. Water is used for all kinds of activities, including bathing, cooking, washing, etc., making water—the Abosom—indispensable to human survival. Indeed, most of the popular Abosom in Ghana are river deities. Ghana, for example, generates most of its electricity from the twin Abosom called Senchāy Aba and Senchāy Yaw, who, together, are known as the Volta River. For decades the Volta has yielded its water in abundance for Ghanaians to enjoy limitless use of electricity, yet successive governments after the builder of the hydroelectric dam, Kwame Nkrumah, the first leader of Ghana who acted in accordance with tradition relative to the Abosom, have abandoned the Abosom in place of foreign ones and refused to propitiate the Abosom of our ancestors. In consequence, the Akosombo Dam is drying up in spite of the heavy rains annually and now Ghanaians are up in arms forgetting that they have abandoned their Abosom saying that they are obsolete because we now live in modern times. In response the Abosom too have turned their backs on us, withholding the very essence of life—water—from us until such time as Ghana acknowledges the primacy of the Abosom and propitiate them. The problem is that anyone who attempts to offer a spiritual causality to issues like that of the lowering water level at the Akosombo Dam is eviscerated by those claiming to be "civilized," educated, and modern, and so the hard social and economic conditions continue unabated. What people sometimes, especially those espousing superiority of foreign values over traditional ones wholly, fail to realize is that African spiritual logic is as different and unique as the human body is solid and finite.

Nature is the manifestation of God as expressed by the Abosom in every respect. Even so, every Ɔbosom is a distinct and separate agency—with its own unique name, features, qualities, and character attributes—as every human being is. All humans, in fact, living things, are the Abosom revealed. As explained elsewhere, "an *Ɔbosom*, like God, is an immoveable primeval being, force, power, or energy of some sort, sometimes expressed symbolically as a rock, river, moon, or ocean, because these objects are perpetually *There*." As water, living beings are Abosom, too. What this suggests is that living things are, in essence, the Abosom in action corporeally, reflecting the character attributes of the Abosom.

FIRE

It would seem at first glance that water is antithetical to fire because water may be used to extinguish fire, but, as we have seen, water generates electricity. In this sense, the two are essentially the same. Fire is the powerhouse, engine of the cosmos, making life possible existentially. We know from ancient Egyptian cosmology that the first creative act of God was fire (*Ra/Re*), which emerged from the primeval mass of water (*Nu/Nunu*), which made possible the corporeal order. There is fire in every corporeal and incorporeal being or force, just as there is water in the creative universe. The emergence of fire from water reveals one essential nature of fire, and that is, fire (and heat) by its nature, rises or shoots up in order to give rise to its life-giving, eternal nature. While fire is very potent, it is when it blazes that its full power is displayed. And so when fire is started, the goal is to see it blaze, otherwise one has to continue fanning pieces of logs until ignition and a blaze is achieved.

For the Akan and other African peoples, all witches are thought to possess fire, spiritual fire enabling them to glow, blaze at night and help propel them to and from their nocturnal escapades.[23] Generally thought to be spiritual in nature, witchcraft fire is real enough to be spewed defensively on those who approach witches nefariously. It may be said in reference to someone suspected of having paranormal sighting and therefore thought to be a witch or warlock as possessing fire (*Ogya*); or, that one's Ogya (fire) is believed to be huge. The Āwutu-ābe of Simpa (Winneba), for example, refer to a witch and witchcraft in general as *Ogya-pah* (possessor of fire) to stress home the point that witchcraft is the ability to acquire spiritual fire for nefarious intentions. It takes special eyes to enable one to sight the kinds of fire, spiritual fire, that witches, warlocks, and highly developed or spiritualized individuals possess. The individuals thought to possess spiritual eyes may travel after midnight and come upon a community that is well "lit" from a distance but upon getting closer discover that there is no light in the community after all. On the contrary, an ordinary person with no "sight," would only see darkness all along. This phenomenon is generally interpreted to mean that witches are feasting en masse, and since nights in Africa are pitch-black, witches turn on their fires but quickly turn them off upon the approach of vehicles or non-witches, or even the Abosom. Fire, then, "powers witches in flight and announces their presence to potential intruders. The size of the fire depends on how powerful a witchcraft is." Fire and witchcraft are sometimes used interchangeably in regard to witchcraft. One cannot be a witch or warlock and not possess fire, spiritual or otherwise.

For the Akan, the source of fire is the Abosom (gods and goddess). As for the Yoruba, for example, Segun Gbadegesin maintains that the source of witchcraft power enabling witches to fly away to attend nocturnal meeting actually emanates from God, Olodumare.[24] Whether originating with God or the Abosom, the fact is witchcraft has a divine source. Yet the general belief is that witchcraft is corporeal, meaning it cannot be taken to the ancestral world upon death. By their very nature, the Abosom are beings of fire (light) and therefore have fires that are massively huge and powerful. The fires of the Abosom easily eclipse those of witches and certain individuals also thought to possess fire although they may not be witches or warlocks. Therefore, in terms of source, fires that are acquired by humans are derived from the Abosom as sources of spiritual power, although by definition, witchcraft is used to cause harm to others without any physical contact.

First, spiritual power—of fire—may be acquired via knowledge of the Abosom and God when people devote themselves to studying the Abosom and God. Some individuals, too, acquire spiritual fire at birth through inheritance, and so those with similar fires recognize immediately neonates susceptible to spiritual influences and bewitch them at birth. Occasionally, a witch may abandon her child because she realizes that her baby possesses a huge fire, fire that is more powerful than a mother's. In one such case, the grandmother of the baby—the source of the baby's witchcraft—had to intervene and take care of the baby.

Theologically, then, all that is known of God is revealed by the Abosom to those who devote themselves to God, thus to study the Abosom is to study God. The Abosom have been with God from the very beginning, if there was ever a beginning at all, because the Abosom have infinitely existed; that is, they have always been *there*. In acknowledgment of one's devotion, an Ɔbosom may reveal itself in the form of fire. While fire is not the only form of a hierophany, fire is the most primal of epiphanies, since no deity is seen in its original nature or form by any human. Such hierophanies may be spectacular, as they are dramatic, occurring when one least expected them, because an individual has been favored by an Ɔbosom. A similar event after a night of divination was recorded as follow:

> Actually, all spiritual agents, including the *Abosom* possess fireballs, such as what I observed in the mid-1990s at about midnight. As I drove home about to make a turn onto the road that led to my house, my headlights went dead. I looked straight up and about one hundred yards in front of me, was a huge, reddish or yellow sinking sun-like fireball on the horizon, dripping ambers that did not burn the forest (either). The ball of fire hovered on top of the trees about fifty feet from the ground in a spectacular fashion. As I watched for some minutes not really knowing what it was, suddenly my lights came back on, so I turned and drove home without thinking much about it. Days later, I learned about the nature of the hierophany and then I became afraid. At the same time, I wished I had moved closer to examine it.[25]

To say that the Abosom are of fire in addition to water is to assert that they are unapproachable, because to get close, too close, and one is burned to death irrespective of whatever relationship that one might have with an Ɔbosom (God or Goddess). It follows that often warnings accompany hierophanies, to the extent that no Ɔbosom should be taken for granted. Sometimes those who take care of sacred objects and symbols are warned not to approach certain sacred objects at certain times because they may witness the transformation of those objects into fireballs and that may not be beneficial to them. Those who take these warnings seriously approached sacred objects associated with the kingship, for instance, with extreme care, caution, and fear. It does not mean that they were reckless before, but sometimes naïve and take things for granted, especially after performing certain rituals repeatedly. For one thing, the Abosom are not respecters of human beings, and therefore no one should be cocky when dealing with such extremely powerful forces. Any dealings with the holy must be characterized by fear and trepidation because, after all, a human is only a mortal being. Yet fire—the Abosom—is the very engine of life which must be utilized existentially in order for life to be sustained. However, if utilized correctly then the power and indispensability of fire is achieved beneficially. Even so, one must not lose sight of the pernicious nature of fire. In itself, it is a delicate balance.

And secondly, spiritual power—of fire—may be attained through education because the attainment of higher education enlightens by focusing the mind on higher essentials. By education I do not necessarily mean attending Western-style institutions, but rather an epistemological focus on the spiritual and how that knowledge is gained. Indeed, knowledge is power, but of which power? It will not be presumptuous to assume that it is the power of fire. If the premise that knowledge is power—whether the power is defined as energy, force, authority, or the ability to control and cause others to do one's will politically, socially, religiously, physically, psychologically, or otherwise—is accepted, then we are speaking of the exertion of energy. But irrespective of the definition of knowledge, the most important singular nature of knowledge is that it must be acquired—and there may be several ways of acquiring knowledge. Since knowledge must be acquired, it is also said that the acquisition of knowledge is not cheap, emotionally, psychologically, physically, intellectually, and, above all, fiscally. Moreover, at every stage of development—whether the stage is based on chronological age, set of years during which time students must accrue certain body of knowledge, or intellectually based on mastery of certain principles, assumptions, or a set of tasks to be completed—students must be tested on certain basic "facts," knowledge, and truisms about what they study. Furthermore, since knowledge has to do with the mind, it means that power is intellectual in essence and therefore spiritual, although the extrinsic effects, whether physical, psychological, or brute force, are clearly on display unceasingly.

In acknowledgement of the expression that knowledge is power and expensive, and that knowledge is derived from fire, the Akan refer to the highest "educated" individuals among them as *Abengfo*—those well-baked or well-done in the crucible of higher learning, such as those who have acquired mystical powers. Thus, an *Ɔbengfo* (singular of Abengfo) is someone thought to be enlightened intellectually by virtue of being a highly learned person, which makes his or her entire personhood impervious to malign forces. Expatiating on concept of *beng* as "well-done or baked in fire" and those seen as embodiments of fire relative to spirituality, the following summarizes what the Akan believe:

> Akan in general . . . measure and judge the degree of spiritual and intellectual prowess in the context of fire, literally and figuratively. For the Akan the highly developed individuals, like kings, elders, and the clergy (akomfo) are described as having been *baked* or *cooked* extremely well-done (*Woa beng*). Thus, they equate intellectual brilliance and mental acumen with spiritual development and consequently address highly educated persons, such as those holding Ph.D. degrees, as *abengfo*.[26]

Above all, the group of people who epitomize spirituality relative to fire, literally, are the *Akɔmfo* (diviners), together with kings and queen mothers. The Akɔmfo are a special class of clerics called by the Abosom who have undergone intense training, graduated in the highest order as Akɔmfo (diviners, healers, and priests), and are set aside for the Abosom to alight on them, to prophecy by announcing the will of the Abosom, perform priestly duties, and lead in rites of propitiation for the ancestors and Abosom. Thus they are more than mediums: they are clerics wholly. As Akɔmfo, they embody spiritual fire; but in addition to what is inherently their nature, they undergo fire baptisms or emersions, literally.

Writing about by fire "baptism" as one of graduating rites in the 1880s among some Fanti (an Akan group) Akɔmfo in Cape Coast in what was then the Gold Coast, now Ghana, Ellis writes:

> The fire test was described to me by five people, who professed to have been eye-witnesses of it, and whose different accounts agreed in the main. The *modus operandi,* it appears, is to kindle a large fire of wood, and, when it has burned to a red glow, without much flame, the burning embers are arranged in a circle of from two and a half to three yards in diameter, the enclosed area being left clear. Each priest or priestess then submits in turn to the ordeal, which is supposed to show whether they have remained pure, and refrained from sexual intercourse, during the period of retirement, and so are worthy of inspiration by the gods. If they are pure they will receive no injury and suffer no pain from the fire. Into the central space left in the circle of fire steps the priest, and, immediately, rum, kerosene oil, and other inflammable liquids are thrown upon the embers, so that the flames leap in the air sometimes as high as a man's head. The flames last, perhaps, twenty seconds, and the priest then steps out. After an interval he repeats the process a second and a third time, and the ordeal is over. If he has been able to stay in the circle each time till the flames have subsided, and has sustained no injury, it is believed that he is pure, and that the gods, being pleased with him, have protected him from the fire. If he has been compelled by the intense heat to leap out, or if he has sustained a burn of any kind, he is not

> pure. This test is not submitted to naked, and the persons subjected to it always wrap themselves up closely in their cloths.[27]

While Ellis was not an eyewitness to what he described, there is no reason to doubt the veracity of his accounts, as I witnessed a similar ceremony in 1999 in the town of Farmanya, also in the Central Region of Ghana.[28]

Graduation ceremonies take place in the evenings reaching their climax at midnight or thereafter, because that is the time that fire initiation of the Akɔmfo take place. The highlights of nocturnal rites include the "jumping over" of a huge bonfire that may be liken to the Christian concept of "baptism by fire." These fire ceremonies are of particular interest to me because it conjured up for me, as a theologian, Christian teachings, and so I anxiously awaited its commencement. Weeks before the ceremony, Essoun, the Ɔkɔmfo to be, had gathered together the special *Issa* wood lit specifically for this ceremony. As the fire was lit and blazed, I thought Essoun would suddenly appear and jump over the fire, because none of the clergy gathered for the ceremony said or explained anything to me and I did not think it was appropriate for me to ask questions as events were unfolding before my eyes. I was just being anxious and a bit presumptuous. After midnight the blaze subsided at which point some of the elder Akɔmfo parted the fire into two heaps in order to widen the jump and make it more difficult during the jump. Still naïve, I thought that Essoun would be required to walk across or run through the middle of the heaped fires. Then, dramatically from one end of the heap, Essoun jumped across both heaps just as the flames leap high when kerosene was thrown on the heaps. She was caught on the other side by a male companion. Upon her third jump, she was hailed by all those present for having successfully completed one major hurdle. Of course, failure would have been interpreted as having broken a taboo, such as engaging in sexual activity while in training, etc., and which would have required her to repeat the ceremony after rites of purification had been performed.

The differences between Ellis' account and my direct observation of Ɔkɔmfo Essoun undergoing the fire test are minor. The way the fires were configured in both accounts were different, in that while Ellis' had the fire "arranged in a circle" and the "enclosed area" left opened and the Ɔkɔmfo seated in the center; in mine, the fire was heaped into two while my Ɔkɔmfo jumped over the heaps through the flames three times, each time kerosene being poured on the fire to increase the height of the flames. There is also a sense in Ellis' account that the Ɔkɔmfo is wrapped tight in her cloths giving the impression that she is protected from the shooting flames as flammable liquids are poured in the fire. This is far from the truth. My observation revealed a thinly covered Ɔkɔmfo. The Ɔkɔmfo had two pieces of cloths—two yards apiece—that the Akan refer to as *Ahatado* wrapped around her chest and waist, otherwise there was nothing really on her. The whole idea of a fire test is to go through fire and not be burned, because if one is chaste, as Ellis points out, then the Abosom will protect the Ɔkɔmfo.

The bonfires that are jumped over or having candidates seated in the center of are real—nothing that I have seen or read about anywhere and no amount of cloths are capable of protecting Akɔmfo (plural of Ɔkɔmfo) from the heat and flames shooting from the fires. The protections that they have are the Abosom themselves who called the Akɔmfo into the clerical vocation because the Abosom themselves are fires. Even those of us who happened to be witnesses to some of these ceremonies stand some distances away from the heat of the fires. The fire tests are ultimate tests for those called by the Abosom, convincing evidence that indeed an Ɔkɔmfo is not a fraud.

It also happens that fire plays a major role in the deaths of those called by the Abosom, the Akɔmfo, as a last rite. As if to say that Akɔmfo commenced their practices as priests wholly through the empowerment of fire, in death too they must also end their clerical vocation by fire. Thus from the period that their corpses are lying in state (*Fuundahɔ*), fire is lit by members of the clerical order in honor of their dead colleagues, not to be extinguished until several weeks after burial. Meanwhile, for their fallen colleagues, members of the clerical order nightly repeat the jumps over fires that they first performed before being admitted into the clerical profession.

Anyone who goes through fire, literally or spiritually, is baked and therefore hardened to the extent of one becoming impervious to negative forces. As evidence, people in general are afraid—or rather respectful—of those who have aspired to the highest mystical, educational, and socio-political and spiritual estates. For example, those holding Ph.D. degrees are appropriately called *abengfo* (those well-done or baked). The Āwutu-ābe (Effutu) also refer specifically to their diviners as *Abrɛwo* (singular is *Ɔbrɛwo*) or those well-baked or done. Obviously, we are not speaking of physical properties that are baked but rather the spiritual prowess gained by going through fire, literally. Fire, then, has an indispensable role in the attainment of spirituality. This must be understood paradoxically, however. Physically, food or meat that is well-done, cooked or baked is perfect for human consumption. Therefore, how are those baptized by fire thought to be impervious to evil powers? The answer is that anyone who has risen to the highest temporal and spiritual estate has become a deity, an Ɔbosom, and has therefore achieved eternal life. In order to achieve immortality the physical body must die and the way to achieving spirituality (or immortality), at least for the clergy, is by going through fire to kill the body. To achieve immortality means that the body has already gone through fire and survived, forever.

The relationship between the attainment of enlightenment (spirituality)—insofar as immortality is concerned—and fire—as having been baked—is old African mystic practice. In ancient Egypt, for instance, the goddess Auset (Isis) undertook the same rite for a prince entrusted to her care. In a bid to immortalize the infant, according to Budge, "Isis . . . was made nurse to one of the king's sons. Instead of nursing the child in the ordinary way, Isis gave him her finger to suck, and each night she put him into the fire to consume his mortal parts. . . . But the queen once happened to see her son in flames, and cried out, and thus deprived him of immortality."[29] Obviously Auset never intended to harm the prince physically, only riding the body of certain "film" that only fire could dispose of. So, from ancient Africa to contemporary societies in Africa like the Akan, in order to achieve immortality (spirituality), the physical body must undergo some sort of fire "baptism" or immersion in order to identify with the Abosom. For Akan clergy then baptism of fire is as real as it can get.

Is the body then an impediment to spirituality? No; because a physical body (*Honam*) is needed in the corporeal in order for it to serve as the basis for a spiritual personality and "body" (*Ɔsaman*), in an afterworld meant only for those with such personalities, as we have seen in the previous chapter. An Ɔsaman is an imprint of an Ɔbosom created after the demise of a human being. We need to remember that Abosom do not have bodies or flesh like humans, because they are not humans even though as human beings our frame of reference is to think of the Abosom, especially apotheosized beings, in anthropomorphic terms. The Abosom are rather strange creatures, with odd shapes, forms, and features, who, together with God, created a human being, which upon death has enough spiritual imprint of the Abosom to constitute a life-form called Ɔsaman.

Yet another distinct group of people emblematic of fire, although they do not undergo as dramatic fire immersions as the Akɔmfo but have their own extensive ritual ablution tantamount to fire baptisms of the Akɔmfo, are kings and queen mothers. On the nature of African kings and queen mothers, one of the courses that I teach is called "African Kingship," which, among other things, examines Western contact with African kingdoms, colonialism, and how colonial policies—assimilation, association, and direct and indirect rules—rendered divine kingship in Africa ineffective as viable political institutions. In addition, it explores the origin and development of divine kingship, systems of succession, and rites of king-making. But in examining some of the taboos for kings and queen mothers, one of the statements that I make in relation to royalty is: Fire does not walk alone. Usually, curious students ask: With whom then does fire walk, and who is the fire?

Fire is a metaphor for Akan kings and queen mothers, as such one of the taboos is for a king or queen mother to walk alone, but each must always be accompanied by someone even if that someone is a minor. A fire without its accompaniment is stationary and only rises up into the sky, and so a ruler without a retinue must not be allowed to travel. Any king or queen mother contravening this rule is subject to citizen's arrest.

A king of Simpa (Winneba), Ghartey V, was once "arrested" for traveling alone when he visited the town of Swedru secretly. Someone spotted him and placed him under arrest for walking alone and took him to the court of the king of Swedru, a neighboring town about fifteen miles north of Simpa, until King Ghartey's family paid a fine and the king was released. Researching the veracity of the story, the elders were informed that he secretly visited the mother of his only son and child, an Agona woman, who resided in Swedru. The reason was that the king was married and did not want his wife to discover his trip to his "baby mama." The fact is that some rulers do not always travel with accompaniments and so try as much as possible to avoid being detected. Still, they are recognized by some citizens, although nowadays citizen's arrests are rare.

What does it mean, then, to embody fire as the Abosom when one is elected ruler? Some enlightened individuals—whether their enlightenments are achieved intellectually through obtaining the highest educational credential in their respective fields, due to years of austere training culminating in fire immersions like the Akɔmfo, or like kings and queen mothers who undergo a series of rites of fortification tantamount to fire baptism—all emit and glow fire around them. They exude heat, spiritual fire that protects them from harm and others who may wish them ill. They glow and blaze to the extent that they are not easily approached, especially by those with less or negative heats like witches and warlocks. Most importantly, these spiritually enlightened individuals must be aware of their own auras and energies in order to sustain their potency, because power—any power—loses its potency if diluted through, say, defilement. This is important in order to project, accordingly, one's positive heat or energy unto someone of less energy, otherwise one may be drained of the source of one's spiritual power. Unfortunately, some enlightened people are not even aware of their spiritual prowess, or that they engage in such prolonged profane acts that they are beyond spiritual awakening. For the Akɔmfo, this is when the Abosom that called them into the clerical vocation leave them, because their defilements prevent the Abosom from approaching them. As for kings and queen mothers, for example, whenever there is reason to believe that they have been defiled, they are purified and divine–human equilibration restored. The point is that spiritual fire must be replenished and sustained periodically, because fire that is stationary extinguishes quickly, and the more reason why fire must have a companion if the full extent of its fury, power, perniciousness, as well as its life-giving beneficence are to be felt. After all, the Abosom, as fires, are always moving like whirlwinds; that is, no spirit ever stands still. Ultimately, all enlightened individuals are transformed persons when they go through fire, but it is up to them to use the fire, spiritual power for societal benefit or for ill. The point is that both witches and warlocks, on the one hand, and the Akɔmfo, on the other, all possess fire, literally and spiritually, but it is the Akɔmfo who are called, trained, and set aside as diviners-prophets-priests-doctors to heal and ensure the well-being of society, while witches-warlocks are perceived as enemies of society.

AIR

Fire travels with air (or wind), which, in turn, travels or moves on water, and so another essence of the Abosom, as we try to decipher their essence, is air. What this means, most importantly, is that air *moves*, and it does so on water and land too. For the Akan, *Mframa* is wind or air, while *Ahom* is breath, as in breathing. While Mframa and Ahom are the same, each, however, is unique in context and function. The Ahom gives ethereal evidence to the *Ɔkra* (soul) through the incessant palpitation of the heart, which offers tangible evidence to the Ɔkra. Furthermore, while the Ahom by itself is not the soul, entirely, it is one of three symbiotically related essences constituting the Ɔkra or soul—the others being the *Nkrabea* (existential career or professional blueprint) and the *Dzin* (name). The Ɔkra (soul) is symbiotically linked to the palpitation of the heart which is enabled by the Ahom (breath). By virtue of its incessant activity which causes the heart to palpitate and makes living possible, the Ahom, though air—because when exhaled joins the undifferentiated air without—is unique and hence its name, Ahom. Thus, the Ahom only refers to the differentiated but incessant air within living organisms that must be exhaled in order to be regenerated without as if the Ahom is contaminated or rendered heavier for circulating in the body. This being the case, it must be exhaled and replaced with a more pristine Mframa from without, following blood circulation in the body.

The ethereal distinction between the Ahom and the Mframa is simple: The Mframa is the body of undifferentiated air without from which the Ahom is derived and from which all life-forms depend. Yet the Mframa is not normally thought of as an Ɔkra (soul), only an Ɔkra when it is in vivo. When exhaled as Ahom, it is perceived as one continuous act of the Mframa. Interestingly, while the Ɔkra is inextricably linked to God and therefore emanates from God, the Mframa is, generally speaking, not considered an Ɔkra. And yet there is an embryonic link between God and the Ɔkra; in fact, God is Ɔkra.

First, there is the relationship between the Mframa and the Abosom (spirits) as spirits of God. The Abosom are of essence Mframa (wind or air), because they are of the same essence as God; that is, the Abosom are unseen spiritual (*Āsunsum*) creatures or forces. The basis of this is the notion that, for the Akan, God (Nyame) is Mframa, because the Akan equate God with wind (Mframa), making the Abosom too Mframa, like God. Unlike God, however, the Abosom are creatures of distinct Mframa and yet inseparable winds linked to, in support and praise of God at the center or middle of an infinite universe, hence the name Abosom (beings of worship of God). The Abosom are expressions of God without making both God and the Abosom one massive Mframa force, which they are indeed. Relationally, the Mframa symbiosis between God and the Abosom is described thus: God is the incomparably gargantuan tree in the center or middle of the universe with its roots deeply embedded in the bottomless abyss, and the Abosom are the branches spread across the universe or universes—with the fruits on the branches being the known and unknown planets and worlds. This is exactly one of the ways that the Akan conceptualize God, as *Tweduapon*—the Dependable Tree. However, the exact location of God in the center or middle of the cosmos, which could be likened to the eye of a massive storm, is—and will—remain enigmatic to humans. Attempts at discovering the center of this singular force that humanity has assigned the term God comes with a warning, that humanity would long be extinct before God could be discovered. Hence, the sarcastic statement: Nyame *bɔwu no, nna maewu* (I will long be dead, before God dies). In other words, none will be alive to witness the demise of God, if it ever came to that because God never dies because God is Ɔdomankoma (God Everlasting).

Second and most definitely, the Akan assert that for anyone to converse with God, one only needs to speak to the air or wind (Mframa). This is in acknowledgement of God's omnipresence, ubiquity, knowledge, and nature in Akan socio-political and religious life and thought. Moreover, it goes to confirm the notion that anyone can converse with God anywhere and at any moment. For this reason anyone who claims to be the only mouthpiece of God is a liar. Furthermore, it affirms the belief that God is accessible to all and therefore not the private property of, or under the control of any single individual or persons. Thus throughout Africa—from time immemorial to the present—God has never had temples or clerics, as Bosman observed in 1704 in West Africa. But even though God is omnipresent and ubiquitous—in the air—still people in general must be taught about the nature of God and the proper ways to fear God.

In addition to God's omnipresence, God's accessibility and knowledge is contained in an often-cited philosophical statement: *Obi nkyirɛ abofra* Nyame (literally, no one points out God to a child). But how are children knowledgeable about God without being taught? First, *Obi nkyirɛ abofra* Nyame simply means that God is accessible to all; in fact, the statement could be taken sarcastically to reject those who purport to know everything about God. And second, the key to deciphering the statement has to do with the essence of God as air or wind (Mframa) and when a child first experiences God. At the very moment of parturition when a neonate emerges from the womb, it must inhale its first Mframa—the gift of life—if it is to survive as a living being. God, then, is the first to enter a child (abofra) as Ahom (breath) in order to make it a living being. By the same token, the Ahom is the last essence to depart a living entity to cause a death. Thus a neonate's inhalation of air is its first unilateral psychosocial act evidenced by its first speech, cry. Similarly, any abeyance of the inhalation-crying act raises extreme concerns of midwives who assist by administering gentle but sharp slaps to neonates. Generally the assistance is enough to trigger crying. With God now within and without, hope is restored in the community of faith.

The notion that God is self-revealing (*Obi nkyirɛ abofra* Nyame) is a phenomenon extending to all societies and peoples, because God is the very air that sustains all of life. Therefore, the idea that God could be introduced to any group of people because they do not have any conception of God is false and arrogance on the part of those who claim to know God more than any other people.[30] As evidence, Europeans and Arabs could only use force to impose their gods on Africans, not because Africans had no ideas of God, but because Europeans and Arabs wanted psychological control in addition to physical control of Africans as slaves. Both Europeans and Arabs realized that once the gods of Africans have been supplanted by foreign gods, then whatever religious pronouncements in the names of European and Arab gods would be accepted without question by Africans since the African gods have been defeated, just like the Africans who worshipped non-Africans as masters. Today, it is pathetic and even shameful to see churches at every corner of Ghanaian streets and what and who they try to imitate: our non-African masters. Only now, non-Africans do not have to enslave and force Africans to worship them once the mechanism of psychological control has been set in motion; Africans clerics are now the ones enforcing what our colonial overlords programmed us to carry out in the name of non-African religions for hours rather than put those productive hours to work and ameliorate our lives. And so the perpetual cycle of poverty and depravation continue unabated for Africans while the non-African societies that we worship and glorify prosper immensely.

In addition to breathing, speaking involves air which is compressed to produce words and sound. Although sounds made are unseen, words produced achieve their desired effects on those intended. To speak is to produce air in a manner that produces creative sound, a unique sound understood by a group of likeminded persons. In itself, it suggests that the spoken word has dynamically transformative, magical powers beyond the world of tangibility. Communicating via this mode with one another as human beings is magical, because words used from person to person result in certain actions without actual physical contact. People know too well the caustic, piercing, poignant, and vituperative nature of words emanating from our mouths when people are angry. Indeed, we do not see the words that we speak, but we certainly know of their pernicious effects on others, physically, emotionally, and psychologically. Yes, we are speaking of the ability to cause harm to others without any physical contact—witchcraft. In this sense, all human beings possess power. So when people speak to one another, or even to God, they use compressed air manipulated to make sounds and intonations that express innermost desires for a people. Conversely, the lack of sound, speech, may suggest that nothing creatively transformative may occur; but, should the absence of speech be interpreted as inertia? For one thing, the absence of speech suggests that no one hears or is a party to an active endeavor, which may suggest that no one carries out the wishes of anyone. However, the lack of sound certainly does not mean inertia, because living things still continue to breathe even in the absence of speech, further suggesting that intrinsically something transformative is still taking place.

Spoken words have power, even for humans, but for God words are creative. For instance, God, we know from King Shabaka of Nubia (r. 716–701 BCE), said words that resulted in the creation of the world. This African king found an ancient sacred text in inner Africa and had it copied, which stated, among other things, that in the beginning God Ptah said words and the world came into being.[31] The Shabaka Stone, now at the British Museum, makes it quite clear that God Ptah spoke in order for the world to come into existence. But exactly what the words of God sounded like, in what mode they were delivered, or even in which language or languages—if God in fact uses any of the languages that humans speak at all—no human being knows because the words were obviously said long before the world came into being; meaning, no human was present to bear witness to them. The Akan will only maintain that God hid creation away from humans (Nyame *bɔɔ wiadzie suma adasa*). The corporeal world then owes its existence to the intangible words, roar, or howling of God. While no human was a witness to the speeches of God, the Abosom were present because they (Abosom) taught humans everything there is—and was—to know about God. We know that God spoke because the Abosom too do speak in languages, some of which are still known to humans. Thus God continues to speak to humans through his Abosom, who, in turn, make the will of God known to God's created order, including humans. One of the modes that the Abosom utilize to reveal the will of God is divination.

Divination is the means through which the Abosom, under the right psychological conditions, alight on Akɔmfo (diviners) in order for seekers to communicate directly with the Abosom (Gods and Goddesses) about existential concerns of the living. For this reason, God, among the Akan or Africans in general, has never had temples or structures where people congregate in order to worship God; clergy who claim to have been called by God directly; or representation of God in any kind, form, or fashion since Africans have always thought of God as spirit. Therefore, anyone who claims to be God's clergyman or woman, because he or she is called by a god, is not only false but foreign to traditional Africa. On the contrary, the Akɔmfo are the ones called by specific Abosom in different parts of the world to specific peoples, because they speak the same language as their Abosom. Since the Abosom know and operate at the behest of God, they speak of God via the Akɔmfo, not because the Akɔmfo are called by God but because the Akɔmfo are called by the Abosom.

MOGYA (BLOOD)

Could a spirit have blood since it does not have a physical form, flesh? Specifically, do the Abosom have what the Akan call *Mogya* (blood) since a body is required to encase blood? Traditionally God does not require blood sacrifices because God does not reside in the corporeal Wiadzie. The Abosom, however, crave blood because the assumption is that they do not have blood. Such cravings may be explained by the fact that only those who are deficient in something crave for that which they lack. Therefore the premium placed on blood by the Abosom could only be attributed to their insatiable appetite for blood. While this reasoning is logical from a human standpoint, it is incorrect spiritually, because it is based on how blood circulates in the body and since spirits do not have bodies the assumption is that the Abosom could not have blood. Therefore, it came as a surprise to me when the Abosom corrected me by saying that they too have blood.

Once during a divination rite, the question came up as to whether or not the Abosom have blood and the Ɔbosom answered in the affirmative. An Ɔbosom went on to explain the nature of their blood, that the blood that the Abosom have is pristinely pure, not to be compared to anything temporal or corporeal. Moreover, their blood does not have an iota of anything impure, or contain any pathogenic agency capable of making them sick. For this reason, the Abosom are incapable of falling sick, becoming ill, or dying. On the contrary, all corporeal diseases and illness are blood borne, explaining why human beings get sick. If all illnesses are blood borne, then it may explain why there is a transitional period for the Ɔsaman of a deceased person before making its final journey to the Samanadzie as a resurrected abstract personality of a dead person. The transitional period of approximately forty days that the Akan designate as the culturally defined waiting period for an Ɔsaman in the corporeal is designed for an Ɔsaman to be "cured" of all corporeal concomitants—in the same way that a neonate is cleansed of all Samanadzie accompaniments immediately upon parturition for the next eight days. After the forty-day spiritual curing or regeneration, the posthumous spiritual personality, the Ɔsaman, proceeds to its idealized existence as a regular Ɔsaman or apotheosized Ɔsaman incapable of death or ever falling ill again. Saliently, the Ɔsaman now does not have a physical body, as all corporeal concomitants have been shed and left behind in the temporal realm. Though relegated to the corporeal environment, the physical remains and attributes, the *fuun* (corpse), are kept at safe places at the cemetery (*Ɛsiāye*) to be reused ethereally whenever an Ɔsaman makes an appearance in the corporeal world.

As the Abosom have pristinely pure blood and since human beings descended from them directly—as we will see in the next chapter—why then is corporeal blood "contaminated" and the source of all illnesses and diseases? What happens to blood that the Abosom pass on to corporeal beings? Unlike the Abosom or even the Nsamanfo (plural of Ɔsaman), corporeal beings fall ill and die because all kind of diseases are found in the blood of corporeal beings. Perhaps the most tantalizing debates that I have had with friends are that since the Abosom have such pristinely pure blood, why are they still interested in human and animal blood, which is not as pristine or pure as that of the Abosom? Another way of asking the same question is: Can invisible agencies like the Abosom partake of corporeal things like sacrifices offered by humankind when everything found on earth is found in the spiritual realm? If the spiritual is the ultimate reality and therefore the blood of the Abosom is pristinely superior to corporeal blood, then why would the Abosom be interested in what might be considered inferior or contaminated blood? From this perspective, the answer is really simple, in that spiritual agencies only partake of the essences of tangible things, leaving behind only nonessentials for human and animal consumption. But why then are the nonessentials not as pristine as the Abosom's?

The mystery certainly lies with the transformation of intangibles to tangibles, from spiritual to material. There is a transformation at the very moment when the spiritual weds the material. As long as blood is spiritual it retains its purity, but once it becomes materialized and circulation begins it loses it purity due to the flesh and corporeal influences. One capability of the Abosom is that they can transform themselves into pseudo material beings. An Ɔbosom changing into, say, a female human being does not lose its divine nature and attributes, including its pristine blood. But a human being would have a material substance of flesh (Honam), which is composed of the very blood of a mother. That is, blood becomes flesh as it is transformed in utero. It is precisely this uterine consanguinity that is the basis of the Akan family unit (the Ābusua), defined as a mother and her uterine children. Though the spirit (Sunsum) will be dealt with in the next chapter, it's worth noting that what is unseen—insofar as a father is Sunsum (spirit)—could not be the basis of sociology—only a mother (blood) and her children constitute a family. Subsequently, there are seven of these uterine consanguineous groupings (the Ābusua) that every single Akan must belong to, namely, the *Asona, Tweedan, Kona, Anana, Abradzie, Asakyir,* and *Asenee*. The Akan position is consistent with the scientific view of mitochondrial DNA and the notion that humanity descended from a single woman in Africa. In other words, in the beginning was the primordial woman, the Old Woman and her children, as the Akan maintain.

Clearly, the blood of the Abosom is transformed when it becomes flesh (Honam). The Honam (skin, flesh) encompasses an outer covering (*nohu*) of the entire physical human personality, *Onyimpa,* who, structurally, is likened to a tree, *dua*, and hence *Onyimpa dua*. The tree (dua) metaphor is meant to describe the human being as a living, structurally upright being (*Onyimpa dasanyi*), as opposed to a fallen (human) dead tree (*fuun*), because upon death a person (*Onyimpa dasanyi*) is no longer a human but rather a *fuun* (corpse).

Subcutaneously, the *nam* (meat) is thought to be the edible part of a body although most meats are sold whole. However, most fish are sold with scales which are removed before the meat proper is reached. So, meat refers to the fleshy part of a body minus bones. Most importantly, meat is blood covered by the skin. Another salient point is that to have Honam (flesh) is to have a body, meaning a corporeal being, because Jesus, for example, makes it clear to his disciples that a spirit has no flesh and bones (Lk. 24:39 RSV). So the answer to the question as to why the blood of the Abosom is pure and free of illness, while human blood and therefore human beings are subject to all kinds of illnesses and diseases, is because the otherwise pristine blood of the Abosom has been materialized in the flesh. The Abosom have no flesh or bones and therefore no reason for them to fall ill or even die since they are incorruptible.

Finally, how then do the Abosom crave for blood, to the extent that blood sacrifices pervade African cultures? Parenthetically, God does not require any blood sacrifice, in the same way that God does not have temples or clergies because God is the One Ultimate Invisible Sunsum (Spirit). And as explained to William Bosman by the peoples of West Africa in 1704 that since ". . . God is Invisible, they say, it would be absurd to make any Corporeal Representation of him, for it is impossible to make any Image of what we never saw."[32] Furthermore, the Africans pointed out to Bosman that even though the Abosom are spirits as God, they (Abosom), as lieutenants of God, have apparitional capabilities—with temples and priests and are therefore worshipped directly in place of God.

When it comes to why the Abosom desire blood ambrosia, one does not need to look out any farther for answers, because the answer may lie with living things' craving for sustenance. Human beings, like the Abosom, crave blood. But unlike the Abosom who do not die even without blood because they are eternal beings, human beings do not live without food, specifically blood, or, actually, milk. Whenever living beings feed on meat, flesh, body, or leaves of any living or even dead things, we are feeding on blood. We have already established that the body is blood, and so living beings need to feed on the blood of others in order to survive. And so for Christians, and especially for Roman Catholics, the emphasis on the blood and body of Jesus is paramount, that as long as and as often as Christians eat the body of Jesus and drink his blood, they remember him. So for Jesus, there is no separation of body and blood; but most importantly, Jesus made it clear that both must be partaken, ceremoniously.

Naturally, people do not drink blood as though they were drinking water, nor can even stand the sight of blood, which is quickly covered. However, blood, fresh blood, has its place in many religious ceremonies, and those who usually handle such blood ambrosia are the highly developed members of society, for example, kings and queen mothers and members of the clergy. Blood opens up the links to the spiritual world allowing the Abosom to directly bless, protect, and sanctify those touched by blood sacrifices. And as long as those individuals lived pure lives and remain untouched by anything unclean, they are protected. Subsequently, whenever an Akan ruler goes near an unclean thing like a dead body, blood is used to purify him or her immediately after stepping away from viewing, say, the corpse of another royalty because a king or queen mother is a living ancestor, meaning he or she is already an apotheosized being in human form.

Ritual purification of certain highly developed individuals is simple. A sheep is readied when it is learned that a king or queen mother would be attending a funeral. After the viewing of the corpse of a colleague, the throat of the sheep is cut and the gushing blood poured on the feet of the royal. Thus purified and sanctified, a royal returns home knowing that he or she is right with the Abosom. Failure to perform this ritual renders a king or queen mother unclean and the direct channel and access to the Abosom is blocked because the Abosom do not go near anything unclean. This is the most vulnerable moment of every royalty's life, because the Abosom are unable to protect their king or queen mother if they are defiled. They do not even respond to divinations; in their place, other Abosom may respond in attempts to plead a king or queen mother's case, especially if he or she unknowingly rendered himself or herself unclean. Having withdrawn their presence from a king or queen mother due to uncleanness, it may take a series of purification rites to get them back. Still, blood must be shed.

The position of a king or queen mother as a living ancestor makes the personality of the royal vis-à-vis the ancestors and the Abosom in general more interesting. To have blood smeared all over a body or have it poured on the feet of certain individuals not only sanctifies the body and therefore the person but also transforms the entire personality into a sacred ambrosia for the Abosom and ancestors. The ambrosia is certainly not the body or blood of the king (or queen mother), but rather the blood of the animal whose blood now is poured or smeared on a king or queen mother. In this context, blood, more than any other offering or sacrifice, atones for mistakes and evil deeds of people. Thus atoned, a king is restored to the aegis of the Abosom and ancestors, offering propitiatory rites to the Abosom and ancestors as their representatives on earth.

As for the Abosom, sacred blood runs through them as the source of their immortality. Therefore, when they spot blood, especially flesh blood, they are reminded of their immortality—in the same way that human beings are reminded of their mortality when blood is exposed—and salivate and delightfully partake of the essence of blood that invigorate them tremendously. Thus revitalized, the Abosom are feistier and ready to accede to demands of adherents.

Conversely, coagulated blood (or even uncoagulated blood) left behind after Abosom partake of the offerings of blood, is for human consumption as holy meat. This applies to all offerings and sacrifices for the Abosom and ancestors; the Abosom and ancestors partake of the essences of sacrifices offered to them and what remains, the chaff, so to speak, is what human beings consume. What is different about the remainder of sacrifices offered to the Abosom and consumed by humans is that the leftovers are consecrated ambrosia because they have been shared with the Abosom and ancestors. In other words, what is good for the ancestors and Abosom is also good for humans, in the same way that food offered to an infant by its mother is also good for a mother to eat.

We know offerings to the Abosom and ancestors are ready for human consumption when certain hours have elapsed after the initial offerings.

However, there are exceptions. If, for example, a sheep is killed and its blood poured on feet of royals attending a funeral, the meat could be eaten right away by those who handled the ritual. After all, only the blood is needed for the occasion. If, however, an offering involves a meal, then it is left at the altar from, say, morning to about late afternoon, after which attendants may eat the meal. Sometimes—and depending on the offering or sacrifice—an offering could be left on an altar for days.

While blood is a source of immortality for spiritual agencies because it is a refreshingly regenerative "drink," it also gives life to corporeal existence up to a point because corporeal existence is finite. Aware of blood as a lifesaving element, the Akan equate blood to life and place a prohibition on the taking of life; that is, spilling of another human being's blood. Therefore, to kill is to spill blood, which is a contravention of divine and natural laws against killing other human beings. But how then is spilling the blood of fellow human beings different from human sacrifices to the Abosom and ancestors when they both are the same: spilling of blood? There is a fine distinction between the two, however: intentionality. The indiscriminate spilling of blood of any kind is a contravention of divine and natural laws; however, spilling blood for sacrificial purposes when an intent is clearly spelled out may be proper. That is, sacrifices may only take place if the intention is expressly for a higher power and cause for a group. But even here, a group's intentions and reasons must be unambiguously stated publicly, otherwise one is guilty of murder. Sacrificing animals, leaves, and gifts of various kinds must be addressed prayerfully as to why they were being sacrificed and messages transmitted through them to the intended spiritual destinations. In common practice, it suffices to offer a sacrificial animal a message and water to drink before killing it.

The Abosom do not always choose the conventional approach of taking blood, as described already. They can suck blood out of living beings while those beings are still alive.[33] This phenomenon is very common because it may involve animal sacrifices organized by a community like the Āwutu-ābe of Simpa (Winneba) during their annual deer festivities. It also applies to people, especially those cursed for one reason or another, murderers, thieves, and very bad people in general. Such individuals have lost their spiritual guidance and protection and are therefore subject to the whims of spiritual forces looking for blood without having to actually kill their prey. Like mosquitoes, the Abosom suck the blood of their victims just to the point of death, allowing some human beings to take the fall for them when they engage in altercations or accidents. Sometimes even minor accidents may result in their deaths, so that the blame is put on others and not on the Abosom. What this suggests is that blood is what the Abosom and ancestors (the Nananom Nsamanfo) want and they make sure that they get it one way or another.

An Ɔbosom, Yaw Dɛnsu, revealed during a divination rite that whenever he feels he needs to drink blood, he takes two cars or buses—which look like small toys to him—from opposite directions and smash them together. Albeit spiritual acts, they invariably cause accidents. He would then squeeze and drink the blood of the bad people, which he could easily identify. When asked as to what happens to the good people during accidents, his response was that he does not kill the good people, as he examines those in the vehicles prior to his actions. But he admitted that some might be injured, although they always recover. And, finally, when asked as to why blood, the emphatic response was "Blood is what we like."

NOTES

1. I told her to start reading Kofi Appiah-Kubi, *Man Cures, God Heals.* (New York: Friendship Press, 1981).
2. Konadu, Kwasi. *Indigenous Medicine and Knowledge in African Society.* (New York: Routledge, 2007), pp. 37–180.
3. Ephirim-Donkor, Anthony. *African Spirituality: On Becoming Ancestors.* (Trenton, NJ: Africa World Press, Inc., 1997), p. 51.
4. Rattray, R. S. *Religion and Art in Ashanti*, (Oxford: Oxford University Press, 1927), p. 154.
5. Ibid.
6. Bosman, William. *A New and Accurate Description of the Coast of Guinea: Divided into The Gold, The Slave, and The Ivory Coasts.* (New York: Barnes & Noble, Inc., [1705] 1967), p. 454.
7. Ibid.
8. Ellis, A. B. *The Tshi-speaking Peoples of the Gold Coast of West Africa: their religion, manners, customs, laws, language, etc.* (Anthropological Publications, Oosterhout N.B.: The Netherlands, [1887] 1970), p. 23.
9. Lipinski, Jed. *A Visit From the Devil: Feared Traditional Priest From Ghana Spends a Year in the Bronx* (http://www.nytimes.com/2013/07/21/nyregion/feared-traditional-priest-from-ghana-spends-a-year-in-the-bronx.html), last accessed on April 12, 2015.
10. Ellis, A. B. *The Tshi-speaking Peoples of the Gold Coast of West Africa: their religion, manners, customs, laws, language, etc.* (Anthropological Publications, Oosterhout N.B. The Netherlands, [1887] 1970), pp. 122–123.
11. Bosman, William. op. cit., p. 146.
12. Ellis, A. B. op. cit., p. 26.
13. Idowu, E. Bolaji. *Olodumare: God in Yoruba Belief.* (London: Longmans, 1962), p. 2.
14. Ibid.
15. Ellis, A. B. op. cit., 31.
16. Joel E. Tishken, Toyin Falola, and Akintude Akinyemi. *Sango in Africa and the African Diaspora.* (Bloomington: Indiana Univ. Press, 2009), p. 1.

17. For the concept of *There* or *Thereness,* see Ephirim-Donkor, Anthony. *African Religion Defined, a Systematic Study of ancestor Worship among the Akan, Second Edition.* (Lanham, MD: University Press of America, 2013), p. 15ff.

18. Budge, Wallis E. A. *From Fetish to God in Ancient Egypt.* (New York: Benjamin Blom, Inc. 1972). p. 16.

19. Emeagwali, Gloria and Walter, Mariko Namba. "Ancient Egyptian Shamanism." In *Shamanism: An Encyclopedia of World Beliefs, Practices, and Culture.* Ed. by Mariko Namba Walter and Eva Neumann Fridman. (Santa Barbara, CA: ABC-CLIO, 2004), pp. 908–909.

20. See Rattray's chapter titled "Birth" in his book, *Religion and Art in Ashanti,* (Oxford, Oxford University Press, 1927), pp. 51–68.

21. Ibid. p.57.

22. Ephirim-Donkor, Anthony. *African Spirituality: on Becoming Ancestors, Revised Edition.* (Lanham, MD: University Press of America, 2013), pp. 45–49.

23. For the fire phenomenon in witches and warlocks, see Ephirim-Donkor, Anthony. *African Religion Defined, a Systematic Study of ancestor Worship among the Akan, Second Edition.* (Lanham, MD: University Press of America, 2013), pp. 80ff.

24. Gbadegesin, Segun. "Eniyan: The Yoruba concept of a person." In P. H. Coetzee and A. P. J. Roux, eds., *The African Philosophy Reader, second edition* (New York: Routledge: Taylor &Francis Group, 2003), p. 179.

25. Ephirim-Donkor, Anthony. *African Religion Defined, a Systematic Study of ancestor Worship among the Akan, Second Edition.* (Lanham, MD: University Press of America, 2013), pp. 80ff.

26. Ephirim-Donkor, Anthony. "Akom: The Ultimate Mediumship Experience Among the Akan," *Journal of the American Academy of Religion* 76, 1, 2008: p. 67.

27. Ellis, A. B. *The Tshi-speaking Peoples of the Gold Coast of West Africa: their religion, manners, customs, laws, language, etc.* (Anthropological Publications, Oosterhout N.B. The Netherlands, [1887] 1970), pp. 138–139.

28. For full account of what I observed and participated in, see Ephirim-Donkor, Anthony. "Akom: The Ultimate Mediumship Experience Among the Akan," *Journal of the American Academy of Religion* 76, 1, 2008: p. 67.

29. Budge, E. A. Wallis. *The Egyptian Book of the Dead: the Papyrus of Ani.* (New York: Dover [1895] 1967), p. l.

30. Bosman, William. Op. cit.

31. Ephirim-Donkor, Anthony. *African Religion Defined, a Systematic Study of Ancestor Worship among the Akan, Second Edition.* (Lanham, MD: University Press of America, 2013), pp. 41–43.

32. Bosman, William. Op. Cit.

33. Ephirim-Donkor, Anthony. *African Religion Defined, a Systematic Study of Ancestor Worship among the Akan, Second Edition.* (Lanham, MD: University Press of America, 2013), pp.121–122.

Chapter Three

The Spirit Incarnate

The Abosom (Gods and Goddesses), as we have seen, are composed of water, air, fire, and blood as the core essentials. These essences enable them, for instance, to rejuvenate themselves by accepting blood of corporeal beings sacrificially. What this chapter does is examine how the Abosom, as spiritual agents of God, link up corporeally on earth to create a species that the Akan called *Onyimpa dasanyi* (a living person). The chapter examines the capabilities of the Abosom, as to when the Abosom intrinsically take hold of material subjects conjugationally resulting in deposition of active essential attributes in living things which ultimately becomes the basis for ethical living (*Ɔbra bɔ*).

The belief in and praxis of what the Akan refer to as *Ɔbra bɔ* is so common a concept that most people take it for granted and yet it seems to govern the way people live socially. Still, the way people discuss Ɔbra bɔ suggests that it has a lot to do with successes and failures in life. Kwasi Konadu, for example, defines Ɔbra bɔ as: "attitude, way of life, praxis . . . living, physical existence,"[1] and as we will see below, indeed Ɔbra bɔ encompasses all aspects of living during adulthood. But most importantly, Konadu asserts that the concept of Ɔbra bɔ is "coming into this world with a sense of mission and an emphasis on the realization of that mission."[2] For J. B. Danquah, "obara" is "ethical existence,"[3] and as we will see in chapter 5, he relates "obara" to immortality. So how is it possible then that a spiritual agency would take hold of a material being in a union? Conversely, how can a spiritual agency as an Ɔbosom produce a corporeal being as an offspring?

Theologically for the Akan, all speculative thoughts about the origin of humanity begin with God. Thus there is a divine pronouncement that the Akan are absolutely convinced about, and that is God is the progenitor of all human beings; in fact, none is the child of the earth (*Nyimpa nyinaa ara yɛ* Nyame *mma; obiara nnyɛ Asasi ba*). What this means, most importantly, is that every human being has a divine origin, not corporeal in nature and therefore the notion that the human being is made of earth is false. But also inherent in this dictum is an enigmatic problem having to do with the physical property of human beings. If all of humanity descended from God, who is spirit, then God's offspring must also be of the same spiritual substance or essence as God, without material properties, as the Abosom. So then, how do we explain the material substance of humanity? Did the earth (Asasi) also contest the human being, and if so, what is the basis for the earth's claim as the progenitor of humanity?

The Akan believe the earth to be female. Actually, the earth is not a single female but two goddesses, namely, Asasi Āfua and Asasi Yaa,[4] for the simple reason that the two separate names denote females one born on a Thursday and the other on a Friday. As female Abosom they are by their very nature spirits (Āsunsum) who are acknowledged as such during libations, but they as earth do not transmit spirit or Sunsum as an active agent. Instead they transmit blood (*Mogya*). Meaning females are incapable of producing offspring. God, on the other hand, is thought of as Father (Āgya) and therefore male. As such, he is not only Sunsum but also capable of producing and transmitting the Sunsum that causes an inactive agent, like blood, to be active, and thus making God the Father of creation. But if God is the progenitor of all human beings, then is earth the mother, at least, of human beings? The naming of earth, Asasi, by God is interesting, suggesting that, perhaps, the earth thought she too may have some claim to humanity. However, any claim to any part of humanity by earth is emphatically rejected by God, as the statement *obiara nnyɛ Asasi ba* clearly states. If human beings are children of the earth then there will be no afterlife because when people die that will be the end since females do not transmit Sunsum. But since human beings are children of God, it means that there is life after death because the Sunsum survives death and the basis for ancestor worship proved. Ancestor worship, indeed, is the religion of Africans, because people believe their relatives survive death to watch over and influence the lives of the living, their posterity. In response, the living propitiate the ancestors and the Abosom. Among the Akan, for instance, the Nananom Nsamanfo (Ancestors) and Abosom are propitiated forty days during the festival called Akwasidai as their way of informing the ancestors and Abosom that they, the living, are alive and well. So, asserting his right as Father (Āgyȧ) of all creation (*Ɔbɔadzie*), God is proclaiming that he is sole owner and therefore giver and taker of life.

The notion that the dead continue to live on as spiritual personalities that must be worshipped is at the core of African religion. Worship ceremonies are rituals that have been made into festivals for the dead or actually for the spiritual personalities surviving death. When I was growing up in Simpa, for example, I and other children who slept with my paternal grandmother in her room were awakened about 4 a.m. by the dirge and wailing of our grandmother. She was wailing for my father, her last born who died a few months earlier, because my father, her son, had appeared to her. But since this was not the first time that my father had appeared to her, why would she wail at this particular time? What we (grandchildren and great-grandchildren) did not understand was that her dirges and wailing were part of a much larger annual ritual among the Āwutu-ābe of Simpa (Winneba), Ghana, for the dead-alive (Nsamanfo).

Annually in the month of August the Āwutu-ābe of Simpa celebrate the Akomasi festival. Early in the month on a Tuesday (because as a fishing community no fishing is carried out on that day), women of an agnatic household who lost members during the year would gather at the agnatic household, the Pramma, after 3 a.m. and sing dirges and wail for all who were lost during the year until about 6 a.m. Then they disperse until about noon when they start bringing meals to the Pramma for agnatic members (and the dead) to consume. It was in this context that my grandmother was wailing for my father, her last born. Sadly, this ancient ritual for the dead has largely been ignored because people now say that they are Christian.

When it comes to following some non-African ritual practices, the trend nowadays is for the Akan and Ghanaians in general to blindly follow foreign traditions at the expense of our own cultural traditions. Yet in the United States, for example, there is national day for the dead on the last Monday of the month of May called Memorial Day. So why would Africans like the Akan refuse to commemorate their dead? No wonder Ghanaian youths are now growing up untruthful, insolent—with no sense of morality—confused, addicted to drugs, and easily influenced by strange lifestyles and values, because they are not sufficiently anchored in African and Akan ritual traditions. This is symptomatic of a society that has lost its core values due to an inferiority complex resulting from slavery and colonialism. Psychologically, it has created fear, and corrupt and intellectual paralysis that has caused us to behave as though our non-African masters were still watching us.

What is known about the Abosom is that they are of the same essence as God because they are immaterial although capable of putting on pseudo material form. However, the same could not be said of corporeal beings, including human beings. Living things have material properties, not spiritual properties as the Abosom, or even divine essence as God whose offspring include human beings via the Abosom. Thus, the question is: How exactly is a human being a divine creature as God, entitling a person to be a son or daughter of God and yet remain a material being? Can the divine, God, who is infinite, produce a material or tangible offspring who turns out to be finite? What, then, does it mean when the Akan say that everyone is a child of God, and none a child of the earth? Meaning, in spite of having material properties that tie a corporeal being to the earth, the metaphor for a mother, God, the divine, the invisible one, is still father of a visible, material being.

To answer these questions, we need to, first, focus on God and God's relationship to the Abosom. The Akan believe that God works through the Abosom, making the Abosom custodians of the vast limitless universe at the behest of God. By nature the Abosom are God's spirits in action, meaning what God wills or proclaims, the Abosom undertake on behalf of God. The relationship between God and the Abosom is clearly stated by Job when he explains that: "The spirit of God has made me, and the breath of the Almighty gives me life" (Job 33:4 RSV). But long before Job, however, ancient Egyptian priests had promulgated that the Abosom (Gods and Goddesses) were the very thoughts and motions of God Ptah. In other words, whatever God thought of and whatever motions God made, those thoughts came into being as gods and goddesses (Abosom). For the Akan therefore the Abosom are the first children of God; as such, the Abosom have always been *there* with God, long before human beings, and before that, corporeal existence. Indeed the Abosom are the creators of human beings, as we see among the Akan that the god of wisdom, Kwɛku Anansi, created the first inanimate human body.[5]

Secondly, the Akan believe that human beings are willed directly by the Abosom—and not God—making every person an *Ɔbosom ba* (child of a deity or Ɔbosom). To be willed by an Ɔbosom (God or Goddess) is for an Ɔbosom to *yeu* (select or choose) a person to become a human being, hence divine selection. The notion is that before an Ɔbosom becomes a human being, the head, or father, of an Abosom Kuu (group, pack, family) selects or appoints the Ɔbosom to relocate to the corporeal. Now whether or not the divine selection is a unilateral decision by the head of an Abosom Kuu, a collective decision of the whole family of Abosom, or an individual decision first made by an Ɔbosom and later confirmed by the father of the Abosom Kuu is not clear. Nonetheless, the "Father" of an Abosom family or group makes the appointment as the sponsoring deity to the extent that later success or failure of the Ɔbosom who becomes a human being directly affects the father-deity (Āgya-bosom) in heaven, so much so that upon death the Āgya-bosom decides to not allow an evil person who was his child to reincarnate. In other words, the Ɔbosom who became a person failed them all by not achieving what he or she set out to achieve in the mundane by leading an unethical life. If, however, a person's life was cut short through no fault of his or her own then the Sunsum of the deceased person—which returns to the collective upon death—is allowed to reincarnate.

The belief in the Āgya-bosom should not be confused with the notion of NaSaman, ruler of the Samanadzie, the realm of the Nsamanfo (resurrected posthumous abstract personalities). Apparently in competition with the Abosom, the NaSaman also wills children to the corporeal world from the Samanadzie with the sole aim of taunting and extracting wealth from parents. Unlike an Āgya-bosom who sponsors another Ɔbosom into the corporeal Wiadzie with the aim of protecting and guiding it into adulthood, the NaSaman manipulates children in the hopes of preventing them from reaching adulthood. Babies who succumb to her power, influence and control become her servants and work at her behest by being reincarnated repeatedly. The cycle of birth, death, and reincarnation is only ended when parents seek spiritual protection for their infants. Sometimes parents take a ritually extreme step of mutilating their babies upon death, in the hope that the babies would be rejected upon their return to the NaSaman. Reacting angrily to the bodily marks on the children that she sent to earthly parents, the NaSaman sends them back to earth, never to return (die) to her again until old age. Seeking protection for and inflicting bodily marks on babies upon death are the ways that, the Akan believe, end the NaSaman's intrigue and manipulation of babies.[6]

On the contrary, every person has an Ɔbosom as father.[7] According to Christensen when he studied the priesthood among the Fanti, an Akan group, "Every person enters the world under the aegis of his father's guardian spirit (*egyabosom*, literally, 'father's deity'), which is usually a nature deity and may be appealed to like other gods."[8] This Ɔbosom father serves as a sponsor to an earthbound Ɔbosom who later becomes a human. Thus people speak of the *Āgya-bosom* (father deity) who not only escorts a human in transit from a spiritual realm to the temporal sphere, but who has the added responsibility of ensuring that a person gets through existence safely, provided an individual acknowledges his or her Āgya-bosom. Hence, the role of an Āgya-bosom in a person's life is one of spiritual protector. As a patron deity, an Āgya-bosom provides guidance and protection for his offspring, warding off evil and other malign forces that may attempt to harm the person under its aegis.

The term *Āgya-bosom* suggests that an Ɔbosom, whether male or female, always expresses itself in masculine terms vis-à-vis a human being and hence Āgya (father). But there is no question as to which Ɔbosom wills other Abosom to the corporeal Wiadzie: gods. Singularly important to the idea of Āgya is the fact that the Akan are absolutely convinced that a father is the progenitor and therefore protector of his offspring, in the same way that an Āgya-bosom wills his offspring into the world and protects him or her. Above all, God is the ultimate Āgya of all of creation, including the Abosom, hence God as Āgya Nyame. In this vein, a human father usurps the roles of both an

Āgya-bosom and God, to the extent that a father (Āgya) is Sunsum (spirit)—albeit a physical being—to his offspring, as a father assumes the spiritual role of the Abosom (and God) while still remaining a physical entity.

During one of my regular meetings with some of my elders as their king in 2013 during a naming rite, the consensus was that nowadays, urbanization has led to the decline in the notion of Āgya-bosom due to the hustling and bustling life in the cities. City life has created situations where parents are less concerned with seeking spiritual protection for their children than making ends meet economically on a daily basis. Consequently, the Abosom too have left people to their own devises, which makes people vulnerable to the whims of nature and evil forces. In the past, parents were genuinely interested in the spiritual well-being of their children and would go as far as to ascertain the purpose of their children's destinies as they placed them under the care and protection of the deities that willed the children. Some parents argue that they are now Christian or Islamic and therefore see no need to seek out tradition clergy equipped in mediumistic expertise to ascertain the whereabouts of Abosom responsible for their children being born. And yet in my own community of Mprumem, some parents who denounce traditional clergy have children who fall ill and do not respond to hospital treatments run to me for loans to send their children for healing to the traditional clerics that they earlier denounced.

If a child is believed to be willed by an Ɔbosom, which the Akan affirm, then how is it possible for an Ɔbosom to be turned into a human being? Here is where the mystery begins because we are not just speaking of copulation but the transformation and transmission of spiritual attributes of the Abosom willing humans to the mundane. Having already decided on the parents and home that a potential human being still spiritual would like to *sojourn* to as a human being, copulation—or rather semen (*huaba*/*ntoro*)—then becomes the means, mode of delivery of an Ɔbosom. In the act, the penis only serves as a conduit. I choose the word "sojourn" (*Suɛɛ*) rather very carefully, because the Akan speak of neonates as strangers and sojourners, intending to move on during adulthood to undertake their *Abrabɔ* (ethical existences and generativity), which may potentially lead to the realization of their *Nkrabea* (existential career or professional blueprint). Children are born as guests to host parents making parents and society temporary custodians of children with the responsibility of nurturing, equipping and educating children until they are ready to engage the world on their own. But going against the notion that neonates are sojourners, soon parents take ownership of their children and behave toward them as though children are not strangers. This is when the reality of having to be responsible for children for a long time sets in, to the extent that sometimes it is very hard for some parents to let go of their children during adulthood.

A FATHER AS *SUNSUM*

As we have already established that the Sunsum is spirit (also shadow and image), it so happens that the same spirit dwells in human beings although only males are bearers of the Sunsum making males progenitors of life, their offspring. In terms of the changing dynamic of a spiritual agency to a physical being, a male becomes the transmitting agency. That is, an Ɔbosom, as Sunsum (spirit) is transmitted through a father's semen (*huaba/ntoro*) during a sexual act analogous to spirit alightment during divination rites, as we see in the next chapter. By spirit alightment I mean the descent of Abosom on the heads of mediums during divination rites.[9] In "Akom: The Ultimate Mediumship Experience among the Akan," scholars are urged to rethink their use of "spirit possession" meant to dismiss and demean genuine African divination religious experiences, as alightment clearly reflects the way Africans describe the encounter between the Abosom and diviners. In the context of an Ɔbosom becoming a human, the resultant agency is a uniquely masculine agency called the *Su* (essential nature), which is an Ɔbosom willed by the Āgya-bosom as an individual. For J. B. Danquah, an Ɔbosom breaks off from the collective Abosom family as "Esu." Clearly for Danquah, the "*sunsum* . . . is basically the *e-su*"[10] meaning the Sunsum is incarnated as the Su in human beings. Everyone then is exactly the Ɔbosom willed into the corporeal environment. Since Abosom are masculine agencies, it happens that what they transmit retains their masculine essential attributes in terms of activity.

By nature the Abosom are active, never remaining still during alightment, for instance, and so it is during copulation that the Sunsum triggers an activity that transforms an otherwise inactive *Mogya* (blood) or egg of a female into what becomes a human being.[11] Therefore, in the same way that an Ɔbosom wills his offspring into the temporal environment, a father is also the one who wills his offspring into the world. And, like an Ɔbosom, a father is supposed to provide protection, ethical principles and guidance, and serve as a role model for his offspring throughout their existence. So a child is said to have two spiritual progenitors: a biological father and an Ɔbosom. Albeit a physical being, a father is regarded as a spiritual protector to his offspring, because his is the physical representation of the Sunsum, the very Ɔbosom who first willed his offspring through a biological father into the world. Subsequently, the role and responsibility of a father to his children are nonmaterialistic since he is Sunsum. If anything, they are psychological. As such, the first psychosocial ritual that a father performs for his neonate is to bestow a name on his child on the eighth day or thereafter. In itself, a name is also spiritual in the sense that names are intangible, only sounds that people respond to. But by naming his offspring, a child comes under the aegis of his or her father who controls his child psychologically—the mother controlling her child physically, emotionally, and socially. Spiritually, a name is an intangible agency passed on from one spiritual agency, an Ɔbosom, to a father, who in turn passes it to his offspring. From the moment a name is pronounced to a neonate, it not only identifies with the name, but the name forever becomes the child wholly. From that moment on a child hears its name as a unique sound and responds to it, forever. Hence, the Akan maintain that a father is the progenitor of his children—not his wife, knowing full well that gestation, parturition, and lactation are all female biological phenomena. The explanation for this seemingly contradictory notion that a father is the one who begets children has to do with the fact that life is seen as spiritual and the father as Sunsum, because it is he alone who transmits semen. As Rattray was emphatically told by one of his female discussants: "If a male transmitted his blood through the penis he could not beget a child." Men then transmit an active agency called Sunsum. The simple truth is that it takes life to give birth to another life.

Ritually, the spiritual control and ownership of a father over his offspring starts with a naming rite (*Dzin-to*). Ideally the rite must commence before sunrise and end with the rising sun, so that the first light a neonate sees is the sun. A neonate may remain in a maternal household or is taken stealthily to the paternal household. Occasionally, the child's maternal family would petition a neonate's patrikin for the right to name a child, but the request may or may not be granted since the right to name is exclusively a father's prerogative. A father, by right, names his own children, but he usually yields to older siblings of his paternal household who may wish to perform the rite. R. S. Rattray correctly points out that "the infant's own father, paternal grandfather, father's brother, father's brother's son, father's brother's daughter, father's sister, and so on" have the honor of naming a child. Occasionally, a father forfeits his right to name his child because he denies fathering a child in the first place, in which case an infant's matrikin bestows a name. However, if at some point the father admits to fathering the child, then a heavy fine is levied against him, the paying of which paves the way for the father to reclaim his child, although he may not rename the child, because one may not perform a naming rite twice. The reason is that a Dzin-to (naming rite) must be performed on the eighth day of birth with water and liquor, in accordance with ancient tradition. In other words, a neonate must survive to see its next natal day, a complete cycle of eight days when citizenship is bestowed with a name. Symbolically though, a naming rite may be performed at any time and on any person, especially on persons wishing to be "reborn" into new groups or even acquire new identities.

Sometimes, an elder that a neonate is named for may perform a ritual using saliva in order to transmit its spiritual properties to the neonate physically.

Saliva is discreetly transmitted by kissing or spitting into the mouth of the neonate and thereby imparting in a neonate essence of the kisser. For example, saliva contains the DNA of a person, but more than that it is the very Sunsum of a person so that the ritual is meant to offer a neonate a Sunsum of the elder. Still, saliva has antigens, such as to clean the eyes or even to cause harm.

The symbolic elements of water and liquor used in the Dzin-to are ancient and therefore not subject to any change because they have specific didactic and symbolic significance psychosocially.[12] This is important because some fundamentalist Christian groups have actually replaced the liquor with soft drinks—a foreign drink—instead, arguing that they do not want to get babies drunk. In fact, the Dzin-to rite has never gotten any neonate drunk, because no one who dips a finger in liquor and then touches the lip of a baby gets the baby drunk, especially when the same ritual is immediately repeated using water to dilute the hard taste of the liquor. The ancestors of the Akan were not so stupid so as to get an eight-day-old neonate drunk, because in the ancient days a mildly alcoholic palm wine was used and absolutely no one would say that a dip of a finger in a wine on the lip of a baby gets it drunk. Interestingly, those claiming to be Christians all went through the same Dzin-to and never got drunk as neonates or even as adults, but now the same adults cede their parental rights to pastors who dream up rituals that have absolutely nothing to do with Christian or Jewish traditions while claiming that their conjured-up rites are biblical.

Another reason offered for the switch is that the use of liquor is "not Christian," yet, as a theologian myself, I find no scriptural basis for the claims made by those now claiming to be Christian. As such, neonates are denied their first psychosocial rite of sharing in the long continuum of an ancient Akan rite. All peoples adhere to their cultural traditions with pride alongside their religious faiths, but when it comes to many Africans and Ghanaians in particular they are the ones who view their traditions and rituals shamefacedly and refuse to carry them out because they now claim to be Christian or Muslim.

One of the reasons why the elements for the Dzin-to (naming rite) are not subject to change is that the remainder of the ritual liquor is shared with all attendees when an elder moves from person to person announcing the name of the neonate, after which a recipient drinks to the well-being of the neonate. This continues until everyone has partaken of the drink. If a person arrived late, the ritual of sharing the drink is repeated until all attendees have partaken some of the liquor. In this way, a father earns his spiritual and psychological rights over his offspring. A neonate first hears and responds to a specific sound that permeates its inner being from its father and spiritual kind. Since all names are spiritual in origin because they originate with the Abosom, as a child grows up it associates and identifies with its name long before it learns how to write it—or never learns how to write it at all if born into an oral community.

The salient point is that the person who names, also owns; and, for this reason, a father psychologically owns and controls his offspring by naming and blessing them. Every person lives his or her name; that is, one exists in name only. Long after a death and in the absence of physical remains, only names are remembered. Thus, it makes no difference as to whether or not a person loves or hates one's father, because a person is his or her father in action and deeds. Therefore, to have and actually know one's father is to be anchored spiritually, otherwise one traverses the world aimlessly in search of one's spiritual kind, a father's. Without this bonding an individual is spiritually dead, and for this reason an Akan child does not exist until named by the patrikin on the eighth day unless a father denies fathering a child, in which case his rights are terminated. Thus terminated, a child's matrikin names the child.

As a vehicle and representative of an Ɔbosom, a father exercises psychological control over his offspring throughout their lives, reflected psychosocially by his right to name his offspring, bearing in mind that names are spiritual in origin. Also, to say that a father is the progenitor of his offspring is to accept the double entendre the statement carries, that a father imparts as well as takes away life, spiritually. A father's anger, for example, may cause the death of his child by depriving it of a spiritual identity or force. Thus vulnerable, a child may succumb to spiritual attacks. An angry father need not speak because his silence is tantamount to death. In this vein, it is important to maintain a good relationship with one's patrikin in order to ensure spiritual tutelage.

A father's spiritual protection is far greater than one would think: it encompasses his entire household. Everyone living in a space owned by a father comes under the aegis of a father's Sunsum. This includes the parameters of his property, because his Sunsum extends over the space that a father claims to be his and everyone and everything in it. It must be emphasized that this protection is spiritual (Sunsum), meaning the Sunsum of a father hovers over all things physical as well as spiritual (Āgya *ni sunsum hata biribiara do*).

Next, a father's Sunsum, while hovering over his household and compound, is also very dynamic, to the extent that it could be transported and transferred. A father's Sunsum serves as an accompaniment to anyone that a father blesses prior to undertaking a journey or any endeavor away from his immediate protection. In this way a father's Sunsum serves to guide his offspring embarking on a journey until one has successfully reached one's final destination. It is prudent therefore for a child to seek a father's approval in certain endeavors if a child wishes to be successful and blessed. For the young, then, it is prudent to be in the good graces of one's father, sometimes even when a father has been less than kind or responsible.

If a father can send along his Sunsum with an offspring, then he can certainly withhold it. Usually this occurs when a father is angry because he has been wronged by someone, particularly his own offspring. When this happens an apology from a contrite son or daughter usually causes a father to mellow and forgive his son or daughter. In this way, a father's Sunsum is restored to protecting his offspring. But sometimes a father may withdraw his Sunsum not because of anger but due to dereliction of his responsibilities to his offspring. For example, a child whose father denies fathering might grow up very angry with his or her father for denying spiritual security and stability. Sometimes a father may later claim his offspring after he admits his mistake and cause his Sunsum to protect his offspring.

The protective nature of a father's Sunsum is on display in the very clothing he puts on. An imprint of our Sunsum is left on everything that we touch or use as living beings, as such, a father's Sunsum is embedded in his clothes which provide a protective shield for his children, especially neonates. In this sense, the Sunsum may be likened to DNA, residue that people leave behind on anything touched or used, so much so that the residual Sunsum is powerful enough to protect a neonate, especially in the absence of a father. A new mother, for instance, would often ask for her husband's clean but used cloth to be used as a protective buttress for their child's weak Sunsum. A sister-in-law of mine will always wear her deceased father's attire whenever ill saying that she feels the presence of her father's Sunsum, which helps her to recover quickly. Occasionally, I complain to an elder brother of mine about a velvet cloth that I purchased for our father but which apparently ended up with another brother after our father died. Since I purchased it for our father I thought the cloth should have been reserved for me, because I wanted to inherit our father's Sunsum imbued in the cloth he wore. But then it was a gift to my father so any of his children had the right to inherit the same Sunsum that I was after, especially since I was not in Ghana when our father passed away. Evidence of the Sunsum as residual imprint is further demonstrated by offering a piece of cloth belonging to a fugitive to a dog to smell and then asking the dog to chase after the fugitive. Or, visiting a psychopomp with a cloth of a deceased person and asking her to contact the deceased through the item belonging to a deceased person because it contains the Sunsum of the dead.[13]

The question is: How can a finite, corporeal being like a father still exercise spiritual power as an extrinsic agency, to the extent of even using it to protect others from a distance, as well as within as an imprint protecting his neonates? First, a father has a more well-developed and therefore a more powerful

Sunsum than any of his offspring. As children are born very weak, a father's Sunsum, though intangible, protects his offspring just by a father being around because his spirit pervades everything that he owns and controls. Moreover, spirits know their kind and bond together even without any physical contact. Furthermore, a father does not need to be around physically for his Sunsum to protect his weak child, as a father's Sunsum permeates his personal belongings used to shield his own kind, his child.

And secondly, a father's spirituality is only as powerful as he himself is under the tutelage of his own Āgya-bosom (paternal deity). In other words, the source of a father's spiritual prowess is actually his Āgya-bosom who first willed him as his child and to whom he acknowledges and serves. As an Āgya-bosom is transmitter of Sunsum to his offspring, so a father is indeed the biological father to his children, although the real spiritual father of any child is the Ɔbosom who wills a child into the corporeal environment. An Āgya-bosom protects a father under its tutelage just as it protects a father's entire household and parameters of his property. For certain elders, especially kings and queen mothers, the Āgya-bosom of the ancestors' stool occupied by the royals is the one who protects the royals by hiding the souls of the king and queen mother. This is why every genuine ancestors' stool has a patron deity, because it is the duty of the patron Ɔbosom to protect the soul of the ancestors' stool,[14] which is the soul of an entire people. In this way, if anyone divines a king, for instance, it is the patron Ɔbosom who shows up to ascertain as to why a particular king or queen mother is being sought, because the soul of a king or queen mother is hidden with him, the leading Ɔbosom of a people in God. This is how a father protects his offspring even as he is also protected by his Āgya-bosom.

Anyone protected is spiritually marked. The marking is to inform other spiritual forces about the ownership of an elder warning those forces to stay away from the specially marked person. Even if a marked person is involved in a group accident, for instance, he or she is usually spared. The reality is that one's soul is hidden making them incapable of premature deaths. What is interesting is that usually other Abosom join in to protect those royals under the protection of a particular group of Abosom, because they recognize the special status of a king or queen mother. The reason is that the elders propitiate the Abosom and so the Abosom in turn protect those who offer them ambrosia. This also explain why the Nsamanfo (resurrected personalities) of dead kings are the most powerful of the ancestors, because they were apotheosized long before they suffered physical deaths. The point is that as long as a father or an elder serves his own Āgya-bosom, the Āgya-bosom in turn protects him and his household, including his friends.

Socially the basis for a father's influence is his Sunsum, interpreted as something unseen, invisible or immaterial and therefore a spirit. Though a spirit, the Sunsum nevertheless manifests itself psychologically as characteristic traits in every person. For this reason, the Sunsum becomes an intrinsic quality inherited from a father, although it invariably finds expression as an outward trait of individual temperament and basis of ethic (Ɔbra). Still, as spirit, the Sunsum is one's shadow or double existing independently of a human being and having a spiritual being of its own, especially during the dream state. The Sunsum is genetically tied to a person and must return to a body if a person asleep is to wake up. Sometimes a person dreaming may be conscious but unable to wake up because a dreamer may not be in full control of his or her wandering Sunsum. This phenomenon occurs because the Sunsum was originally an Ɔbosom and must be reminded of its new mode of existence as a human being by making every effort to wake up. In the final analysis, the Sunsum is expressed tangibly through human actions inherited from the Abosom through fathers, no matter how unconventional those actions might be. So, not only is every father a Sunsum; in fact, all responsible fathers are Abosom (Gods and Goddesses).

THE *SU*

The *Su* is an Ɔbosom materialized as the raw essence and drive in human beings. It is the intangible Sunsum (Ɔbosom) transformed miraculously in the flesh; the imprint of a spiritual agency on a material being, an egg, or as the Akan put it, the *Mogya* (blood) of a female. The vehicle for this miraculous act in which an Ɔbosom as Sunsum (spirit) makes its entry into the mundane is the male, making a father not only the transmitter of semen (*ntoro/huaba*), but the conduit through whom the Abosom undertake their creative acts. This alone is the basis of a father's spirituality because a father is the bearer of Su (Ɔbosom). Through a father an Ɔbosom deposits its imprint in a female's mogya in the form of the Su, defined as the raw nature or essence of the potential human. Thus, a potential human being is essentially the Ɔbosom wishing to be human and willed or sponsored by its Āgya-bosom into the corporeal environment. As a result, every child is wholly the offspring of the Āgya-bosom that willed it, meaning one is never alone in the mundane. The test is finding and acknowledging the Āgya-bosom as one's protector in a capriciously harsh and dangerous world.

The Su is unique in that it is wildly active and unchanging—although it is sublimated in most parts during childhood—because it is the core basis of behavioral and characteristic traits and ethical principles. So fundamental is the Su that developmentally all ethical and behavioral patterns are explained in the context of the Su. This makes the Su the very essence of the Ɔbosom before it is willed as a child into the mundane. In other words, every human being is not only the Ɔbosom that was willed into the corporeal environment, but also the Āgya-bosom who is now the sponsor of the Ɔbosom turned a person in the corporeal. The reason for this phenomenon, as explained above, is that the Abosom exist as family groups with each family group known for their unique character attributes and capabilities. As such, the way a person behaves is not really different from the Āgya-bosom that willed a person.

Most importantly, the Su is the basis for ethics (*Abra bɔ*) during adulthood when people undertake ethical pathways and become directly responsible for their own actions in pursuance of Nkrabea (existential career or professional blueprint). In recognition of the wild nature of the Su, parents and society as a whole sublimate the Su through a series of culturally designed rituals aimed at bringing the Su in line with accepted norms until the ethical phase of human existence in adulthood when the responsibilities of parenthood ends and an individual is responsible for one's own actions. This means that fathers do not pass on their Su to their offspring, because ethically the Su is unique to every individual. The only time that a father might be said to have transmitted his Su to an offspring of his is when both father and son or daughter are willed by the same Ɔbosom in which case both father and son or daughter may behave similarly. But even here, each person is responsible for one's own ethic (Ɔbra) as each person embarks on one's own ethical life in pursuance of one's own existential career or professional blueprint (Nkrabea). Since the Abosom each has its own unique nature, it also means that every human is unique in every aspect of living.

By nature, the Su is raw essence and basis for all character traits and ethical principles. After all, it is a spiritual agency in the flesh; meaning, the freedom once experienced spiritually is now limited as a human being. In fact, the nature of a spirit is to move and so the freedom of movement is put to test during infancy when the Su is at its highest expression. For instance, crawling of children cause parents and society to circumscribe the movements of toddlers by setting parameters to limit children within the confines of homes. The Su then is best expressed in infancy; for example, an infant has an urge to move toward an item it is fixated upon. Clearly, the Su has propensity to act in freedom, which, most importantly, must be anchored and refined, if not controlled.

THE *SUBAN*

The primary task of parents is to nurture children into becoming good and well-behaved children in the hopes that they grow up to become responsible adults. This task begins in infancy at the very moment neonates give us hope at birth when they offer their first speech (cry) at parturition. Psychosocially, parents begin to inculcate rituals and values peculiar to any group as to what it means to belong to a particular group of people; that is, what it means to be a human being. So while people are aware of the Su, it is the *Suban* (dispositional or character formation), the first cultured stage of the Su that they are most concerned with. Thus the first psychosocial ritual is the malleability of the Su into Suban as the basis for societal sustainability. The Su develops into the Suban (essential character formation) at the moment when a child is first aware of itself as a child or *self*. This is when a child begins to *want* and *demand* without reason and tests the limits of its confines and societal tolerance or the lack thereof. Essentially, a group is dealing with character formation of its children, which extends to the onset of education. During the maturational processes the Suban is expressed in the context of what is proper and acceptable and what is not within the larger societal norm. Thus, the Suban is an intention behind outward expressions, whether an intention is good or unethical.

Inherently then the Suban is very dualistic in its expressions, although socially right or proper ways of behaving are those normally encouraged. In this way the Su is sublimated psychosocially as Suban, but due to its agitated nature, ripples into dos and don'ts, accepted or unaccepted character traits. The dualistic tendencies are on display when a person is said to display *Suban-pa* (good temperament or disposition) within the context of what a group accepts as proper, or *Suban-bɔn* (bad or unethical disposition) when an individual behaves antisocially. Naturally, this is the result of limitations placed on certain proclivities the Su exhibits. What this suggests is that constant vigilance must be paid to infants otherwise they endanger themselves. In the process, children learn to inhibit those negative tendencies because they lead them into trouble and so children instead try to cultivate the positive proclivities. However, as one matures, an individual's attitude relationally determines a person's Suban, as to whether a person is thought to be a good, agreeable, respectful person, or ill-tempered, antisocial, or even a bad person. During the maturational processes and throughout life the Suban expresses itself as either Suban-pa (good-natured person) most times, or Suban-bɔn (bad or temperamental person), although socially the Suban-pa is what is displayed generally. Developmentally then the Suban must be civilized, cultivated, and refined, with the Suban-pa encouraged and nurtured, while the Suban-bɔn is eschewed. Though latent, Suban-bɔn grows alongside Suban-pa nonetheless, because in adulthood we discover that the Suban-bɔn temperament thought to be under control reappears intermittently when people are angry or under some sort of attack.

A person is said to have Suban-pa when exhibiting grace, obedience, humility, respect for elders, gratitude, and patience and discipline, because ultimately Suban-pa results in acts meant to benefit and ameliorate society.

Even though the expression of Suban-pa is individualistic in nature, its lasting effects and benefits are relational and long-lasting, because people are remembered long after their deaths in accordance with the kinds of Suban-pa that they exhibited when they were alive. For the Akan this remembrance is not a nostalgic pastime but rather an active awareness that Suban-pa may be revisited upon the families of a deceased person. Therefore, the development of individual Suban—and specifically Suban-pa—is central to the well-being of a family and to the Akan sense of community and belonging. Thus since Suban has to do with what is proper and therefore an acceptable social practice as well as what is contrary to social norms, Suban is the basis of ethics (Abra bɔ).

In adulthood, we find that the Suban, once again, determines the kind of ethic (Ɔbra) that an individual leads, as to whether one leads an Ɔbra-pa (ethical life) or Ɔbra-bɔn (unethical life). If during young adulthood an individual has been cultured at the previous education stage and inculcated in what it means to cultivate an ideal life—the prerequisite for Ɔbra-pa (ethical life)—then chances are that an individual would invariably master the art of living and be elected to the position of elder (Nana). After all, the goal of educating children is to mold them into developing good character attributes in the hope of children becoming model citizens as adults. However, an uneducated (cultured) young male adult, the *Abrantsi*, or the female, the *Akataesia*, might not be able to make the transition into adulthood and end up delinquent, petulant, and antisocial, because such an individual lives by the whims of his or her impulses because of one's unethical behavior (Suban-bɔn). To avoid this behavior, the Su must be cultured early on in order to prepare the groundwork for the ethical principles that young adults need for ideal citizenship and eldership.

THE *WEERI*

If the Suban is society's way of controlling, refining, and then sublimating the Su and forcing a child to conform to societal norms, then the *Weeri* (pronounced WEE-RY) is the inherent willpower or energy of the Su. In fact, the Weeri is the cathectic transformation of the Su into an active mode; as such, the Weeri manifests itself in a variety of psychological and affective actions. Still, the affectivities are expected to conform to the socially acceptable range of functionality.

Literally, *Weeri* means "skin" or "hide" of a person or animal; suggesting that the Weeri is tough, tenacious, impervious, and strong and therefore an inexhaustible energy closely associated with the heart (Akoma) and the soul (Ɔkra), enabling a person, for example, to face incredible odds with courage and resilience. Its quality is thus measured in terms of strengths and weaknesses, or highs and lows. A person has a strong Weeri or willpower when in the face of incredible physical pain one is still able to cling on to life tenaciously. Its influence pervades the living world, yet it is also understood that excessive display of Weeri can be violent, even dangerous if not controlled or sublimated. That is to say, that there is a raw (violent) side to every human being or animal, the recognition of which leads to the cultivation of discretion, patience, control, and discipline. By its very nature, the Weeri is an agitated and excited agency, making its relationship with the soul quite interesting because its normal functionality is tantamount to the happiness of the soul and the well-being of the heart (Akoma).

The reason why the excitation of the Weeri influences the soul is that the soul (Ɔkra) depends on the Weeri for its bliss which, in turn, affects the proper function of the heart. After all, we are speaking of two spiritual agencies (the Su and the Ɔkra) that are symbiotically related and recognize each other. Functionally, the Weeri is subject to the emotional fluctuations associated with the heart and the soul. A person's Weeri is said to be low or weak when experiencing profound grief, melancholy, rejection, and dejection (*No werɛ ahow*). One is sad or sorrowful (*No werɛ ahow*) because the Weeri is grieving for all kinds of reasons, but whatever the reasons, grieving is unhealthy and must be ended. When the Weeri grieves it means one's energy level is low, very low. The low ebb of the Weeri as a cathartic energy means a slow functionality, which in turn saddens the soul because there is not enough cathectic activity of the Weeri to excite or propel the Ɔkra to healthy functionality. In turn, the sadness of the Ɔkra affects the way the heart palpitates by slowing it, in the same way that excessive excitation increases heart palpitation.

Restoration of holistic health means that the Weeri is elevated or excited to a healthy level that balances an individual's energy level to a state comparable to the happiness of the soul and the heart. In other words, the Weeri of a grieving person, for example, must be raised up through consistent counseling, encouragement, and visitations by friends and family members until holistic energy level is achieved for a healthy life, otherwise the person experiencing depression could die (*Awerɛhow kum nyimpa*). In fact, sadness or sorrow kills (*Awerɛhow kum nyimpa*). That is, a Weeri must be brought under control (balance) in order for any human being to function normally in any society. Indeed, the best period to learn to sublimate the Weeri is during childhood.

THE *AWEREKYIKYIR*

Intrinsically there is a more benign, comforting, and uplifting side to the Weeri called *Awerɛkyikyir* (pronounced A-WE-RƐ-CHI-CHIL). And insofar as a person experiencing depression or profound grief is concerned, this innate quality is essential in lifting up a person from a melancholic state to good health. The Awerɛkyikyir is affectively triggered in response to depression in order to restore balance to the Weeri and make the soul blissful. Often the Akan would say that to show or display affectivity (Awerɛkyikyir) is to be human, because they believe that the Awerɛkyikyir emanates from person to person (*Awerɛkyikyir fir onyimpa hon*). When people hug one another there is transference of energies, when usually a higher or superior energy flows to a person with low energy, with the aim of uplifting the Weeri of the one with low Weeri energy due to depression or bereavement. Similarly if an unclean person were to hug a highly developed person, the highly developed person is defiled during the exchange or transference of energies, especially if the hug was not solicited. For this reason, highly developed persons like elders and traditional rulers are usually protected by people whose duty is it to make sure that no one gets too close to such persons. So when the Akan say that Awerɛkyikyir emanates from person to person in the proper context, they mean so therapeutically.

Everyone is thought to have a gentle, counseling, consoling, comforting and uplifting spirit needed to alleviate the state of melancholia, especially when shown toward the bereaved. This capacity in human beings and animals should be extended to include others in need of spiritual, emotional, and psychological help. The reason is that the Awerɛkyikyir in living beings is meant to help lift up the spirit or Weeri of anyone facing psychological help, when one literally transfers one's balanced spiritual energy (Weeri) to another person's low Weeri level. For the Akan, whenever there is a bereavement it is customary that women, especially elderly women, spend days and weeks with the bereaved family until a culturally defined time of three months, sometimes not saying anything to the bereaved. In the ancient times, it took a whole year; nowadays, the period of visitations where elderly women sit with the bereaved has been reduced significantly due to the difficult economic times, as it is the responsibility of the bereaved family to feed the mourners during the duration of their stay. However, the larger point is that those experiencing profound grief and depression must not be left alone in their depressed or bereaved moments. It is expected that after the duration of the Awerɛkyikyir period where people reside with the bereaved, that he or she recovers, or else the goodwill turns into frustration, anger, and even insults, as to why the bereaved does not respond to treatment. This meant to get the bereaved or the depressed to snap from such a dangerous state. In Job 2:11–13 (RSV), we read the following:

> Now when Job's three friends heard of all this evil that had come upon him, they came each from his own place. . . . They made an appointment together to come to console with him and comfort him. And when they saw him from afar, they did not recognize him; and they raised their voices and wept; and they rent their robes and sprinkled dust upon their heads toward heaven. And they sat with him on the ground seven days and seven nights, and no one spoke a word to him, for they saw that his suffering was very great.

The salient point is that Job's friends came to be with him, and at the end of the culturally defined period of mourning Job started speaking. From the Akan perspective, Job should have snapped out of his suffering and accepted the inevitability of the death of his children because it had gone on for far too long. When that was not forthcoming, his friends responded to Job's claim to innocence and actually became angry at Job.

Etymologically, the Awerɛkyikyir is a conjugation of *Weeri* (skin or hide, energy) and *kyikyir* (to bind up or tie together). In practice, Awerɛkyikyir is the human propensity to care, physically and spiritually, making Awerɛkyikyir a dual-faceted phenomenon capable of offering psychosomatic healing. Conceptually, the Awerɛkyikyir restores the energy of the Weeri to a normal level by physically elevating a low Weeri energy level to an acceptable level, otherwise a death could occur as a result of a person's inability to lift oneself from a depressed state. The Akan are adamant in their belief that sadness, indeed, profound sorrow, could kill (*Awerɛhow bɔkum onyimpa*). This is because prolong states of sorrow or sadness, depression, and suffering do not make a healthy state and one should not be allowed to drown in one's sorrow alone. Hence Awerɛkyikyir is meant to arrest a state of low morale by elevating one to a healthy state of living.

If the practical side of Awerɛkyikyir is actually taking steps to bind the brokenhearted by physically offering assistance to the sick, bereaved, the depressed, or melancholic, then the spiritual side, though also physical, is unseen but just as effective as the former. Since the nature of the spirit (*Sunsum*) is actively requiring energy, it follows that the inactivity of a spirit due to the cessation of the Weeri or activity can lead to death. Therapeutically, it is incumbent upon relatives, the clergy, counselors, and actually the duty of everyone to bind the brokenhearted and console the needy and the poor in order to restore wellness, wholeness and bliss to a person or group, because, as said already, *Awerɛkyikyir fir onyimpa hon* (affectivity emanates from a person), making the Awerɛkyikyir emotionally and sympathetically contagious. That there is an active transference of spiritual energy whenever one hugs another person and hence *Awerɛkyikyir fir onyimpa hon*. Even though men are not traditionally inclined to display affectivity publicly, it is precisely when they do so that the effects are sentimentally transforming and healthy.

THE *AYEMHYIHYI*

To show Awerɛkyikyir, an individual must have first gone through three cathartic steps. The first is what the Akan called *Ayɛmhyihyi* (pronounced A-YEM-SHI-SHI), or the burning, churning, or gnawing sensation within the stomach. The term *Ayɛmhyihyi* is a conjugation of the terms *Yɛm* (bowel, stomach), and *Hyihyi* (burning). In other words, Ayɛmhyihyi is the cathectic sensation felt when one is confronted with human suffering engendered by deprivation and desolation, such as the pernicious devastation of war or a disaster. It is like the sensation felt within the stomach when one panics; meaning, this state applies to a specific area of the stomach—diaphragm—which emits sensationalism during moments of extreme pain and anguish.[15] According to Nketia, during the singing of dirges at funerals, "A band or a piece of cloth may be found tied round the body, in the region of the diaphragm—symbolic of anguish as well as a support to the diaphragm and a relief of physical pain."[16] This suggests that Ayɛmhyihyi may be triggered by sad news or events. We already know that sadness (*Awerɛhow*) kills because it saddens the Ɔkra (soul), meaning Ayɛmhyihyi triggers sadness if a situation is not arrested. The good news is that the source of Ayɛmhyihyi is localized, and while it is strong enough to emit cathectic sensations that can lead to paralysis, it can be controlled, in the same way that mourners tie pieces of cloth round their midsections in order to relieve the pressure and anguish on the diaphragm. As pointed out by Nketia, pressure must be applied on the area exhibiting Ayɛmhyihyi in order to relieve the situation. The paralysis of Ayɛmhyihyi occurs when some people are unable to even eat due to the emotional and physical pain they may experiencing. That is, the effects of Ayɛmhyihyi could be experienced physiologically.

Though its physiological effects are felt and seen, the psychological effects of Ayɛmhyihyi must be discerned rather carefully. Sometimes, even without any observable causality, suddenly one may experience Ayɛmhyihyi. Speaking to a number of elders and elderly women in two communities in Ghana (Winneba and Mprumem) in 2013 after I invited them to discuss this phenomenon and other spiritual issues,[17] my discussants asserted that there is a spiritual causality to Ayɛmhyihyi when one picks up sensations about events occurring far away from one's geographical location. Furthermore, the sensation could be about events that have already transpired but which are yet to be known by persons easily influenced by spirits; or, that Ayɛmhyihyi could be experienced as premonitions about unpleasant events long before they actually occur, especially if a person is one who is spiritually in tune with or a vehicle for the Abosom, like a diviner, priest, or a person the Akan describe as having a "light head." Experiences of Ayɛmhyihyi as premonitions do not last long, lasting from few seconds to minutes. The key here is being aware enough to know what is taking place and learning how to bring the situation under control, otherwise it could lead to temporary discomfort or even momentary paralysis. The simple way to arrest such sensations—in addition to pressurizing the area of the diaphragm—is controlled breathing; that is, breathing or exhaling "upwards" in attempts to "empty" the lungs. It is similar to breathing into a paper bag when one is experiencing fear or having fainting spells. The point is that Ayɛmhyihyi, like Awerɛkyikyir, emanates from the Weeri, an intrinsic cathectic force, power, or energy, and one way to mitigate the Weeri is through controlled breathing.

THE *ĀHUMMƆBƆR*

Secondly, many people, especially women, are usually moved to Ayɛmhyihyi, which, in turn, propels them to perform Awerɛkyikyir because they first display a higher level of dispensation called *Āhummɔbɔr* (Ā-WHOM-MO-BOL) or compassion. The act of Āhummɔbɔr is more a disposition than affectivity because one may have compassion and not be moved to Ayɛmhyihyi or Awerɛkyikyir. Conversely, one cannot be moved to Ayɛmhyihyi, which may compel a person to undertake Awerɛkyikyir and not have Āhummɔbɔr in the first place. For example, when a person comes in contact with a dying or hungry person—as found in the Gospel of Luke (10:30–35) where a Samaritan was moved to compassion and offered assistance to a dying man, while both a priest and a Levite moved on without offering any help—the first reaction is to have compassion or Āhummɔbɔr on the individual, which may trigger Ayɛmhyihyi because of the pathos of the situation. Human nature is such that many people would be inclined to offer assistance in attempt to help alleviate the situation (Awerɛkyikyir), but occasionally some people would be inclined to move on without offering assistance; meaning, they stop at Ayɛmhyihyi because they are unable or unwilling to offer assistance, or simply do not care enough to actually offer assistance. Yet others may be willing to offer assistance (Awerɛkyikyir) but may be hindered by circumstances beyond their control. Ideally while Āhummɔbɔr, Ayɛmhyihyi, and Awerɛkyikyir function together to achieve the ultimate result, each may be displayed or acted out independently. For instance, a person may have Āhummɔbɔr and not have Ayɛmhyihyi; similarly, one may perform an Awerɛkyikyir task and not have any sense of Āhummɔbɔr or Ayɛmhyihyi because it may only be his or her job. However, one must transcend the Āhummɔbɔr if the situation is to be arrested, otherwise, like Ayɛmhyihyi, Āhummɔbɔr becomes just another selfish, apathetic state.

THE *ABADAI*

Finally, an individual must also exhibit *Abadai* (A-BA-DA-I) or beneficence in order to relieve a state of want. It is only then that one proceeds to Āhummɔbɔr, Ayɛmhyihyi, and Awerɛkyikyi and tends to the state of want. While most people may stop at Abadai by their altruism or philanthropic act, Awerɛkyikyir is a step beyond Abadai, because Awerɛkyikyir entails personally getting involved in the caring and tending to a need.

These intrinsic attributes, although masculine in nature because they are manifestations of the Sunsum, are actually feminine in their outward expressions. Hence, God is the ultimate Beneficent One (*Ɔbaatan*), the only one who epitomizes all these essential qualities toward his creation. Although an Ɔbaatan is generally thought of as motherliness—as in only a mother would know what her children would eat—most royal positions among the Akan are occupied by men. Still, anyone elected to position of Ɔbaatan (beneficent one) is expected to act by exhibiting the qualities and attributes of a mother—maternal love and kindness to all citizens. Therefore, anyone who consciously demonstrates these qualities is being Godlike; indeed, there are people who assiduously try to make a difference in the lot of humanity. Unfortunately, there are also some people who really do not care one way or another.

THE *SASU*

I have held many private meetings through the years with elders to discuss range of research interests, including the last one that I held in 2013 after the funeral of my queen mother in early September of that year. Of all the discussions that I have convened, the one that generated the most lively debate between the women and men was one on the concept of *Sasu*. The elderly women passionately blamed the men for being responsible for the negative Sasu that they pass on to their offspring, which puts undue burden on women, especially when fathers shirk their responsibilities. So, what is the Sasu that my discussants ascribe to men, actually fathers?

Sasu is the attitude that makes up a person, meaning Sasu could be a learned behavior, pseudo personality displayed to effect a result. As such the Sasu has to do with the unique way that a person speaks, walks, pretends, and comports oneself so as to be admired or even hated. Therefore the Sasu is the contrived outwardly expression of a self. In other words, the Sasu could be conscious pretenses that people put out in order to impress as well as deceive the larger society. Indeed, the Sasu encompasses mannerisms, the kind of mannerism clearly on display when potential lovers meet for the first time. It does not mean that the Sasu is negative, rather it means that human beings have the tendency and even the capacity to express certain innate dispositions that affect others in ways that may be beneficial or adversely inimical, meaning the absence of the Sasu reveals the true character of a person. When my mother refused to allow a sister of mine to marry a man that she wanted to marry, my sister went ahead and had children with the man anyway and when all the children took after him, my mother would occasionally remind my sister in a negative way as to how she did not heed her warnings and has given birth children who took after the man's Sasu. So, Sasu could be good or bad traits depending on a particular character stance.

In the context of likeness, the Sasu is an image or reflection, and strangely, it could be transmitted, or that children could copy the likenesses of their parents, especially fathers. One day another sister of mine brought the man that she had been seeing home to greet our mother. Both our mother and I took a look at the man and said nothing. After the man left our mother humorously asked my sister: "Is this the type of man that you will be giving birth to his Sasu into my family?" Our mother had made her intentions known: She did not want my sister marrying her boyfriend because our mother did not want the man's likeness or kind as grandchildren as the man did not meet the criteria mother had set for us, her children.

As a unique persona, the Sasu is closely aligned with the Su, as an essential nature of a person, as well as the Suban, which deals with behavioral and character patterns. Yet the Sasu is different from the Suban in that it deals specifically with mannerisms and how one does things uniquely when need be, no matter how falsely. For this reason the Sasu is not a ritual, which is performed routinely and repeated among certain groups; meaning, whereas a ritual is group-oriented and understood by all, the Sasu is uniquely individualistic. Even so, the Sasu is the routine, idiosyncratic, ritualized, and stylized way of doing things by an individual in a manner that sets one apart from others. And like the Suban, the Sasu may be impressive and admired or annoyingly abhorrent. For example, as my discussants pointed out, a woman may say to a man whose Sasu she admired that she may want to have his child in order that the child may take after the man's Sasu. Another woman may refuse the advances of a man because she does not want to have a child who may take after his bad Sasu. The suggestion is that children reflect the Sasu of their parents, particularly their fathers. During divorces, for example, a wife may take solace from the fact that she would never again have children who took after her husband's bad Sasu. By the same token, children too may be warned not to emulate the Sasu of some friends or even certain adult relatives; rather, they are encouraged to emulate the Sasu of certain idealized individuals in the hope of forming permanent relationships that could lead them to better futures. It was in this context that my elderly female discussants were annoyed at their male counterparts, blaming them—men in general—for the way children behave nowadays. The Sasu, then, is an adult lifestyle, appearing when one is morally and ethically concerned with existential and spiritual matters and their social ramifications. Meaning, the Sasu is ethical in its application because it is a learned behavior although it could be hereditary too.

The human being is a spiritual being, claimed by the Abosom who intrinsically make possible all human actions. How one speaks, walks, displays mannerisms, and acts reflects the nature of the Ɔbosom that willed an individual into the corporeal wholly. The role of parents is to influence children as much as possible psychosocially, but in the end each child is his or her Su in toto. There is the illusion that children take after or must reflect their parents. Sometimes, it may be said of a child who is completely different from his or her parents that the child is the opposite of his or her parents behaviorally. Or, children may turn out so differently from their parents during adulthood that people may even question whether or not the children (now adults) are the same children they used to know growing up.

All these remarks attest to the unchanging nature of the Su, which for a while during childhood through adolescence and even young adulthood is sublimated in conformity with societal norms. But with the freedom and independence of adulthood also comes the need to express one's innermost self or one's true nature or character. Some youths may not even wait until adulthood to express their innermost personalities; they rebel against authority because they would not conform to societal structures and boundaries. This is actually the result of the Weeri not fully modulated or the inability to sublimate the Weeri. The Weeri is the driving force in all that a person does and therefore the Weeri must not be perceived negatively, because it is only when parents or society fails to modulate the Weeri and allows certain aspects of it to be displayed excessively that the Weeri may be destructive. Reaction or lack of reaction to the influence of the Weeri is key to actions taken, as to whether one moves beyond Ayɛmhyihyi and actually take steps toward Awerɛkyikyir, or even shows compassion because one is first disposed to Abadai.

THE *TSIR*

The head is certainly the most fascinating of all spiritual agencies of this study because the head appears to be a tangible entity unlike the other agencies already discussed, which are only expressed through actions of persons. According to Gbadegesin, for example, the Yoruba speak of inner (spiritual) and outer (symbolic or physical) heads.[18] In addition to the brain, the *Ori* (head), Gbadegesin asserts, is the bearer of destiny because it is where "individual destinies are wound up," and picked up by each newly formed person not knowing which destinies the heads contain as a person enters the world.[19]

As for the Akan, the *Tsir* (head) is the source of all spiritual (Sunsum) or psychological activities, including mediumship rites. To the Akan this is because the Tsir contains the *Adwen* (brain) making the head the seal and nerve center of all the intrinsic quality attributes described already. The notion is that the bigger a head, the more brains (*Tsir kɛsi na adwen wɔm*) to a person and therefore the more intelligent and knowledgeable. There is, however, a distinct difference between wisdom and intelligence (*nyansa*) and knowledge or brains (*Adwen nkon, Nyansa nkon*) even though the two are inseparably one. There are people who are very knowledgeable and are quick to offer answers about a range of issues, yet they lack the wisdom of thoughtfulness and reflection enabling them to think and analyze issues before offering opinions. Wisdom and intelligence are mutually dependent on knowledge, the accrued body of life's experiences from which intelligence and wisdom emanate. No wonder wisdom is the hallmark of eldership.

The head is thought to be the essence of a human being. A person is defined by his or her head; that is, what is actually *in* a person's head because it directs all activities. A good person with clear intentions is said to have "good head" (*Tsir papaa*) or "good brains" (*adwen papaa*). To congratulate a person for whatever achievement or accomplishment, it is said to the individual: *Wo tsir nkwa* (literally, life to your head). The response usually is: *Metsir daasi* (My head thanks you). Sometimes an anxious couple may want to know about the destiny of their child and may consult an *Ɔkɔmfo* (diviner). During such a consultation it is said that: "We are going to consult the child's head" (*Yɛri kɛbisa abofra ni tsir*), making the head an oracle, so to speak. In actuality, it is the soul, Ɔkra, that is divined and not necessarily the head. It does not mean that the soul is the head, although Gyekye is of the opinion that the Ɔkra is lodged in the head.[20] However, the Akan believe the shoulders are the seat of the Ɔkra, because they refer to the shoulders as *Krado*, meaning seat of the soul or Ɔkra; and as such, the head sits well balanced on the soul (shoulders).

On the other hand, when one fails in life then it is thought that the head is unsuccessful or did not fare well (*Ni tsir annyɛyae*). An individual thought to be a miser is said to have a "hard head," literally (*Ni tsir yɛ dzin*); and by the same token a beneficent individual is said to have a "soft or loose head" (*Ni tsir mu goow*), literally. Clearly every human being is the head in action.

On the contrary, an evil person or anyone who harbors bad thoughts secretly may be described as having dark head (*Tsir mu yɛsum*); while a crazy person is one whose head or brain does not work or operate. Conversely, a young person who demonstrates all the right social etiquette and decorum characterized by respect for the elders and those in position of authority is said to be a thoughtful person (*Ɔbadwenmafo*). Therefore the thoughtful person's brain is thought of as being good (*adwen pa, papaa*) or evil or bad (*adwen bɔn*). What we see here is a head that acts as the source of all of human actions and thoughts. No wonder for the ancient Egyptians the head acted as a referee hovering over the scale of ultimate judgment observing the precedence during the weighing of the dead human's heart against a feather of the goddess Maat to determine if one lived a worthy life or died a second time for living an unethical life.

Indeed, what makes a human being is the Tsir (head) and what is within it makes the head the seat of the Abosom during divinations. As the Tsir is positioned and balanced perfectly on the Krado (shoulders, or seat of the soul), it makes it possible for the Abosom to alight on during divinations and mediumship rites. Even the hair on the head, especially that of a woman and particularly of a diviner, is of such significance that during divinations the hair becomes a landing magnet for the Abosom as it attracts them, as we will see in the next chapter. Therefore the idea that during a divination rite the entire human being (body) is possessed is false[21] because a body, unlike the mind (brain), is not pure enough for the indwelling of a deity (Ɔbosom).

The Tsir is subject to all kinds of spiritual influences although not every person comes under such influences. To be a candidate for spiritual influences one must have a "light" head—meaning, one is susceptible to certain spiritual swings because the head and hair attract all kinds of spirits. Such an individual is supposed to carry anything on his or her head to prevent spirits alighting on it and subjecting the person to all kinds of exploits. To have a light head or Tsir (*Tsir yɛhar*) simply means that a person has a "head," making one naturally very sensitive to spiritual chatters and activities. It means that the head is a receptor for spiritual energies. In itself, the extra sensibility is strange and scary, worrisome, and overwhelming, as the head—acting as antennas—easily picks up all kinds of inter-agency activities, including visions and dreams. Initially, the information and visions that individuals receive may appear not to pertain to them until days, months, or even years later, but no matter how long they take, the messages received are certainly fulfilled. To have a light head, or head, also includes the ability to "hear" as well as "see." Usually, these categories of individuals are the ones called into the clerical (priesthood, prophetic-mediumship, medical, and even kingship) vocations.

Conversely, a person with a "heavy head" (*Tsir ayɛdru*) is usually one who is drunk, in which case nothing could be carried on a head. Normally, such a person, if he is an elder, is encouraged to sleep. So, it is not uncommon to visit an elder and be told that he is asleep when he is not supposed to be sleeping at that time. An astute individual will know right away that the elder has a heavy head, a metaphor for being drunk and therefore unavailable. A person with a heavy head normally speaks gibberish and an elder is not supposed to be in such a condition in public or in private and hence the advice for him to have a nap until such time as he is sober.

African women and children carry foodstuffs and all kinds of merchandize on their heads, and so the logical question is: Are they then susceptible to alightment? For most adult women, scarves are used to tie their heads when carrying loads, or they have some sort of pads on their heads to cushion and balance loads. Children who carry items to marketplaces to sell also use pieces of cloth folded into pads on their heads, as did I when growing up selling bread in trays. From experience, sometimes the loads were so heavy and the trays wide that the pads were needed to cushion and balance the trays. Those thought to have "light heads" and carry loads are not summarily alighted upon, however. The reason is that spirits too are aware of the subsistence and economic needs of people, and so spirits make it easier for their wards selling items on the heads for those items to be bought quickly. The point is that those thought to have light heads sell things quickly, but most importantly, as long as the head is covered when carrying loads, the head is free of spiritual influences. In the end, whether or not a person is alighted upon depended on the Ɔbosom thought to have willed an individual and whether the Ɔbosom wanted to be known through a particular individual. But above all, alighting on any person also depended on the destiny or existential career or professional blueprint (*Nkrabea*) of a person and whether an individual was willed to be a medium or not and for an Ɔbosom to decide to manifest itself.

Becoming an adult is being aware of one's inner attributes in terms of strengths (qualities) and limitations (modulations), or highs (impulsiveness) and lows (judiciousness, patience). Ideally eldership is where these intrinsic qualities are on display, especially when elders are discussing matters affecting their communities. However, it is during adulthood—young adulthood in particular—that the praxis of ideal attributes as the basis for eldership are

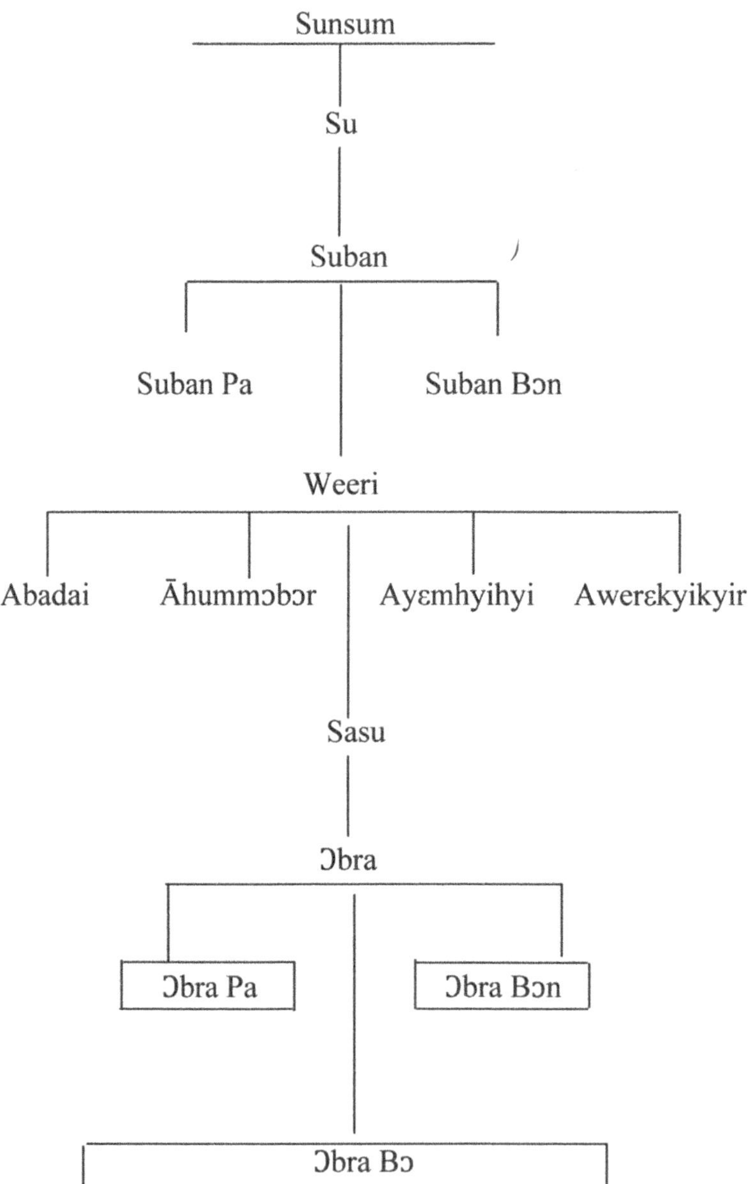

Spirit Incarnate
Sunsum
Su
Suban
Suban Pa
Suban Bɔn
Weeri
Abadai
Āhummɔbɔr
Ayɛmhyihyi
Awerɛkyikyir
Sasu
Ɔbra
Ɔbra Pa
Ɔbra Bɔn
Ɔbra Bɔ

Figure 3.1.

exhibited. Earlier, still as a youth, signs of potential eldership are first shown when an obedient, humble, and respectful youth accompanies elders to deliberations. These qualities and attributes must be nurtured and cultivated for generativity (procreation, production, and creativity).[22]

THE *ƆKRA*

The term or name *Ɔkra* has been defined as *soul* by most Akan scholars, including Rattray (1923), Kofi Antubam (1963), Opoku (1978), Gyekye (1987), Konadu (2007), to name only a few. Even though the Akan maintain that all persons are willed by Abosom and are indeed children of the Abosom due to the notion that the Abosom impart their intrinsic qualities and attributes to the children, they still make the claim that all human beings are children of God, and none are the children of the earth (*Nyimpa nyinaa ara yɛ* Nyame *mma; obiara nnyɛ Asasi ba*), as seen already. But how can the Akan give credit to both God and the Abosom as progenitors of humankind as it seems? The double entendre statement is not a contradiction at all but rather an acknowledgement of a human being as divine originating in heaven with God, as opposed to one with a corporeal source. The statement presents us with a creative view in which God is above as Father (Āgya), and earth (Asasi) as Mother is depicted as being below, and that life could only emanate from above from a heavenly source and not below from earth. That is, in the same way that earth without rain or water is a desert and therefore incapable of sustaining life, so life cannot originate on earth without first the impartation of spiritual life from above. Literally, the assertion, *Nyimpa nyinaa ara yɛ* Nyame *mma; obiara nnyɛ Asasi ba*, first, may be interpreted as an "argument" between God and earth, Asasi, to establish paternity, so to speak, of children born to Asasi (earth). In other words, it takes life to create life and only God (*Gyidɛ* Nyame) is the giver of life (*Ɔkra*). On the contrary, Asasi (earth) is unable to produce offspring because she is incapable of generating life on her own.

Second, the Abosom are progenitors of the created order, including human beings, because they are co-creators with God. As agents of God, the Abosom are the ones who actually begin the creative process of making human beings by activating an otherwise inactive *Mogya* (blood) of women and imbuing them with intrinsic attributes that serve as the basis for moral and ethical principles. Spiritually, however, while the Abosom will people into the world individually, collectively only God claims all of humanity as his own for the unique reason that only God is the giver of life. The Abosom are individually responsible for the protection and guidance of each and every person that they will into the corporeal, while God has the overall responsibility of the created order. However, how one remains under the aegis of an Ɔbosom depends solely on one's relationship with the Ɔbosom (God or Goddess) that willed one into corporeal existence. If one does not know the Āgya-bosom that willed one into the world, then ethically one only needs to lead a good life.

The Akan are absolute in the belief that only God is the giver of life called Ɔkra (soul). The Ɔkra is readily and unconditionally available at the moment of birth when it takes in its first breath of air outside the womb. In the womb a fetus depends entirely on its mother's Ɔkra for its viability through the activity of inhaling and exhaling of its host, the mother. Parturition starts the individuation processes insofar as a neonate becoming a living entity separate and apart from its host. It starts the very moment a neonate offers its first speech—cry. This is the instant that a neonate first experiences God (air) without and when it becomes a living being, and after the Ɔkra is believed to be seated within as *Ɔkratseasifo* (the Ɔkra-in-residence). Therefore, it is imperative that a neonate cries immediately upon expulsion from the womb.

The precise characteristic nature of the Ɔkra can be inferred from certain socio-political thoughts among the Akan, which point to the Ɔkra as being more feminine or at best one of an equilibrator, because God balances the spiritual and material components of a human being. Since the Akan practice matrilineal kinship descent, it follows that their rulers are always female and male although the male rules as king on behalf of his female counterpart, who happens to be the real power on the basis of the matrilineal kinship descent system. Also, the seating arrangement in a palanquin reflects the dual nature of the Akan kingship. Seated in front of a king in a palanquin is a premenstrual girl regarded as the Ɔkra or soul and therefore symbolic wife of the king. As a female she balances the male ruler as his Ɔkra. In the past, she was sacrificed alongside a decedent king, because an Ɔkra must accompany its owner, the king, in death. As the Ɔkra and symbolic wife of a king, she must be of a royal lineage and receive a pampered treatment. From a king's perspective, she becomes his responsibility and he must support her materially and financially as long as she is unmarried. Ideally, before she marries, the groom-to-be performs certain rites for the ruler before he releases his "wife" to be married. In other words, the ruler must be ritually compensated by the groom-to-be before a king allows his Ɔkra-wife to be taken away in marriage.

The notion that the Ɔkra is an ever-seated (*Ɔkratseasifo*) agency *balancing* the spiritual and material components of a living person reveals the location of the Ɔkra. For the Akan, the shoulders are referred to as *Krado* (seat or place of the Ɔkra), because the shoulders balance a person, particularly the head. Although the precise location of the Ɔkra may be lodged in the head, according to Kwame Gyekye,[23] from the rite of restoration there is no doubt that the Ɔkra is located on the shoulders. As evidence during rites intended to re-establish balance for persons suffering from psychosis, the shoulders are touched with eggs during the ceremony. Other indications of the location of the Ɔkra are the prohibitions the Akan place on the shoulders. One must not lean on another person's shoulders, or when a shoulder is touched by mistake, then the other shoulder must be touched for symmetry. Another example is found during attempts to "de-possess" one "possessed" by a spirit. The ways out of spirit possession or alighting that I have observed on several occasions working with diviners for decades in the Central Region of Ghana is to tap the shoulders of the possessed person with special vines. Similarly, for example, during a ceremony for knighthood that I have watched on television, a sword is introduced to the Ɔkra when it is touched on either side of the shoulders of the knight for balance and valor precisely because it is the seat of the soul, as the Akan hold. Socio-culturally, the left shoulder is thought to be feminine, while the right is masculine.

From the political standpoint, the relationship between the left shoulder and the right shoulder is on display during seating arrangements for a king (*Ɔhen*) and his queen mother (*Ɔhenmaa*). Whenever both are seated in public, the king sits on the right-hand side of his queen mother, while the queen mother in turn sits on the left-hand side of the king. However, this seating arrangement is not uniquely Akan. In the Christian Apostles Creed, for example, Jesus is depicted as sitting at the right side of God, meaning Jesus now rules on behalf of God as the ultimate Christian judge, because God has ceded all power to him in an obviously patriarchal kingdom. In this context, God is the feminine Ɔkra of Jesus, while Jesus becomes the masculine king and therefore the ruler. However, unlike the Akan system of two parallel linear systems of succession—one male and the other female—and where real power resides with the queen mother by virtue of her ability to transmit bloodlines, Christianity has a system comprising of the same sex hierarchal system of a Father, Son (and Spirit).

THE *AHOM*

We have already seen how the Ɔkra enters the body of a neonate at the very moment it inhales its first breath of air. The unique breath of air is what the Akan refer to as *Ahom,* which serves as an intangible attestation to the presence of the Ɔkra in the person. The Akan view the continuous activity of inhaling and exhaling to be unquestionably God; that, no matter how deeply one exhales, there remains within a residual breath attesting to the fact that the Ɔkra is eternally seated in an individual as *Ɔkratseasifo*. When exhaled, the breath of air joins the atmosphere, that body of air that is God without. Therefore God is the air, because air is synonymous with God forming the basis for the saying: "To speak with God, converse with the wind" (*Sɛ pɛdɛ kasa kyerɛ* Nyame *a kakyerɛ mframa*). For this reason, God could not be aloof or distant when experienced both within and without as the very air that sustains life. By extension, this is the sense behind another aphorism: "God is self-revealing even to a child" (*Obi nkyerɛ abofra* Nyame). If God is self-evident and accessible to all, then the irrelevance of clergy, temples, and images for God has been revealed. Subsequently, God is never worshipped,[24] at least not directly, although God is the first to be complained to when things go wrong, contrary to Bosman's claim that God is not called upon in times of need. Most importantly above all, the Ahom is free for all of God's creation and acquired unconditionally.

The only thing required of everyone is to just breathe in the first breath and God does the rest automatically and involuntarily outside of the womb. The Ahom, however, must not be taken for granted, because as with all finite beings, at some point there is cessation of breath. As breath indicates life, so the cessation of breath indicates death. At a time decreed only by God, the Ɔkra as a living agency (the *Ɔkratseasifo*), terminates the body when the last puff of breath is exhaled, giving way to death. Nevertheless, the Ahom alone does not constitute the phenomenon of Ɔkra as a seated agency in a human being, even though the two were intrinsically and symbiotically related, because the Ahom (breath) attests to the presence of the Ɔkra within, which returns to God at death via the Ahom.

THE *DZIN*

The person who names also owns that which one names; and for the Akan, God is the first Namer, bestowing a name the very instant a child is born, followed on the eighth day by the Abosom, as we have already seen. In other words, every human being first has a divine name originating with God, and then a spiritual name derived from the Abosom via fathers as representatives of the Abosom. An Akan mother does not get to name her offspring, because, as we have already established, no one is a child of the earth. This makes a human being more a spiritual than a corporeal being. As the Father of creation, God asserts his right to name all of his offspring on the day that one comes into being, including the Abosom together with their qualities and essences of the day they came into being. Thus the Akan have seven pairs of divine names after the days of the week for boys and girls.

These names are further evidence of God's direct ownership of the human being. Just as God imbues every person with an Ɔkra, God unconditionally offers every child his or her first name immediately upon birth based on the day that a child is born. Thus, the Ɔkra is also the bearer of a divine name called *Kra-dzin* (soul name) or *Da-dzin* (day name), which, like the Ahom, is assumed automatically, freely, and without any formal ceremony. In fact, the divine or day name is the very name of the Ɔkra, derived directly from God based on the seven soul essences of God in operation on each given day of the week. Therefore, a neonate inherits the very essence of God at work on the day that a child is born. As a result, children born on any particular day of the week all share the same core divine essence together. However, the very nature of the Ɔkra as a harmonizing agency means that the Ɔkra balances equally names that are shared by the sexes. This is why there are equal names for girls and boys.

The divine names with their accompanying essences are inherently different from the spiritual or psychological character attributes inherited from the Abosom through fathers, in that people willed by the Abosom via fathers collectively display the same inherent strengths and psychological attributes originating with the Abosom. Similarly, those born on any day of the week also collectively inherit from God seven primary tendencies that enable them to gravitate toward the same intrinsic values and ideals, and they exhibit similar discernments and predilections. However, what separates them individually is the psychological character attributes inherited from sources other than God, the Abosom, which ultimately make all individuals unique. What ultimately makes every individual uniquely special is the kind of Nkrabea willed before God.

THE *NKRABEA*

The Nkrabea is the sum total of all spiritual and physical activities undertaken as an adult to the very moment of death. Every person is born with a unique blueprint of what will be achieved existentially and so it is up to every single person to discover what the blueprint is in order to build on it starting at adulthood. Thus, as a person's existential career or professional blueprint, Nkrabea must be achieved when one discovers and engages in the kind of career or profession that is meaningful, fulfilling, and satisfying as an adult, as we will see in the final chapter. It also means that conceptually, there is a deliberate taught praxis to achieving Nkrabea, which has everything to do with ethics, referred to by the Akan as (Abra bɔ). Precisely, they believe that Ɔbra bɔ (ethic) commences at adulthood, making ethical existence a generative activity.

The term *generativity* is used technically from the perspective of Erik Erikson[25] in three ways. First is procreativity, when an adult is expected to marry and have children in order to augment his or her group. Procreation is the basis of an adult's worth or value existentially, because having children determines one's station in the community. As one scholar puts it, in West Africa, it is not necessarily if one is married, but rather if a person has children. That is, in setting out in search of one's own Nkrabea, one must not do it alone. In fact, society expects the young adult to marry and have children.

The second use and understanding of generativity has to do with productivity. The expectation and concern here is for adults to sustain parents and the community that first nurtured them into becoming responsible adults by giving back to the community and taking care of one's parents. One is obliged to support one's family, and for those of us who happen to reside abroad, remittances to family and community in support of various projects and causes in Africa is commonplace. Many people take these remittances and support of community as their duty and obligation, because it lays the foundation for altruism, the requisite for becoming an elder.

And finally, generativity is used in the context of creativity; that is, "primarily . . . concerned with establishing and guiding the next generation." This includes senior elders inculcating and bequeathing to succeeding generations the wisdom accrued throughout life in the face of death. Hence, for Erikson—and as it applies to the Akan—generativity, or rather the concept of *bɔ* (to shape, create, mold or form, as well as to destroy or break) has to do with the way in which adults carefully meander their Abra bɔ (ethics) during adulthood in order to avoid destructive and delinquent pitfalls. In this vein, Ɔbra bɔ is not only an ethic (Ɔbra), but an ethical existence and generativity.

Etymologically, the term Nkrabea is derived from *nkra* (message/s) and *bea* (place, residence, journey or destination). However, it would be wrong to base the meaning solely on this conjugation, because when people discuss the Nkrabea as an achievable objective such a conjugation is far from their thoughts. The Nkrabea is the personalized decree or career blueprint accompanying the Ɔkra as an existential career of professional mission or an objective to be accomplished. There is a reason and a purpose for being born; a sense of duty and mission that must be accomplished existentially, and until that divinely decreed purpose is achieved one feels unfulfilled professionally. Really, life has no meaning or purpose for anyone who has not discovered his or her Nkrabea, and so one must pursue life, so to speak, until death.

In the final analysis, the Nkrabea and its role in human activity might be a matter of trial and error, because the Akan maintain that *Ɔbra wɔ dan mu* (meaning an ethic could be altered or changed). That is to say, that if a particular ethical path proves unsuccessful, then it is incumbent on a person to change one's attitude, profession or career, or even an abusive spouse. Similarly, if an individual enjoys a considerable degree of prosperity, then it may be interpreted as having found one's Nkrabea. Likewise, if a person finds oneself in a perpetual cycle of failures, then the culprit is almost always the non-realization of Nkrabea. This does not mean, however, that an individual is resigned to one state of existence, because only death, the eschatological component of Nkrabea, puts an end to life's goals. Yet, even this may have been decreed by an individual's Nkrabea. The inherently good thing about Nkrabea is its universal message of salvation for adherents, because an individual may have many chances of starting over again until everyone has attained his or her existential objective, ultimately. Therefore African-Akan soteriology has a built-in mechanism of reincarnation to enable everyone to be "saved" from existing at a lower orbit to the abode of the ancestors. The good news existentially is that one should not resign oneself to any unproductive state or Ɔbra (ethic), but rather must move on and work indefatigably to improve on one's existential condition. This is what the concept and praxis of Nkrabea are all about.

The fact is both the Ɔkra (soul) and the Nkrabea (existential career or professional blueprint) are divine in origin and so they have everything to do with existential conditions, although the Nkrabea is the personalized career blueprint for life's journey, making life meaningful and worth living. But life can also be a living hell when all possibilities seem to elude an individual's search of a meaningful life. So, rather than live as a generative person dexterously to ensure an ideal life, one becomes a delinquent and lives a life of stagnation, despair, and regrets. Yet regardless of how one lives, the goal is to become ethically responsible for one's own actions as well as the actions of the collective during adulthood; most importantly, finding one's own ethical and spiritual niches professionally within the matrix of human family. Consequently, a person must maintain a delicate balance between the spiritual and physical worlds, which are emblematic of a generative personality leading to the discovery of an Nkrabea.

OWU

Often left out of the discussion about the nature of the Nkrabea is Owu (death), because culturally, people have been conditioned to view death as an unpleasant enemy. In the words of J. H. Nketia, "Death is not regarded as a happy or welcome event. The pathos of mortality and the vanity of some of those beliefs are expressed in some dirges and song. 'To be in the hands of Death is to be in the hands of someone indeed.' 'If the Departed could send gifts, they would surely send something to their children.'"[26] But death is an integral part of Nkrabea as breath is to the Ɔkra (soul), because Owu accompanies Nkrabea as an existential career blueprint. Owu awaits everyone during moments when life seems to have run its course, regardless of whether one has achieved one's Nkrabea or not. Subsequently, Owu is on the minds of people all the time, but unlike the Nkrabea, which a departing Ɔbosom tells God regarding its existential goals and objectives to be accomplished, Owu originates with God as an accompaniment of the Nkrabea, making Owu divine, while Nkrabea is finite insofar as unaccomplished Nkrabea is concerned. Every Nkrabea then has with it the manner of death for every living thing, thus Owu is God's return ticket guaranteeing that every living entity returns to the collective spirituality (immortality). And, as the author of Owu, only God is the one who knows exactly the time and manner of everyone's death. And while the Abosom are aware of Owu, like life or Ɔkra, they are not the authors of it and therefore incapable of stopping death from occurring, although they are capable prolonging life.

While Owu is borne by the Nkrabea, an indestructibly divine aspect of God in all living things, Ɔkra (soul), is also the bearer of Nkrabea and in this respect makes an Nkrabea divine. Hence Owu is a symbiotic part of Nkrabea, although people fail to make the connection until death because Owu is viewed negatively, as that which is bad and could not therefore have originated with God. But the fact is that Owu is a part of a complete package called Ɔkra, and so at a time only known to God, death (Owu) ends corporeal existence in order to usher a deceased person's abstract personality (Ɔsaman) into a life of immortality.

A holistic human being then is a spiritual person. First, the characteristic attributes that enable a person to act and behave uniquely originate with the Abosom, making every person an Ɔbosom in human form. As evidence, the Abosom utilize the head when making themselves known during divinations, with the head (Tsir) serving as the nerve center. Moreover, the Abosom lay claim to every person as being those that they willed into the corporeal. In consequence, each child is said to have an Ɔbosom as an Āgya (father). However, the ultimate claim to parenthood is made by God. God is the father of every single individual in the corporeal environment, as the giver of the very life that sustains existence. Most importantly, as giver of life in the agency of Ɔkra, God is also the one alone who takes away life in the agency of death, Owu. Thus life and death are exclusively God's rights, making him alone the progenitor of life, and not the earth, Asasi.

Finally, who is a human being, the product of both the Abosom and God? How must a person identify himself or herself? Who is a person? One thing that both God and the Abosom have in common for a human being is that each bestows a name on the agency that becomes a person. Relationally, as progenitor of all of humanity, God assigns each potential human to an Ɔbosom who, in turn, wills a person into the mundane as a spiritual father, and therefore it is an Ɔbosom's right to name a child on the eighth day via a child's biological father, after a child has already acquired its first name, *Kra-dzin*, on the day of birth from God. The one who names is the owner of that which is named, thus a person is a child of God, first, and of the Abosom, second. Every person then is the name that one bears. One lives one's name, and called by that name, forever. Most importantly, one's name is also the name of one's soul, the Ɔkra. Thus to have a name is to have a soul, and to have a soul is to have a name, otherwise one does not exist. Religion, ancient Egyptian and therefore African religion, according to Wallis Budge, is the worship of the souls of the dead, otherwise called ancestor worship. Indeed, all religions are about the souls (names) of dead ancestors.

Since God is the first to name his offspring on the day of one's birth when a neonate inhales its first breath, the Ɔkra, to enable it to live as a child of God, it also happens that during a divination rite the name first called is one's divine name, the *Kra-dzin*, acquired on the day of one's birth. This is followed by one's spiritual (Abosom) name acquired on the eighth day of birth and given by the father. Thus names are spiritual in that they are not seen but heard; that is, we only respond to unique sounds that we identify with, forever. For the Akan, then, existence is all about living an ideal life and bequeathing to succeeding generations a name worthy of evocation. So when asked: who are you? Just say your name, because, as for the ancient Egyptians, a name is the seal of the total human economy.

NOTES

1. Konadu, Kwasi. *Indigenous Medicine and Knowledge in African Society*, (New York: Routledge, 2007), p. 44.
2. Ibid.
3. Danquah, J. B. *The Akan Doctrine of God* (London: Frank Cass & Co., Ltd., 1968), p. 162.
4. Konadu, op. cit, p. xvii.
5. Bosman, William. *A New and Accurate Description of the Coast of Guinea: Divided into The Gold, The Slave, and Then Ivory Coasts.* (New York: Barnes & Noble, 1967 [1704]), 146.
6. Ephirim-Donkor, Anthony. *African Spirituality: On Becoming Ancestors, Revised Edition.* (Lanham, MD: University Press of America, 2011), pp. 15–16, 20–23.
7. Christensen, James Boyd. "The Adaptive Functions of Fanti Priesthood." In William Bascom and Melville Herskovits, ed., *Continuity and Change in African Culture.* (Chicago: Univ. of Chicago Press, 1959), 257–278.
8. Ibid, p. 260.

9. Ephirim-Donkor, Anthony. "Akom: the Ultimate Mediumship Experience Among the Akan." *Journal of the American Academy of Religion* (2008) 76/1, pp. 71–74.

10. Danquah, J. B. *The Akan Doctrine of God* (London: Frank Cass & Co., Ltd., 1968), p. 66.

11. Rattray, R. S. *Religion and Art in Ashanti*, (Oxford: Oxford University Press, 1927), p. 51

12. For specific details of the naming rite, please see Ephirim-Donkor, Anthony. *African Spirituality: On Becoming Ancestors, Revised Edition.* (Lanham, MD: University Press of America, 2011), pp. 91–94.

13. For thorough discussion of the notion of psychopomp, see Ephirim-Donkor, Anthony. "Akom: the Ultimate Mediumship Experience Among the Akan." *Journal of the American Academy of Religion* (2008) 76/1, pp. 74–76.

14. Ephirim-Donkor, Anthony. *African Religion Defined, a Systematic Study of ancestor Worship among the Akan, Second Edition,* (Lanham, MD: University Press of America, 2013), p. 181.

15. Nketia, J. H. *Funeral Dirges of the Akan Peoples.* (Ghana, Achimota: 1955), p. 9.

16. Ibid.

17. As the traditional ruler of Gomoa Mprumem, I periodically invite some of my elders to talk about all kinds of religious and philosophical issues. It was in this context in 2013 during the months of September and October that I invited some women and elders in Winneba and Mprumem to discuss, among other thing, how one could sense the presence of spirits and other agencies.

18. Gbadegesin, Segun. "Eniyan: The Yoruba concept of a person." In P. H. Coetzee and A. P. J. Roux, eds., *The African Philosophy Reader, second edition* (New York: Routledge: Taylor &Francis Group, 2003), pp. 175–191.

19. Ibid, p. 180.

20. Gyekye, Kwame. *An Essay on African Philosophical Thought: The Akan Conceptual Scheme.* (Cambridge: Cambridge Univ. Press, 1987), p. 100.

21. For my refutation of possession during divinations, please see "Akom: the Ultimate Mediumship Experience Among the Akan." *Journal of the American Academy of Religion* (2008) 76/1

22. Erikson, Erik. *A way of Looking at Things: Selected Papers from 1930–1980.* Ed. Stephen Schlein (New York: W. W. Norton & Company, 1987), p. 607.

23. Gyekye, op. cit., p. 100

24. Bosman, William. Op. cit.

25. Erikson, Erik, Op. Cit.

26. Nketia, J. H. *Funeral Dirges of the Akan Peoples.* (Achimota, 1955), pp. 6–7.

Chapter Four

Manifestations of the Spirit

Divination[1] (*Akɔm*) is one way that the Abosom make themselves known to people, when they—the Abosom—alone fall in love with human beings, call or choose individuals into the clerical profession who go on to train and graduate as diviners for the Abosom who chose them as "wives." Critically important to the Akan is that no human being can choose to be a diviner (an *Ɔkɔmfo*) without being called by an *Ɔbosom* (a God or Goddess), because divination (Akɔm) is a very difficult profession not taken lightly by the Akan. Without being married to a deity (an Ɔbosom), how else can anyone make the will of the Abosom known to people? It will just be a lie then. Certainly, one could learn to be a priest or priestess (an *Ɔsɔfo*) or even a doctor (*Oninsinye*)—although even for these two clerical vocations, one must have descended from a priestly or medical family—but one can never learn how to be a diviner without a call. After all, it is an Ɔbosom who seeks a mouthpiece for divine pronouncements and therefore the need for it to select the person who would best serve its interests, rather than the other way around.

Another way that the Abosom make themselves known is during the conjugational act where the Sunsum descends and transmits the core essence of a human being in the form of the Su, as we have seen previously. Yet another way focuses on the extrinsic ways that the Abosom manifest themselves on human beings under certain physical and psychological conditions during divinations. While the previous chapter dealt with the innate psychological ways that the Abosom manifest themselves behaviorally as a result of the Su, this chapter looks at the Abosom as they dramatically express themselves outwardly by influencing expressions when they alight on subjects and cause them to endeavor in activities that, ordinarily, subjects would not undertake on their own. These outward manifestations, while fleeting, are long lasting enough for the Abosom to have their way as long as subjects remain under their dictates. These outward manifestations take many forms and occur in varied ways. For example, Paul, in his letter to the Corinthian Church, succinctly describes some of the many ways that the spirit is manifested:

> Now there are varieties of gifts, but the same Spirit; and there are varieties of service, but of the same Lord; and there are varieties of working, but it is the same God who inspires them all in every one. To each is given the manifestation of the Spirit for the common good. To one is given through the Spirit the utterance of wisdom, and to another the utterance of knowledge according to the Spirit, to another faith by the same Spirit, to another gifts of healing by the one Spirit, to another the working of miracles, to another prophecy, to another the ability to distinguish between spirits, to another various kinds of tongues, to another the interpretations of tongues. All these are inspired by one and the same Spirit, who apportions to each one individual as he wills. (1 Cor. 12:4–11 RSV).

The quotation of Paul's letter to the Corinthian Church is meant to show the limitless workings of the Spirit of God. Most importantly, the quotation demonstrates how the spirit expresses itself in ways that are universally indiscriminate and unconditional. Within this context, this chapter is about how, through the Abosom, God is revealed in action in human beings.

One advantage that the Abosom (Gods and Goddesses) have over tangibility is that they affect everything solid, including human beings, while the opposite, insofar as humans are concerned, is not the case unless one is specially gifted with paranormal capabilities enabling a person to observe certain phenomena. This advantage makes it possible for an Ɔbosom then to alight on a medium, for example, to express itself in certain human subjects during divinations. Mediumship experiences are fleeting because an Ɔbosom chooses to remain distinctly spiritual and not material, enabling it to depart when it wants. However, the phenomenon whereby a spiritual agency entirely becomes a human being through the process of kenosis is permanent, as we have seen in the previous chapter, lasting until just before the death of a living being.

Regarding the phenomenon whereby spiritual materials become objectified, I discussed (in the second edition of *African Religion Defined*) visitations that my wife and I made to our Mandinka medium friend, Bangali, in Liberia and how Bangali used to snatch tangible objects from the air.[2] But perhaps the most famous of the phenomenon of physical objects emerging from the "nothingness" of the air was when the high priest-medium of the Asante, Ɔkɔmfo Anɔkyi, "brought down the Golden Stool from heaven as the soul of the Asante people."[3] The idea of a priests-diviners commanding something tangible from the air, or they, themselves—priests-diviners—

transforming themselves into animals or vanishing for moments to days or even years is not uncommon in Africa.[4] Akan folklore, for example, talks about the great Ɔkɔmfo Anɔkyi characteristically vanishing and reappearing when he was still a baby to the astonishment of his parents and others, confirming the fact that for Africans, a person is a constituent part of spiritual agencies.[5] This also explains the notion among Africans that life in the corporeal is fleeting; matter, then, is an illusion if real life is spirit. After all, many cosmogonies in Africa, including that of the ancient Egyptians, speak of Gods whose command from their perches in spiritual realms resulted in the formation of corporeal realities as we know them now.

In the late 1980s and early 1990s, I conducted research among the Āwutuābe (Effutu) of Simpa (Winneba), a coastal city in Ghana, and the elder fishermen were absolutely convinced that during major storms, sacks of fish fell from the sky into rivers and the sea. They did not mean fishes jumping up and down in excitement during storms and finding their way on land, but rather fish in placenta-like sacks falling from the sky and bursting open upon hitting the sea and the fish swimming away. And although elders talk about this phenomenon, it was during my research that elders insisted on the veracity of their claims of what children were told.

While listening to the news on television one day on a research trip to Ghana in the fall of 2013, it was reported that some fish has fallen on land rather than in a river nearby causing the townspeople to gather in amazement. Although a bit skeptical, I was still inclined to believe the story wholly because these notions have been around since time immemorial; that is, they are time tested and therefore truthful or even scientific. The elders contend that whenever there was scarcity of fish, God—or rather the Abosom—released some fish into the sea, although this phenomenon is rare these days because of human stubbornness and unfaithfulness. The reason is that contemporary generations tend to dismiss some experiences of earlier generations, as if to suggest that those experiences were somehow false or fantastical. Such skepticisms are typical of the contemporary generations' attempt to view themselves as more civilized and superior to previous generations, failing to realize that traditions are born of antecedent experience. But when about two years later Thailand[6] also experienced fish falling from the sky after heavy rains, there was the sense of affirmation that the elders were—and are—not simply imagining things.

Similar phenomena witnessed by some African children (including me) in their lifetime simply defy explanations, so that it would be hypocritical of them not to accept claims of earlier generations at face value. The elders attribute the contemporary generation's skepticism of the past to hubris, which has led to cessation of the phenomena so common in the past. If there is no faith in the ancestors, Abosom, and the God of their ancestors, then, the elders argue, in turn the spiritual forces would turn blind eyes on the plight of people, for it is only when one has faith enough to worship the ancestors, Abosom, and God that the spiritual agents, in return, bestow their blessings on their posterity. Even where miracles do occur, they occur with less frequency nowadays because of the present generation's worship of foreign Gods and ideas that do not require immediate accountability. This then has led to recalcitrance, disbelief, lack of respect for elders, and callous disregard toward one another, resulting in pillaging of family and national resources, my discussants lamented. For the elders, there is only one explanation for the mean spiritedness and immorality: too much evil as a result of the full embrace of foreign values at the expense of traditional ones.[7]

What contemporary generations fail to understand because they are oblivious of their own cultural histories is that these ideas—the interplay between the spiritual and the corporeal Wiadzie—are perfectly consistent with African cosmological accounts. As we will see in the next chapter, African cosmogonies speak of spiritual worlds "above," and corporeal worlds below, where divine agencies descended and engaged in all kinds of endeavors and ascended to the spiritual abodes when their engagements were over. The trend nowadays among Ghanaians is that they rather proudly recount foreign creation stories as though those cosmogonies were their own, rather than adhere to their own traditional accounts bequeathed to them by their own ancestors. Yet when one juxtaposes those foreign creation stories with those told by Africans, it is discovered that the African versions are very ancient and older.[8] The reason for this attitude, the attitude of bashing African cultural traditions, is explained in the context of slavery, colonialism, and inferiority complex.

Concerning commanding a concrete object like Ɔkɔmfo Anɔkyi's ancestral stool from the sky for the Asante people, the assertions by fishermen that sacks of fish drop from the sky into rivers and sea, or even my Mandinka friend grabbing solid plants and herbs from the air, the question is: Can a spirit (Ɔbosom) materialize and become a concrete object, like the very earth that we live on? Curiously, if tangibles emerge from air, then are those tangibles already in existence but not observable by the human eyes? The answer, it seems, is an absolute yes. Similarly, Gbadegsin also states that among the Yoruba there are those "special human beings" that tradition acknowledges as having the "ability . . . to 'see' and 'communicate' with spirits" not because "such spirits have physical properties" but because "they are supposed to operate beyond ordinary space."[9] For the Akɔmfo, as part of the graduation rites, they are required to swallow the eyes of dogs to enable them to see, similar to what McCall described among the Igbo.[10] The reason why a tiny minority is able to talk about spiritual things in ways that most people do not is because they have special eyes enabling them to see spiritual things. For some, they are born with the eyes to see beyond the ordinary, while others like the Akɔmfo and some traditional rulers like myself have certain herbal concoctions squeezed into the eyes for certain number of days. Sometimes in addition to the eyes, the ears may also receive the herbal drops. For all these rites and rituals to work, they must be energized or activated when the right spells are chanted over them. Even so, we do not see everything most of the time until something has to be revealed in order for one to write or talk about them. Therefore a priest-medium-diviner like Ɔkɔmfo Anɔkyi or Bangali in Liberia is capable of grabbing tangible objects at their choosing from air because they see what most people do not. As the Akan would say: "They have eyes" (*Wɔwɔ enyiwa*).

What people see as empty space is not spacious after all but rather a world that is entirely occupied by beings and "structures" beyond human perception. This is not in reference to the term "junk-space," itself an oxymoronic reference, because it implies that space is congested and yet spacious; rather, it is a world, universe that space does exists, spiritually. Therefore, for some priests-mediums-diviners-prophets like Bangali and Anɔkyi, they only tap into the unobservable world to request and transport to the world of tangibility objects that already exist in their purest forms. It requires a special paranormal capability and friendship with the Abosom willing to grant one access to a world unimaginable. The danger for a human being with such a paranormal gift or capability is hubris, as human beings begin to take such access for granted to demand even more than they can handle. For the great priest-medium Ɔkɔmfo Anɔkyi, for example, he even tried to conquer death. He claimed that he would travel or sleep (depending on which account one heard as a child) for seven days and nights and awaken on the seventh day with the antidote of death. His only caveat was that while he was in a deep sleep no one should cry or wake him up. Listening to the story as a child, one can only imagine my anticipation as to what happened next. But like all who have wrestled with the enigma of death and failed, Ɔkɔmfo Anɔkyi too failed. A few days into his sleep, a woman on a visit to his village and unaware of Anɔkyi's injunction on crying or wailing, and not to awaken him from his sleep because no one remembered to inform her, thought that Anɔkyi had been sleeping for too long and attempted to wake him up and when he did not respond, she raised her voice to cry thinking that Anɔkyi was dead. Unbeknownst to her, she had actually caused the death of the great priest-medium. Perhaps Ɔkɔmfo Anɔkyi was already dead, but we, the youth, blamed the woman. However, we, the children, were reminded of the moral of Ɔkɔmfo Anɔkyi's attempt to defeat death. That Anɔkyi wanted to be God, because only God is the author of death, *owu*, and life, *nkwa*. With so many gifts and so much power—spiritual power—Ɔkɔmfo Anɔkyi overstepped his bounds as a human being by attempting to cheat death. However, his spiritual powers had limits because he was a human being and not God.

DIVINATION

The Abosom (Gods and Goddesses) do "speak" to human beings all the time, but the most direct and certainly dramatic way is through divination. This is what makes African religion a participatory and interactive religion because adherents are able to speak directly to the Abosom and ancestors about their existential problems. In this way both clients and Abosom engage in discussions that address the specific well-being of clients. Naturally there are several kinds of divination, but here I am referring to a direct, face-to-face encounter with a deity in the Akan mode; that is, when an *Ɔkɔmfo* (diviner) is alighted upon by an Ɔbosom (God or Goddess) in order for the Ɔbosom to speak directly with a client or seeker. Anxiously, humans seek direct intervention and answers from their ancestors and deities about existential conditions. Believed to influence the affairs of their posterity, divination is a mode of communication in which humans, the Akan, consult with diviners (*Akɔmfo*) as mediators in order to hear the voices of Abosom and the Nananom Nsamanfo for psychological assurances about their existential ordeals. These ordeals are economic, social, political, and, above all, regard health and well-being.

In general, many Akan Akɔmfo use bells to summon the Abosom after preparing themselves psychologically and physically, making sure that they have not come in contact with anything impure. Ideally they undertake ablutions—if they had not done so already—put on ceremonial attire, and remove wigs, as that would be disposed of prior to the Abosom making their alightments. The head must be free of anything unnatural.

The head of an Ɔkɔmfo is the most important part of the body because the head is where the Abosom alight during divinations. For this reason, the head must not be covered, free of scarves, wigs, pins, and all other unnatural objects during divination. Even where the Abosom make precipitous and unannounced alightments, all and any foreign objects suddenly and dramatically fall down as if someone has taken them down. The head is the seat of all mediumistic rites whether one is alighted upon or not, or whether one is easily influenced by mediumistic activities. In other words, one does not need to be a medium in order to come under the influence of the Abosom although one must have been a spiritual person, meaning such a person is marked by a deity without him or her even knowing it, as we will now see.

The "carrying" (alighting of an Ɔbosom) motif is very important in divination activities because it serves to define true and genuine Ɔkɔmfo from fake ones with regard to whether or not one is capable of being alighted upon. An Ɔkɔmfo's ability or inability to *carry* an Ɔbosom or any spirit may be used to determine if an Ɔkɔmfo is still alighted upon or not. Unlike, say, an ordinary person having a "heavy head" and unable to sell anything in the sense that no one buys from him or her as compared to another having a light head who sells anything that one carries, a genuine Ɔkɔmfo must be able to carry any Ɔbosom who may want to manifest itself, because a true Ɔkɔmfo is trained exactly for that purpose. Years ago some Akɔmfo friends of mine told me that a newly inaugurated Ɔkɔmfo in Simpa (Winneba) could not carry the Ɔbosom that called her into the clerical vocation. When I asked as to how they were able to determine that when all signs pointed to the contrary, their response was simply to affirm what they believed. So years later when the Ɔbosom was thought to have left the Ɔkɔmfo, their stance was that the deity never alighted on her in the first place. Initially, I thought their suspicions were only based on jealousy, but it appeared they were right all along, as I later came to the same conclusion.

If an Ɔkɔmfo used to carry the Ɔbosom but now was unable to do so, then the answer may simply lie with defilement; meaning she may have done something impure to prevent the Ɔbosom from alighting on her. Unable to purify oneself because it is expensive fiscally, first, and secondly, it would alarm the community and potentially end her career, she may delude unsuspecting clients by faking alightment. Even so, some Akɔmfo are readily dismissed by peers for having been abandoned by their Abosom. However, abandonment does not mean that the Akɔmfo are unable to perform the duties as healers. Rather, it means that they may not be able to carry the deities that called them into the clerical vocation initially. Still, they may be able to carry other spirits, as those spirits may fill in the vacuum left by the Abosom. The challenge is certainly being able to discern which Ɔkɔmfo is legitimate.

Another reason why the "carry" metaphor is extremely important spiritually and academically has to do with correcting the mischaracterization of the *Akɔm* (mediumship profession) phenomenon by non-Africans scholars. Unfortunately many African scholars also tend to follow Western scholars in their mischaracterization of a genuine African religious phenomenon of alightment as possession. Carrying any spirit is best described as alightment, not possession, as non-Africans tend to use because they are accustomed to the term *possession*. Or, perhaps, they use it out of ignorance, or arrogance and condescension. On the contrary, the Akan and other African peoples describe their divination experiences as *alightment*, and so the question is: Why is academia in general and Western scholarship in particular still hanging on to the term "possession" when the evidence says otherwise? James Christensen writes in regard to Fanti priesthood that: "The primary requisite to becoming a Fanti priest is possession by a deity (*obosom*) or by the 'little people' of the forest (*mboatia*). This state of possession of or 'call' is the supreme religious experience. It occurs when the deity 'comes down on the head' and may occur at a public ceremony where drumming and singing are conducive to possession."[11] Even though Christensen clearly describes alightment as when a deity alights on the head of a person to be called into the clerical vocation, he is still inclined to refer to the experience as "possession" rather than call it the way it was described to him. In 2008,[12] I argued that "first, the 'carry' description of deities alighting on the heads of Akɔmfo underscores the need to rethink the so-called 'spirit possession' characterization, because it is a misnomer with negative connotations, and also because it does not accurately describe the Akan mediumistic experience. And second, when a deity alights (*Sie*) on a medium, she/he must carry it literally on her head, a clear indication that the head was the locus during trances."

The Akan term *Sie* (to alight, get down) is understood as a descent from above of an agency, so in this context a spirit or an Ɔbosom is thought to be descending from above—the sky—to land on the head of an Ɔkɔmfo (medium-diviner). When landing is achieved, it is said that the Ɔbosom has landed (*Woāsie*) from up high.

In the context of a Christian church service the question is whether or not a Sunsum (spirit) of a congregant has descended or landed (*Ni sunsum aba*). Sometimes in black church services and in a high-spirited, emotionally charged service, some congregants may be "possessed" by spirits, to which observers would say: *Woāsie* (she has been alighted upon). That is, a spirit from up high has descended or alighted upon a congregant. During all these cathectic experiences, it is the Sunsum (spirit) that is thought to have come down on the heads of believers. Like kings and queen mothers whose feet are not supposed to touch the ground, the Abosom too do not touch the ground or earth, and so the head (*Tsir*) serves as the landing pad for them due to what the head encases: the brain.

Along the same lines, the Sunsum of a non-medium person may "alight" during a worship service when it may be asked: *Ni Sunsum aba* (has the spirit descended), for example. However, the distinction here is clear: The Sunsum (spirit) that alights on a person during a church service might not be an Ɔbosom. Such an alightment may be the result of catharsis engendered by and in response to music or incandescent preaching. As such, nothing emanating from such an individual is decipherable, and usually after a while normalcy is restored. However, if anything meaningful is said, then it is understood by members of a church because it is said in the language that everyone understands, not the gibberish that is now associated some fundamentalist churches.[13]

Watching a video of my inauguration (installation) ceremony as the ruler of Mprumem after the ceremony in January 1994, one could see and hear one of the kings who tended to me warning the select women carrying various gifts to be presented to the king in public by the royal wife (my wife), to prevent alightment (*Sie*) during the procession to the durbar ground. This was just before the procession began. My initial reaction to my colleague's instructions to the women was that the women could not control the activities of the Abosom. However, the king was right in that mediumistic activities are psychological and if not warned, especially those thought to have "light heads," then they could open themselves up to mediumistic influences, since the items the women were carrying were in brass trays thought to attract spirits. The point is that alightment can be controlled or switched off during special occasions.

The emphasis on carrying the deities is because the Abosom are thought to be very heavy and weighty, yet the Abosom are creatures of light and air. So how can agencies of air be that heavy? The Abosom do not reckon their age chronologically, as humans do; rather they do so on the basis of weight. Weight in turn is determined on the basis of ascendency of a deity, which in turn determined the "age" of a particular deity. Time of ascendency should not be construed as birth because the Abosom are not born in the same way as humans, rather time of ascendency must be construed as when a deity first appeared in the corporeal. Unlike humans who are born as neonates, the Abosom appear as fully mature creatures and therefore their weight, at the moment of appearance, determines their "age." So, for instance, when an Ɔbosom says that it is heavier than another Ɔbosom, then it means it has been around longer. It does not, however, mean necessarily that it is older because while some "young" deities appeared early in the corporeal, it does not mean that they are necessarily weightier than deities who appeared late. The weightier an Ɔbosom is means that it has been around from the very beginning, making it heavier to carry.

Interestingly, human beings also measure things in weight, as in stones, so that the weightier, heavier a person or thing is the better, as in boxing. As someone who loves boxing, whenever there is a heavyweight fight, there is much excitement and money to be made. It is only in recent decades that the Western world has become obsessed with body weight as something negative and unhealthy, but in Africa heavy people are still admired because one is thought to be living well. The reason for this mindset is that most people are skinny because they walk a lot and so when a person puts on weight then it is interpreted as good living. Unfortunately, it means that heavier people do less walking, suggesting that there is a correlation between walking and being healthy and skinny. It does not mean, however, that the Abosom too must lose weight because the Abosom do not get sick or die; they are who they are—just *there*.

The ability or inability to carry a deity depends entirely on the training—duration and degree of difficulty of training and how true a call may be—an Ɔkɔmfo receives. Ideally any genuine Ɔkɔmfo should be able to carry any Ɔbosom, but the fact is that some Akɔmfo are unable to perform this task at some point during their professional careers. To carry anything one must be strong enough to carry and tow any load, otherwise the weight of the load will collapse on the carrier. The reason is obvious, less-than-adequate training means that the deity being invoked might not respond, and when it shows up the medium's life may be endangered, as was the case when my father and his team, including Joseph Nunoo (secretary for the Effutu Traditional Council under three kings from the 1920s to late 1970s and who confirmed the encounter to me), went to invoke the Ɔbosom Penkyae Otu, the leading deity of Simpa (Winneba). When the elderly Ɔkɔmfo summoned Otu and as the party waited anxiously, suddenly and violently the Ɔkɔmfo was lifted up from her stool and raised until her head hit the ceiling in the room and she was slammed back on her stool, again and again against the ceiling and back on her stool three times. In the state of panic and fear, the party initially thought that the Ɔkɔmfo was injured, because they had never encountered the deity in this manner. Then, just as suddenly, Otu greeted and spoke to them after the third time that he slammed the Ɔkɔmfo on her stool. After Penkyae Otu departed, the elderly Ɔkɔmfo fell from her stool, and for moments the group thought that she was hurt, but she was fine although she was physically and intellectually drained. Thus, divination, insofar as the alighting of Abosom on diviners is concerned, is measured in terms of *weight*, as to how heavy an Ɔbosom is on a diviner. As a result, the Akɔmfo assert that the deities weigh on them heavily during divination in spite of the fact that the deities are agents of light or air. This is exactly why specialized training is needed for anyone called into the mediumship vocation to enable Akɔmfo to be the vehicles of the deities as they are.

The idea of weight of the Abosom may also be understood numinously. The weightier an Ɔbosom is, the holier. This does not mean that some Abosom are not holy, rather it has to do with power of some Abosom over others. Just the mere presence of the holy evokes a sense of awe and fear, as when the Sunsum of an Ɔbosom falls, literally, on an individual. Contextually, it is the holy coming into contact with the profane mortal being that causes the profane to die, take ill, or be unable to speak or move. The un-holiness of a human subject is predicated on the fact that the unholy human is a mere mortal, not to be compared with that which has been *there*, perpetually. Subsequently it is necessary to set aside and train those identified and called by the Abosom themselves to experience hierophanies in a manner safe and desirous for the Abosom and also humans. Normally when those thought to have "heads" or exhibit proclivities thought to be spiritually influenced encounter sacred spaces, they react accordingly by, say, removing their shoes or departing the area for fear of being exposed or alighted upon. In this context, one may be heard saying: *Ha yɛ dru* (this place is heavy) to mean that the site one is standing on is holy. That is to say, that the holy resides there because the Sunsum (spirit) of an Ɔbosom hovers on the spot, which is felt by weighing on those thought to have light heads or easily influenced by spiritual agencies. Physiologically, one may experience chills or goose bumps—a signal to re-orient oneself, intellectually.

If weight determines the "age" of Abosom which, in turn, determines the power of deities because of the eternal existence of Abosom, which cause fear and trembling on the profane and mortal beings to the extent of even causing death, it also follows that power has to do with rank. Rank has to do with how the Abosom are seated when they convene to discuss matters affecting them. Similarly, in human terms, the older a person is, the more powerful spiritually he or she becomes after death. When elders meet, for example, the seating arrangement is based on seniority and rank. If this were not the case then young people would physically manhandle the elderly, but as it were, this is not the case because there is something about the old that prevents those physically stronger from harming them. This is called respect for authority. Of course, some elderly are clearly abused, but there is a general respect for the elderly by virtue of certain individuals living to be very old and explaining why old age is ideal existentially, because the very old are thought to be spiritually powerful. Consequently, most African elderly are accused of being witches because they seem to know everything. Even though the physical atrophy of old age is real, in spiritual terms it accrues into spiritual weight, power; thus, the very old have weightier and powerful spirits. Some elders are so powerful that they are thought to cause death to, say, infants because neonates have such light spirits (*Āsunsum*) that they are easily put to flight. This explains the evil eye phenomenon and why the Akan believe certain elders to possess this capability[14] because their very presence is enough to cause harm to neonates. This power dynamic explains the relationship between the Abosom and mortals and why mortals seek immortality, to be like the Abosom.

Still, on the subject of Akɔmfo (mediums-diviners) being able to carry the Abosom (Gods and Goddesses) on their heads, interestingly in the New Testament, Paul (1 Cor. 11:4–10 RSV) makes a curious observation about women's heads. Paul wants women to cover their heads, and one of his explanations as to why women should veil their head is quite fascinating. In verse 10, Paul offers a revealing reason for the veiling of women, and that is because of angels. For Paul, angels or spirits have keen interests in uncovered heads. Paul, it seems, did not trust—or was suspicious of—angels or spirits in general when it came to women who did not veil their heads. Clearly for Paul, unveiled hair of women attract spirits and so to avoid spirits from alighting on women, he argues that women cover their heads. Indeed, there is a sensual connection between the head (hair) and Abosom of which Paul is clearly aware.

For Akan Akɔmfo—most of whom are women—uncovered heads (hair) of women serve as invitations for spirit alightment. Subsequently, whenever the Akɔmfo are divining privately, invariably they make sure that their heads are not covered; it is only when they do not want to be alighted upon that they wear scarves. Even so, Abosom wishing to alight invariably remove the scarves in dramatic fashion.[15] However, while in a trance during public ceremonies, their heads are always left uncovered for the continued alightment of the Abosom; otherwise their heads are covered during normal everyday activities. In the past, both sexes of the clergy (Akɔmfo and Asɔfo [priests]) wore "white linen caps, which completely covers the hair,"[16] although nowadays female Akɔmfo prefer scarves to caps, while male Akɔmfo and Asɔfo hardly wear any cap at all in public. Obviously, the hair of women, especially of Akɔmfo, is what attracts the Abosom and other spirits. During the graduation rites for a former Ɔkɔmfo friend of mine in 1999, her long hair was divided into five strands of north, south, east, west, and center, and throughout the long procession through the town of Simpa (Winneba) she remained in a trance. I am not sure if her hair had anything to do with her trance, but as long as her hair remained unveiled she opened up herself to spirit alightment.

Many Akɔmfo attend public performances in support of colleagues dressed up with their heads covered, with no intention of being alighted upon. Yet, every Ɔkɔmfo is keenly aware that her Ɔbosom could make precipitous entry. This happens when one begins to sway from side to side, shakes and quivers, and attempts to undress. After observing an Ɔkɔmfo called Awo alighted upon, Appiah-Kubi wrote:

> When the spirit begins to show itself in her, a dramatic physical transformation takes place. In a standing position, she staggers, appears to lose her balance, begins to sway, and may fall onto the ground or into the arms of attendants or bystanders. Her entire body begins to vibrate; her hands are rigid at her sides or stretched out above. Her feet are planted widely apart and she may lurch back and forth from toe to heel. The vibration increases in intensity, somewhat resembling the convulsion of a seizure state. At the same time she emits deep

> grunts and groans. Her jaw begins to protrude, her lips pout and turn down sharply at the corners, her eyes dilate and stare fixedly ahead or into the sky. An impression of masculinity and fierceness envelops her face. She rises from the ground or her special stool, or breaks away from her supporters.[17]

The nature of the Abosom or spirits in general is that when the spirit, any spirit, comes upon anyone, especially on the Akɔmfo in public, no one can sit still because the spirit moves. That is, no one can claim to have been alighted upon and remain still. Public displays are venues for the Abosom to show off the dancing skills, and so such displays invariably involve alightments but without divine pronouncements most times, because the Abosom only wish to dance. If there is any speaking at all, then it usually involves an Ɔbosom attempting to teach musicians new songs. Divine pronouncements occur in private during consultations when an Ɔbosom alights on a Ɔkɔmfo, which does not involve the same movements as during public performances.

Summoning of Abosom during divinations is always filled with anticipation and anxiousness. First there is the preparation of an Ɔkɔmfo which may take few minutes—if she is already engaged in divination rites prior one's arrival—to about an hour or so if she has to take a bath, especially if a visit occurs early in the morning. Sometimes a seeker may visit an Ɔkɔmfo only to be told that she is not divining and must return a few days later. (This may be because she may be having her menses if she is a young Ɔkɔmfo, although a client will not be told this explicitly.) Other times a first-time visitor will be told that he or she came at the wrong day since some Akɔmfo do not divine on certain days of the week. So, to visit any Ɔkɔmfo a seeker may have to do some research, otherwise one may be disappointed. Nowadays, the use of cellphones has made it easier to call before any visit (as I now do with my Akɔmfo, although most of them are elderly or post-menopausal women), if one has access to the number of a particular Ɔkɔmfo. The goal of every genuine Ɔkɔmfo is purification of body and mind before making herself available to her *husband*, the Ɔbosom that called her as its medium. Normally purifications entail taking baths and then putting on the usual Akɔmfo attire, which is white apparel most of the time.

Sometimes the choice of attire for private and, especially, public performances is dictated by an Ɔbosom, especially if the Ɔkɔmfo is already alighted upon. According to Appiah-Kubi, an Ɔkɔmfo would have a "special dressing room where all these garments and the cultic panoplies are kept. She is usually dressed by the female attendants. When . . . the priest-healer rejects the choice of dress, it is interpreted to mean that the attendants have not made the right interpretation concerning the possessing spirit. The attendants must then try one garment after another until . . . right choice has been made."[18] Usually attire worn by Akɔmfo during private consultations is worn by conscious Akɔmfo themselves before divination rites, because they are not alighted upon prior to the rites. That is, an Ɔkɔmfo would usually dress up in a white attire before commencing to call an Ɔbosom. Sometimes, however, a gift of, say, a piece of cloth given to an Ɔbosom during divination and placed around the shoulders of the Ɔbosom (actually the Ɔkɔmfo), may be thrown away when another Ɔbosom alights on the Ɔkɔmfo after the departure of the first. Or, the second Ɔbosom, recognizing that the piece of cloth is not his or hers, would asked that the item be removed. In my years of being involved in divinations, I have sensed some jealousy among some Abosom when gifts are presented to some and not others.

During private consultations, when an Ɔkɔmfo is ready she sits on her priestly stool facing her altar, with her divination pot containing sacred water in front of her or on her side. The stool is her divination stool given to an Ɔkɔmfo, as a "special stool that belongs exclusively to a clergyperson . . . offered to a clergyperson upon graduating from clerical training. This priestly stool is retired upon the death of the clergyperson and referenced by subsequent clergy associated with a founder of a particular shrine." In my own community of Gomoa Mprumem, for instance, a family that arrived in Mprumem from another community called Gyankoma as refugees who placed themselves under the protection of the ruler, Nana Ɔwom, in the second half of the nineteenth century, included a dwarfish Ɔkɔmfo. Now the descendants of the Ɔkɔmfo have turned her priestly stool into a royal stool in that family's desire to appear royal, and they have periodically contested the kingship of Mprumem to no avail.

The sacred water in an Ɔkɔmfo's pot must be replenished at all times, and normally the replenishments take the form of prayers and libations, some offered just before she starts divining. Then orienting herself intellectually toward a fixed point on the altar, an Ɔkɔmfo begins to ring a small bell or a similar instrument unique to her deity. The bells used are unique to the deities and the Akɔmfo who ring them, although there is no doubt that when a bell sounds the Abosom hear and listen as to which direction the ringing is emanating from and whose "wife" may be calling. Furthermore, every ring is unique in that no two bells sound the same, so that an Ɔbosom may get accustomed to a particular ringtone emanating from its Ɔkɔmfo. Yet when Akɔmfo are switched and the same bell is used, the Abosom still know exactly which Ɔkɔmfo is calling. This suggests that it is not so much about the ringtones as it is about the Ɔkɔmfo ringing the bell. After all, the Abosom are married to their human subjects and not ringtones or bells. However, it appears that the person who rings the bell, just by holding it, transmits her kinetic energy and spiritual sound by the exertion made through the ringtones that are heard by her husband who responds hurriedly. After all, sound, like any name, is spiritual and travels in wavelengths, which is heard by the person being called. In other words, people do not see their names but respond to them; meaning, people respond to the unique sounds that parents, friends, instructors, and relatives make that identify us as unique individuals. In the end, though, the Abosom, as infinite spiritual agencies, are omniscient relative to finite beings, as such they do not have any problem knowing who is and who is not calling them.

On the contrary, an Ɔbosom may land or alight on its Ɔkɔmfo with or without a bell being rung. The reason is that the soul of every Ɔkɔmfo is hidden in his or her Ɔbosom, as alluded to already in the previous chapter. For this reason, the Ɔbosom with whom an Ɔkɔmfo's soul is hidden is the first Ɔbosom to respond to the Ɔkɔmfo's divination to ascertain as to why a soul under its aegis being summoned. We would recall that every soul, Ɔkra, has a name and so when a soul is being called, the first person or agency to hear it is naturally the agency which is protecting the soul, the Ɔbosom. So sometimes suddenly an Ɔkɔmfo would be alighted upon by the Ɔbosom that called him or her into the clerical vocation because an Ɔbosom knows exactly where its Ɔkɔmfo is and what she is doing. As evidence, one only attends a public gathering of Akɔmfo to see different Akɔmfo alighted on by different deities. The point is, that the Ɔbosom do not need bells to be rung for them to alight on their Ɔkɔmfo, as they track the movements of their wives; indeed, it is their human subjects, the Akɔmfo, who need special instruments to sound before calling their husbands, the Abosom. Upon hearing its unique ringtone an Ɔbosom would alight on its Ɔkɔmfo first—although other Abosom could alight as well—because the Ɔbosom is married to an Ɔkɔmfo and must ensure that all is right.

The duration of rings usually indicates how close or far away an Ɔbosom is. Usually it takes a few seconds to about a minute for an Ɔbosom to alight. Anything after a minute is too long. Sometimes after a long delay an Ɔkɔmfo will stop and offer more prayers and libation in her pot imploring her Ɔbosom to respond. Generally, an Ɔbosom responds very quickly following the second prayers and libation. Occasionally, an Ɔbosom alights even before a bell is rung, explaining that it happened to be nearby. This happens when an Ɔbosom is expecting a particular guest, meaning it was tracking movements of the guest to the moment when an Ɔkɔmfo is readying herself to summon her Ɔbosom.

There is a strong sense of anticipation as an Ɔbosom approaches because the ringing of the bell becomes faster, quicker, and louder. Clearly an Ɔkɔmfo is in an altered state of mind and sphere. It is as if her mind has been sucked out, a clear indication that an Ɔkɔmfo has already made contact with her Ɔbosom and vice versa. This is even before alightment is actually made; in other words, a subconscious state of mind must be established before the crescendo of actual alightment. Absolute attention and focus is required, as one notices the intensity and focus of an Ɔkɔmfo as well. Then, suddenly and spectacularly, an Ɔbosom alights. Silence follows momentarily as an Ɔkɔmfo loses her individuality and sense of self wholly. The Ɔkɔmfo has become the Ɔbosom who just landed wholly. I use "landed" deliberately, because for those of us who travel by air a lot, there is a vicarious sense of having witnessed the landing of a plane or something huge and the silence felt as the plane moves toward the gate. In this case, it is the Ɔkɔmfo who is the landing pad with her Ɔbosom landing on her from above and taking control of the head (mind) and manipulating the rest of an Ɔkɔmfo's body. At this point there is no longer an Ɔkɔmfo but an Ɔbosom who has wholly taken over its human subject intellectually, speaking in a different voice and language and behaving in a manner utterly different from the Ɔkɔmfo who initiated the call.

The silence is broken by the Ɔbosom as the visiting agency. And invariably the first words spoken by an Ɔbosom are to greet the assistant (*Ɔbrafo*) of the Ɔkɔmfo who usually sits not too far from an Ɔkɔmfo as an interpreter. Sometimes, some of the Ɔbosom are not easily understood because they speak archaic versions of current languages, so the Ɔbrafo (assistant), having been around the Abosom for considerable length of time, is usually in the position to decipher the versions of what the Abosom say. An Ɔbosom must address its Ɔkɔmfo's assistant by name as that confirms the true identity of an Ɔbosom to an Ɔbrafo. An Ɔbrafo once told me that his cue to the identity of his Ɔkɔmfo's deity is when the Ɔbosom addresses him by a special name or nickname, otherwise he knows right away that a different Ɔbosom has arrived. This is important because some Abosom have the tendency to feign their identities as though they are the ones being invoked. After all, human beings do not see the Ɔbosom and so one way to ensure authenticity is through the use of specific names.

Then after the initial exchange of greeting with the Ɔbrafo (assistant), the attention turns to a client or seeker. Seekers are greeted in general terms; however, known clients are greeted by name, nickname or title. This is really assuring as it means intimacy and special connection with the Abosom. Personally, there are Abosom who address me by a specific name of mine and others who call me by my traditional position or title. The difference is that the Abosom who address me as a traditional ruler are Abosom that I have had a relationship with through the years, while those referencing me by a specific name are very personal, including my Āgya-bosom (Ɔbosom father). On my part, the address to every single Ɔbosom is Nana, except those that I have a very personal relationship with. The title or term Nana is neuter and applies to both men and women elders; but above all, Nana is the highest socio-political and spiritual title that an Akan could acquire, as both Ellis and Rattray have pointed out. In this vein, every male and female Akan ruler is a Nana; so is every grandparent, ancestor, Ɔbosom, and above all, God.

The greetings are quite simple and straightforward with two parts. First, an Ɔbosom would say: *Me mahum Omaingya* (My peace to you), or simply, *Omaingya* (Peace), or *Mongyi Omaingya* (I offer you my peace). In other words, the Abosom arrive in peace and therefore bring along not only peace but blessings as well, which they extend to all present to allay any anxiety that anyone might have.

To accept the peace that the Abosom offer, clients respond by saying: *Omaingya 'baa/mbra* (Let peace be or reign). The exchange of peace greetings opens the way for the second part of the divine greetings. Upon hearing a response an Ɔbosom would follow up the peace offer and ask: *Apow mu* (How are you?). An inquirer may reciprocate by ascertaining about the state of the Ɔbosom, to which the reply usually is: *Me wɔhɔ* ("I am there" or "I exist"). The response, *I am there* or *I exist* underscores the fact that Abosom simply *exist*, forever; that is, the Abosom have always been *There,* eternally, making them the Gods that they are.

Like human beings, the Abosom too speak varieties of language depending on the locale where they are found and who shows up during a divination rite, because an Ɔbosom could exist among different ethnic groups. To one group, an Ɔbosom only speaks their language, and to another an entirely different language when invoked. This is explained by the fact that if, for instance, an Ɔbosom is a river, it may flow for hundreds or even thousands of miles among different ethnic nations all speaking different languages. To each group, the same river Ɔbosom may be known under a different name speaking their language making an Ɔbosom speaker of a multiplicity of languages. In *The Making of an African King,* for instance, I offer an example of this phenomenon about the Ɔbosom called Kɔbena Ayɛnsu.[19] This river deity flows through many communities not all of which speak the same language and empties into the sea in Simpa (Winneba). The people of Simpa are Guan speaking so that when the deity Kɔbena Ayɛnsu is invoked in Simpa during divination rites, he speaks fluent Āwutu language. However, when he is invoked by any of the Akan-speaking groups outside of Simpa, the Ɔbosom speaks *Twe* (Akan). When I asked him during a divination as what his "ethnicity" was, he told me that he is an Ɔkyi-ni and therefore speaks Twe. Concerning the Āwutu language, he maintains that he learned the language when the Āwutu-ābe first arrived in Simpa. I recall one day visiting a diviner of the deity outside of Simpa. When I got there the diviner already had a client with her. As I waited, I overhead the client speaking the Āwutu language to the deity, while Ɔbosom Ayɛnsu also only spoke Twe. The client was from Simpa and knew that the Ɔbosom understood the Āwutu language and decided to communicate with him in Āwutu. I thought it was interesting to hear the exchanges in different languages.

Another explanation as to why the Abosom may speak many languages is that as a river flows through many communities, it is joined by several other rivers (deities) as a single river making its way into the sea when, in fact, it made up many distinct rivers. So while a river may appear to have a single name, it may actually have many names because it is made up many Abosom. Therefore, it is highly probable that different deities may indeed speak to different ethnic groups in their own languages because the deities speak the same language as theirs when invoked, and not the deity whose name a river bears, unless an Ɔbosom asserts that it the same river Ɔbosom. Explained thus, an Ɔbosom is whatever an ethnic group believes it to be linguistically. But regardless of where they are invoked, the Abosom invariably communicate in clear languages of understanding; that is, languages understood and spoken by a people, albeit archaic versions of their language.

The Abosom make divine pronouncements in the name of God because God speaks through the Abosom who, in turn, speak in clear and unambiguous languages to humanity. However, speaking in clear languages does not mean that what is spoken is understood in its entirety, as languages continue to evolve to the extent that the Abosom speak ancient versions of language spoken today. Still, most of what the Abosom say is understood. Even where some words are misunderstood, assistants (Abrafo) are present to interpret ambiguous words and their meanings. As for me, such words offer me the opportunity to learn because I always make it a point to ask for clarification and etymology of words and terms, which the Abosom are eager to provide.[20]

The salient point about what the Abosom speak is that every language spoken by humans is—and was—first spoken by the Abosom. Meaning, speech is a spiritual sound first made by a non-human. Speech is spiritual, a compressed air that makes sound, and even though we do not see the sounds we make as tangible instruments, the effect of the sounds we make identify us as unique individuals. Many of these languages are now obsolete, archaic, or no longer known, because some of the humans who first spoke them are no longer around. But no matter how dynamic speech is, what is unchanging is the air without—God and the gods (Abosom). So, for the Akan, God and the Abosom hear everything proceeding out of the mouths of peoples and creatures that do not use the same modes of communication as humans. Scary as it is, people still take what they say out loud for granted, unaware that the moment any sound is uttered, an agency has wind of it and it is no longer a secret. And as long as an Ɔkɔmfo is in the state of alightment, she is not affected by corporeal influences. There is no awareness of time, for instance, because she is under the dictate and influence of a powerful spiritual agency.

When discussions are over, an Ɔbosom would announce its intention to departure. As if standing on the shoulders of an Ɔkɔmfo, it springs upward like a bird, and in the same way that an Ɔbosom connects with an Ɔkɔmfo's mind prior to actual alightment, an Ɔbosom takes along an Ɔkɔmfo's mind momentarily before letting go at some point in flight and consciousness is regained in a matter of seconds. Sometimes, during the transition and just as suddenly, another Ɔbosom may alight. This occurs when several Abosom have been summoned and take their turns alighting, or when other deities want to get their message across.

After regaining full consciousness, an Ɔkɔmfo would ask her assistant as to what transpired. Invariably an Ɔkɔmfo's assistant, the Ɔbrafo, would summarize what transpired to an Ɔkɔmfo, a clear indication that Akɔmfo are not aware or in control of what goes on during divinations, unless, of course, an Ɔkɔmfo was feigning divination. But even she were feigning, she would still demand to know what transpired in order to give credence to the divination.

In all my years of participating in rites of divination—and I have had countless numbers of them in my position as a traditional ruler—there is one that stands out for me in terms of its sensationalism during a departure of the deity. Indeed, it was spectacular as it was scary. After an Ɔbosom informed us that it was departing and thinking that it would follow the routine path of departure, the Ɔbosom suddenly and quickly turned sideways and headed (the Ɔkɔmfo's head) against a wall of the divination room so hard that it vibrated the other walls of the room. The sound created as a result was like two huge rams bumping heads against each other. The experience startled me and my accompaniment because it not only caught us unawares, but that it was the first time that my accompaniment and I had witnessed such a dramatic departure from an Ɔbosom. We actually thought the Ɔkɔmfo was hurt, but when she regained consciousness we realized she was just fine. How can anyone hit his or her head so hard against a wall of cement and not fall unconscious with a very serious head injury or sustain some sort of permanent concussion under similar circumstances? Of course, this is one of those religio-spiritual nonsensicalities that one does not have any rational explanation for. Indeed, for some moments we were being rational human beings, forgetting that what just transpired before us was an irrational religious encounter not subject to rational explanation. Apparently the Ɔkɔmfo's assistant (Ɔbrafo) had encountered this Ɔbosom a few times and told us about the departing style of that particular Ɔbosom from northern Ghana. When the Ɔbosom came again during our next divination rite, we, together with the Ɔkɔmfo's Ɔbrafo (assistant), pleaded with it to find another way of departing but he refused. We, however, persisted and then pleaded with it to depart gently and not hit its head against the wall so hard, which it did. There is no doubt that the Ɔbosom is a ram deity. It also reminded me of the encounter my father and his co-elders had when they divined the leading deity of Simpa (Winneba), Otu, and how Otu lifted and slammed the Ɔkɔmfo three times against the ceiling in her divining room, as described above.

TWINS ALIGHTMENT

There is a common song for twins that people sing during rituals honoring twins among the Āwutu-ābe of Simpa. Indeed, growing up in Simpa, Ghana, I recall singing the same song as we, the youth, also participated in some twin festivities. Even though we sang the song, we never really understood what the song meant until my 96-year-old mother-in-law sang and interpreted the song to me on October 1, 2013, during a research trip to Ghana. The song, in Āwutu and interspersed with Akan (Fantse), is:

Awo Awo Awo Awo oo
Apaa yae, omaingya saa
Ayea ee
Awo ā, awo ā; eyee ɛbien
Amenya mu fulful
Apeae dɔwaa, na apeae brɛw

(Oh birth, birth, birth, birth
Hail, peace
Birthing, birthing; this is two
They are not gotten arbitrarily
It is only when the gods love you,
That the gods bless you with twins)

This song, in addition to glorifying parturition or procreation as worthwhile, points to twins as special children specifically given to those parents whom the Abosom have favored, not as a random act.[21] Thus to have twins is for the Abosom to fall in love with a parent. Most importantly, the song confirms the notion that it is the Abosom who will children to parents in the corporeal, and that every child has an Ɔbosom as a spiritual father, although, as we have seen in the previous chapter, God is the ultimate father of all.

So while divination is obviously the more direct way the Abosom interact with humans, their Akɔmfo, when Abosom and humans speak face-to-face with one another about existential conditions and well-being of humans, it is by no means the only way. As loved children of the Abosom, twins also encounter the Abosom in dramatic fashions during rites commemorating their special births as twins, although not in a manner like divinations. While any Ɔbosom can will twins to a parent that it falls in love with, the overall twin deity is called Abam Kofi. His name means that this Ɔbosom is a Friday deity as the second "born" after the initial twins in what the Akan consider as a set of twins—the first born after the twins being Tawiah. Meaning, Abam Kofi is a twin himself, being one of the set of Abosom twins. But more than a twin, Abam Kofi is the most powerful of the twin deities and hence his cult and worship.

Among the Akan, a set of twins is comprised of five children in successive order: the twins proper, *Panyin* (elder) and *Kakra* (younger). Even though chronologically the Panyin is the older of the two, spiritually the Akan believe that the Kakra (also Kakara) is actually the elder of the two—with the Panyin being an assistant to the Kakra. The Panyin is born first in order that he or she may prepare the way for the elder, the Kakra. Subsequently, the Kakra is thought to be more spiritually powerful than the Panyin. Consequently, if the Panyin were to die, the rationale offered is that he or she was only supposed to accompany the Kakra to the corporeal world and return to whence it came from. In other words, society has a spiritual explanation for the death of a twin rather than face the real possibility that the lack of resources to adequately care for twins could contribute to the death. This should not discount the spiritual causality of such deaths by any means.

One day, I called a "daughter" of mine (actually a daughter of the ruler that I succeeded; that is, my granduncle) to my house because one of her baby twins cried continuously every night after midnight. Since her house was not far from mine, I could hear the baby cry and that disturbed me a lot. When she came to my house, I told her that I was very concerned about her baby and that she and her husband should do something about it. She pressed for more answers but I only urged her to keep an eye on him. Unfortunately, a week later the Kakra—not the Panyin—of her twins died suddenly. So while society has justification for the death of the first born of twins, it seems there is no explanation for the loss of the Kakra, except to blame it on witchcraft. As in almost all cases, the Kakra (the second of twin births) is usually the smaller of twins, so that extra attention is paid to the Kakra. For example, the younger of the twins is fed more to the detriment of the Panyin (elder), which could lead to the neglect of the Panyin. The fact, however, is that more Panyins survive birth than the Kakras (second of the twins), because they are usually bigger and stronger and even healthier at birth, as my own twins confirmed.

The first single child born after twins is called *Tawiah* (or *Tawuah*). As anchor of the twins, the Tawiah is thought to be more spiritually powerful than the twins. Normally this triad may be accepted as "complete" if a parent does not have any more children, but there is always the pressure to have more as the Akan consider the set incomplete. As both my wife and I are first single children after our respective twins, there was pressure on us by relatives after our twins were born to have their Tawiah too. When we finally had our Tawiah, still there was pressure on us to have yet another child until we told our relatives that we have decided not to have any more children. The Tawiah is naturally stronger than the twins because he or she is single and receives full attention during infancy, especially if one of the twins died.

The second single born after twins and the first after the Tawiah is special because he or she bears the name as the twin Ɔbosom, Abam. As such, the Abam, like the Ɔbosom whose name the baby bears, Abam Kofi, is thought to be very powerful spiritually, meaner and stronger than even the Tawiah. The Abam is said to control the complete set of twins and so she or he must be mitigated to prevent him or her from anger.

And finally, the third single child born after the twins, Nyankomagor, is thought to be the weakest and calmest of what the Akan consider to be a set of twins, just like the pinky finger. In other words, a complete set of twins is made up of five children. Having all five means that Abam Kofi has found a special favor with a particular family or parent, especially if the children were not solicited from a deity. The fact is that sometimes a couple experiencing difficulty having children may solicit help from an Ɔbosom. Such children, if the Ɔbosom fulfilled its promise, are also five in total, as we will see below.

During a naming ceremony for twins, each neonate receives raffia-strung beads of white and black (or red), the colors of Abam Kofi, that are tied around a child's wrists to signify the fact that they are twins and identified for the deity. Sometimes a piece of gold is strung together with the black, but regardless of the addition, the rest of the beads on both sides must be white. Henceforth the twins wear the raffia-strung beads throughout their existence unless they choose otherwise. It must be noted that not all parents choose to mark their children for the Abam Kofi. While my mother had beads around my wrists as a baby, I do not recall having them on as a child or youth, except when an elder sister of mine died, when my mother wrapped a vine around my wrists when I arrived at the funeral. However, small effigies of the twins wearing the raffia-strung beads are believed to have been hung-up on a wall in a room in honor of the deity bringing them directly under the aegis of the Ɔbosom.

In addition to being hung on a wall, situational rites may be performed for twins who display neurotic tendencies in order to restore psychosomatic balance. Otherwise, twins wait until the annual festival in the month of August held to coincide with the harvesting of crops, at which time Abam Kofi is propitiated during the Nta Abam festival. It is during the festivities honoring Abam Kofi that twins are alighted upon by Abam Kofi and other Abosom.

The Nta Abam festival begins early in the morning in most households where twins reside. In the community of Simpa where I conducted research in the 1990s, many households have twins born in them but not all participate in the festival due to economic reasons. The festivities begin when an altar and symbolic form of Abam Kofi is taken down from hanging on a wall and laid on a specially prepared bedding. Food items like yams, plantains, eggs, and chickens or sheep are readied for a sumptuous meal, as well as trays containing diluted seawater, into which are placed special vines believed to empower the seawater. Afterwards, chickens or sheep are slaughtered and the blood poured into the water and onto Abam Kofi's symbolic shape.

Preparation and consumption of the main meal is completed by early afternoon for the actual feasting to begin, after selected portions of the meal have been set aside for Abam Kofi. Next, boiled eggs and morsels of *Ɔtɔ* (a sacred meal of yams, one white and the other red) are offered to Abam Kofi when morsels of Ɔtɔ and eggs are placed on the image of the Ɔbosom. Following that, the twins—and anyone who is a twin but not participating in the festival as a twin—congregate around the Ɔtɔ and eggs that are in a white tray and partake of the same sacred meal as for Abam Kofi. This is to say, that twins eat apart from non-twins.

When the feasting is over the kitchen is swept and the trash added to the sacred seawater and readied for the most festive part of the festival: a journey by the twins to dispose of the trash in trays at the beach. Bathed and clothed in white outfits and each twin smeared with white myrrh and marked with double insignia of red (or white and red) myrrh their on joints, forehead, and temples, the twins ready themselves for the ordeal ahead. A priest or priestess or an elder offers prayers and libations in front of each tray to be carried by a twin, after which she takes some of the water and gently rubs each twin while exhorting them about the impending journey to dispose of the trash. Then, beginning with the eldest twin, the Panyin, a priestess lifts up each tray and taps it three times on each twin's head, and on the third count the twin holds the tray in place. Lined up behind the eldest, a priestess again offers final prayers and libations, but this time into the trays now being carried by the twins. Finally, the twins are ready to proceed to dispose of the contents of their trays.

The eventual destination is a community's kitchen midden in non-coastal communities, or the beach if a community is a coastal one, as in those festivals that I observed. Accompanied by members of participating households and joined by spectators singing praise songs of the deity, Abam Kofi, the twins slowly make their way to the beach. Along the way to the beach, twins from other households join in, turning the festival into one long procession of many twins, each group followed by a crowd of family members and spectators. The journey is a struggle as it is spectacular, especially as they all converge at Yɛpimso market (the last central place adjacent to the beach), because Abam Kofi and other deities descend, literally, into the sacred water or actual trays, thereby alighting on the twins. That is, a twin may experience a gradual increase in the weight of the tray, becoming heavier and heavier until such time as a twin is virtually unable to move. In a state of trance a twin is completely under the control and sway of an Ɔbosom.

Thus alighted upon, dazed, with eyes appearing to be dilated, twins react naturally by attempting to dump the trays and their contents away entirely—quite an impossible task because the hands appear to be glued to the tray. Sometimes they succeed in emptying their trays, but are unsuccessful in dumping the trays to the ground because an Ɔbosom is residing in it. Consequently, they turn their heads back and forth and from side to side, stand still momentarily, then sway from side to side erratically, raise and tap the trays on their heads, rub the base of the trays around their heads, run helter-skelter, and then stop. Following the twins, the crowd sings the most popular twin song in the Āwutu language:

Meyae Maawɔ, Tawuah-Abam ā;
Meyae Maawɔ, Omaingya Saa

(They won't proceed; Tawuah, Abam;
They won't proceed, Peace to you.)

What is notable here is the invocation of the names of Tawuah (or Tawiah) and Abam, the most powerful duo of a set of twins, the first- and second-born children after the twins. The song is to encourage and plead with the Abosom, especially Abam Kofi, to proceed, quickly. In the process the water and most of the contents are wasted, while some spectators are even injured as they attempt to avoid the encounter, especially if a spectator is a non-participating twin. The notion is that if a twin in a trance succeeds in hitting a nonparticipant twin with his or her tray, it would trigger alightment on the nonparticipating twin. For this reason, spectators—especially nonparticipating twins—move farther away from twins in a trance. Somehow, Abam Kofi recognizes twins who may be casual observers and tries to pursue them among the throngs of spectators enjoying the festivities. Remarkably very few twins, if any, get injured.

Once at the dumping site on the beach, the contents are thrown into the sea and with the help of their accompaniments each twin is dipped into the sea three times. The ritual bathing effectively ends spirit alightment when the deities depart. Upon their return home more libations are offered and Abam Kofi returned to his altar to await yet another annual festival.

Interestingly, there are some twins who are never alighted upon during the entire journey. Recently, a twin acquaintance of my wife who annually participated in twins festivals remarked that she thought her twin sister was a flirt. Her reason was that she could not understand why the Abosom always alighted on her sister and never once on her during the many years that they participated in the twin rites growing up. Explaining, she said that when her sister was alighted upon, her sister would always fall into the arms of their male accompaniments, and for that, she thought her sister was a fake. Teasing her, my wife explained to her that maybe she had a heavy or weightier head which made it hard for the Abosom to alight on her. On the contrary, her sister may have had a light head and therefore could be easily influenced by the Abosom. But our acquaintance would not accept my wife's explanation and insisted that her sister only pretended to be alighted on just to attract men and not because Abam Kofi descended upon her.

A CALL BY THE ABOSOM

The Abosom can call any human being into the clerical vocation, but there are special children that are of particular attention to them because of their special circumstances. As we have seen, the Abosom call twins because of the oddity of their birth, but most importantly, it is because their parents found favor in the eyes of the Abosom. Others called by the Abosom are those whose births were very difficult, to the extent that their mothers died at childbirth or soon after parturition; or those whose fathers died while they were children, meaning they were orphaned as children requiring the Abosom who willed them to intervene and assume in the direct care and protection of such children. In my own case, my Āgya-bosom told me that he willed me to my biological father—whom he called by his special name to my surprise, a name that very few people knew—but he could not take care of me. It seems that the fact that my father died while I was still a child was not an excuse for him to have left me fatherless.

Finally, a select group of people who encounter the Abosom—or rather are confronted by the Abosom in yet another dramatic fashion—are the

Abosom'ma (divine or Abosom children). The encounter—or confrontation—is usually one-sided, because an Ɔbosom has identified and chosen a person that it wants as a "wife." The reason is that an *Ɔbosom ba* (divine child) is the Ɔbosom's own child as a result of a couple, who after experiencing difficulties conceiving, consults with an Ɔbosom to intervene. During such consultations a couple makes a vow to dedicate any and all potential children born in consequence of an Ɔbosom's intervention to the deity, together with certain prescribed items for a thanksgiving ceremony. Meaning such a child or children would belong to the Ɔbosom and not the biological parents forever. This is exactly what Hannah went through in First Samuel 1:9–11 (RSV):

> After they had eaten and drunk in Shiloh, Hannah rose. Now Eli the priest was sitting on the seat beside the doorpost of the temple of the Lord. She was deeply distressed and prayed to the Lord, and wept bitterly. And she vowed a vow and said, "O Lord of hosts, if thou wilt indeed look on the affliction of thy maidservant, and remember me, and not forget thy maidservant, but wilt give to thy maidservant a son, then I will give him to the Lord all the days of his life, and no razor shall touch his head."

A favorable response from an Ɔbosom may result in as many as five children—just like a set of twins except that they are known as *prɛkɛsaw* (rough hair) because they are of divine births. Such children are considered children of the Ɔbosom who willed them to a parent. And, symbolic of their sacred births, their hair is left uncut and unkempt with strings of beads, cowries or coins tied to segments of the hair. As adults they dress in whitish garments and beg for food or are fed and sustained by society as priests/priestesses. Parents wash the hair of the Abosom'ma (divine or Abosom children) except that the hair is not combed or cut. To cut the hair of an Ɔbosom ba (divine child), for instance, the Ɔbosom which "fathered" the child must first be consulted and propitiatory rites performed for the Ɔbosom. These Abosom'ma (divine or Abosom children) and their descendants, together with twins and those born under special circumstances, like those whose mothers died during childbirth or those children orphaned as babies or children, are the ones *called* into the clerical profession.

The call into the clerical profession is the focus here because it so dramatic and overwhelming that families are often caught unawares when their wards exhibit psychotic tendencies, resulting in sudden behavioral mood swings. Even where the case is obvious, some families are adamant in their refusal to the traditional clerical career path as a viable career choice for the wards due to the negative connotations associated with *Akɔmfa* (the process of being called). In the process, not only are potentially lucrative careers destroyed, but the very well-being and happiness of those called are also destroyed, as was the case of a classmate of mine.

In middle school a classmate of mine experienced what everyone thought was a call into the clerical profession. At one time, for example, she disappeared for about a week but was later found inside a rocky hill not from our middle school and her house. She later claimed to have been abducted by a group of dwarfish men. It was the consensus among us, her classmates, that she would be sent away to train as an Ɔkɔmfo, but her educated parents adamantly refused. Her father, a lecturer at one of the local colleges in Simpa then and a church elder at a local Christian church, never allowed his daughter to become an Ɔkɔmfo, perhaps, for fear of being ostracized by his church. My classmate loved to sing and would sing for hours—some saying that it was her singing that attracted the attention of the *Mmoatia* (invisible dwarfish race). As far as I know, she never turned out like her other siblings. Actually, she was never really the same person after her teenage experiences and could not progress educationally as her other siblings. For example, her younger brother, also a classmate, went on to college and became very successful. Just as the Abosom have their Akɔmfo, the Mmoatia too have their own Akɔmfo.[22] The Mmoatia, unlike the Abosom, reside in trees and rocks and have a world and human race[23] of their own, although in most cases they act at the behest of the Abosom, just as the Abosom act at the behest of God. R. S. Rattray describes the Mmoatia as follows:

> The most characteristic feature of these Ashanti "little folk". . . is their feet, which point backwards. They are said to be about a foot in stature, and to be of three distinct varieties: black, red, and white, and they converse by means of whistling. The black fairies are more or less innocuous, but the white and the red *mmoatia* are up to all kinds of mischief. . . . The light-coloured *mmoatia* are also versed in the making of all manner of *suman* [amulets] which they may at times be persuaded to barter to mortals by means of the "silent trade." . . . Little figures of *mmoatia* of both sexes are often found as appurtenances of the *abosom*, the gods, whose "speedy messengers" they are.[24]

Curiosity with Mmortia as a spiritual or tangible human race may be as ancient as the ancient Egyptians, because we have an account where a captured dwarf from inner Africa was sent north so that the dwarf could entertain King Pepi of ancient Egypt.[25]

When an Ɔbosom confronts a potential Ɔkɔmfo, the experience is such that a family is often left in a quandary as to what to do in spite of the fact that a family is of a priestly ancestry. One reason is the fiscal strain accompanying the whole process of *Akɔmfa* (a call to be a diviner). It is one thing to have a priestly ancestry and quite another to be called, and hence attempts by parents not to answer such divine calls, even to the detriment of the children. One reason may be due to the huge financial cost involved and Western influences that regard traditional systems as uncivilized and primitive.

On the part of individuals experiencing these calls—most of whom are youths or young adults—they do not know or understand what is happening to them behaviorally, as they are innocent victims being used by powerful agencies. Some of these behavioral problems may "include intermittent fits, seizures, and convulsions similar to epilepsy . . . tear off his clothes and cast them off, roll on the ground, groan, and moan."[26] Although an individual experiencing episodic calls exhibits signs of insanity or madness, there is no evidence of any "apparent connection, among established practitioners, between possession and mental aberration."[27]

Another point is that a call into the clerical profession (as a diviner, priest or priestess, or doctor), especially Akɔm, is one-way affair, with a human subject not seeing the spiritual agency pursuing him or her. What this indicates for those being called as diviners is that their experiences could be disruptive and even detrimental to their well-being and psychological, social, and emotional state until an intervention is sought to mitigate the situation. Often subjects hear what appear to be voices of some sort of invisible agents controlling and directing their actions; sometimes, they are awakened to sounds and sights of strange creatures (*Mmoatia*) or find themselves at places far away from home and utterly strange to them when they regain awareness, and yet they are unafraid of their surroundings. Such was the call of Kɔbena Aprɛku, a famous Ɔkɔmfo of Simpa (Winneba).

Ɔbrɛwo[28] Kɔbena Aprɛku was reputed to have performed many spectacular feats. And many decades after his demise in the mid-1960s, he is still talked about. For example, he could fetch water with a basket, stretch his hands up and it rained. However, he may best be remembered for saving the life of a rival "diviner" by the name of Kɔw Boyee[29] after he swallowed a knife but was unable to remove it from his anus as he always did during public performances. Kɔw Boyee would fall dead for an hour or so after swallowing a knife about a foot long, wake up suddenly, dance for a while and remove the knife from his anus amid jubilation from the spectators. One day during a performance, however, the knife got stuck. As he was unable to remove the knife and coughing blood, the intervention of rival Kɔbena Aprɛku was sought by the Abrɛwo (diviners) in attendance. Ɔbrɛwo Kɔbena Aprɛku came and removed the knife in a spectacular fashion, perhaps to prove to all that he was spiritually more powerful than Kɔw Boyee. Following this fiasco, Kɔw Boyee did not perform again for years, some say, until after the death of Aprɛku. The fact is that Kɔw Boyee was never an Ɔbrɛwo (diviner) but rather a medium who carried himself as an Ɔbrɛwo (diviner) because he worked with Mmoatia (dwarfish spiritual agents). This, according to some of the elders, infuriated some of the real Abrɛwo (diviners), including Kɔbena Aprɛku who, from his house, cast a spell on Kɔw Boyee during one of his public displays about a mile away, resulting in the knife getting stuck in Kɔw Boyee's anus. Resuming his public displays in the late 1960s, some of us as youths witnessed him perform the same feats on many occasions in Simpa.

But did Kɔw Boyee just put a moratorium on his public displays because of this onetime accident, or was it caused by fear as a result of Kɔbena Aprɛku's ability to cause harm to him from a distance? Whatever the reason, Kɔw Boyee waited until the death of his nemesis before performing again. If Kɔbena Aprɛku wanted to send a message to Kɔw Boyee that he was not an Ɔbrɛwo (Ɔkɔmfo) and should therefore stop carrying himself as such, then his message was sent loud and clear. In the end, it was all about spiritual power and who among the two men was more powerful.

Fascinated by the spiritual accomplishments of Kɔbena Aprɛku, I researched him for several years, ending in the fall of 2013, with an Ɔbrɛwo by the name of Baaka, a niece and trainee of Kɔbena Aprɛku. My initial research focused on how he, Kɔbena Aprɛku, was called and by whom, because I was intrigued by his feats.

I have known Ɔbrɛwo Baaka since the 1970s and worked with her on various rituals during the years, especially when I became the traditional ruler of my community.[30] Although Ɔbrɛwo Baaka began training under her uncle, Ɔbrɛwo Kɔbena Aprɛku, he sent her away to train under a different diviner when she was called. As a result, Ɔbrɛwo Baaka completed her training under another Ɔkɔmfo (diviner) whose first trainee was Baaka, which means that she was the first trainee of her master and hence the Akan name *Baaka* (from the Akan *Abakan* or firstborn). As the leading Ɔbrɛwo for the Tuawo Asafo (traditional soldiers), she is the Ɔbrɛwo who leads the Tuawo Asafo to the forest to hunt for a live deer annually for the Apeae (Abosom) of the Āwutuābe of Simpa led by Penkyae Otu (the leading deity of the Simpa). In her eighties now, it is always a wonder to see her so energized leading her troops for miles and scouring the forest as though she was still a teenager. But then she would be in a trance during the entire period of the hunt.

Ɔbrɛwo Kɔbena Aprɛku was a priest in training before his deity called him. He was taken and driven by the deity into a thick forest at what is now the community of Attɛtu for days, with no one knowing where he was, but was attended to by the lion Ɔbosom that called him. After days in the forest he was driven about twenty miles to the house of the Ɔkɔmfo who would become his master in the town of Konyanko. Still in a trance, he told the Ɔkɔmfo (his eventual master) that he has arrived to be trained and that he should send word to Simpa (Winneba) about his whereabouts to enable his family to come and perform the necessary rites. This is how his people or anyone else had word about his calling.

There are two very important facts about Ɔbrɛwo Kɔbena Aprɛku's call that confirm what the Akan and their kindred groups assert about the clerical profession in general. That, one, the priesthood (Asɔfodzie) is different from Akɔmfa (the call into divination or mediumship profession). One can actually train to become a priest, as the Ɔbrɛwo Kɔbena Aprɛku was doing before he was called. But still one must have descended from a priestly family, must have priestly ancestry, or be one of those special children already discussed.

And two, one may be a priest and still be called into the Akɔm profession, because Akɔmfa is markedly unique from the priesthood which does not require a call. In other words, one may be a priest and not called because the priesthood is learned. While Akɔmfa is also learned, the difference is what happens before one gets to learn Akɔm (how to become a diviner or an Ɔkɔmfo), a call. For an example, the boy Samuel was already studying the priesthood under Eli, the priest, before he (Samuel) was called (1 Samuel 3). Samuel's birth falls under those already described, meaning he was an *Ɔbosom ba* (divine child).

Calls are always dramatic, and yet another way that a call occurs is after the death of an Ɔkɔmfo. Upon the death of an Ɔkɔmfo (diviner), kola nuts are chewed and morphed into a ball and taken to the divining room where the altar of the Ɔbosom is whose diviner has died. There, prayers and libations are offered to formally inform the Ɔbosom about the death (gone to *Abosomnkyir*). Then the ball of the kola nut is affixed to the altar, an icon or image of the Ɔbosom. This means that the Ɔbosom too is in the state of mourning. All these happen before the Ɔkɔmfo is buried. If the Ɔbosom is determined to choose another "wife" from the Ābusua right away, then it will dramatically seize someone during the entire duration of the funeral. The candidate would be in the state of trance for days, not speaking, eating or drinking anything. Crucially, if the call is authentic, then during the seizure the candidate will be driven by the Ɔbosom into the room where the kola nut ball is affixed to the Ɔbosom's altar or image is and just as dramatically take the ball of kola nut with his or her mouth and swallow it. It is only after these events and others that a candidate begins training as an *Ɔkɔmfo ba* (diviner-in-training).

Ɔbrɛwo Kɔbena Aprɛku's call followed the same pattern as described elsewhere,[31] including one involving a teenage girl who lived not far from my father's house. In late 1980s and early 1990s she started experiencing what was later confirmed to be a "call." Sometimes, Essoun, the name of the teenage girl, would take off alone into the forest for days. One of my interviewees, Elizabeth, asserted that she had gone with Essoun and others to fetch water from a pond near the Winneba Water Works due to the chronic water shortages in the past. In her late teens, Essoun already had a baby, who was on her back when they went to draw water. While they were drawing water, the next thing she and the others realized was that Essoun had disappeared, leaving her baby there alone and crying. Terrified, Elizabeth took the child and ran to Essoun's family and narrated what had just taken place. Initially, people thought that Essoun was insane or in the process of becoming one, in spite of the fact that her grandfather was a noted Ɔbrɛwo, meaning she was a candidate for a call.

These disappearances are common among the Akan and their kindred peoples and they all take on the same or similar patterns. Indeed, anyone could learn to become a priest, but unless one initially hears a distinct but confusing and consistent voice of an Ɔbosom calling an individual, and with subsequent training, one can never become an Ɔkɔmfo (diviner), in accordance with Akan or Āwutu traditions. The reason is that the Abosom make frequent alightments on those that they call, and as Brigid Sackey succinctly explains, the behavior of a person alighted upon by an Ɔbosom undergoes significant changes:

> A possessed candidate goes through a series of mental and physical crises expressed apparently in paranoid behavior and sudden illness, which for a time may defy therapeutic treatment. In other words, the person behaves strangely, but this strangeness is regarded as normal because its symptoms are evidence of a call. Sometimes a person may go to the forest and discover a flaming stone charged with power, the temporary dwelling place of a spirit. The discoverer becomes the priest of the deity that has thus revealed itself. He remains in the forest for several days, and when found, behaves strangely.[32]

Subjects experiencing such hierophanies invariably find their way home under the direction of the spirits that first led them away. While they may be aware of their surroundings, they are unable to do anything about their situation because they would be under the dictates of powerful forces. Some even claim to see those searching for them but are unable to reach out to them. They seem to enter a different world unaffected by the tangibility of corporeal environment. Yet others who disappear maintain that they were unaware of their disappearances because there was no sense of time in the spatial bobble that they existed in, albeit no different from the world of tangibility. This explains why, when those being called re-appear after days or even weeks of being missing, their re-appearances are as dramatic as their "disappearances," which always cause huge commotions. The subjects, it seems, are, strangely enough, unperturbed by the commotions around them, often insisting that they have been treated kindly by their Mmoatia (dwarfish) "captors" who taught them the use of medicine or herbal treatments for all kinds of illnesses.[33] Sometimes it takes days before some of them are able to communicate with loved ones again. These incidences serve as evidence for, sometimes, unconvinced or recalcitrant families seeking answers for their ward's episodic disappearances and strange behavior issues.

One thing is certain when it comes to the Abosom manifesting themselves, and that is movement. Behaviorally, human beings are exactly like the Abosom who willed us into corporeal existence, but periodically they manifest themselves dramatically on some individuals because they want those individual to make their pronouncements known to societies. These encounters are often misunderstood and mischaracterized as insanity, but however mischaracterized when a spirit or Ɔbosom is upon a person because an individual has found favor with a deity, the will of the Ɔbosom reigns supreme as the spirit alters the movements and behavior of the person called. Under the influence of an Ɔbosom, one is compelled to act in a manner consistent with an Ɔbosom seeking a "wife."

A call is, however, the beginning of a long process before a novice actually becomes an Ɔkɔmfo (diviner). Meaning, "Training is an absolute necessity for anyone called into the clerical profession, if such a person is to have a normal life in society. For one thing, training is designed to end the episodically erratic and uncontrollable flights that untrained subjects experience when spirits alight upon them." However, the ultimate goal of a call is to serve society and so one must be disciplined, acquire and refine one's "mental acuities, learning certain physical techniques and skills, and acquisition of medical knowledge, aimed at enabling trainees to perceive and attune themselves to the alighting of spirits." In other words, an Ɔkɔmfo must prepare herself physically and psychologically in such a way as to enable her to receive the Ɔbosom that called her in a controlled, disciplined and refined manner. This then enables a spirit to communicate in a rationally clear language of understanding with clients seeking assistance.

NOTES

1. See Ephirim-Donkor, Anthony. "Akom: The Ultimate Mediumship Experience Among the Akan," *Journal of the American Academy of Religion* 76, 1, 2008.
2. Ephirim-Donkor, Anthony. *African Religion Defined, a Systematic Study of ancestor Worship among the Akan, Second Edition.* (Lanham, MD: University Press of America, 2013), p. 19.
3. Ibid. p. 175ff.
4. Emeagwali, Gloria and Walter, Mariko Namba. "Ancient Egyptian Shamanism." In *Shamanism: An Encyclopedia of World Beliefs, Practices, and Culture.* Ed. by Mariko Namba Walter and Eva Neumann Fridman. (Santa Barbara, CA: ABC-CLIO, 2004), p. 908.
5. See Gbadegesin, Segun. "Eniyan: The Yoruba concept of a person." In P. H. Coetzee and A. P. J. Roux, eds., *The African Philosophy Reader, second edition* (New York: Routledge: Taylor & Francis Group, 2003), pp. 175–191.

6. Genever, Shana. "Fish pour down in Thailand." (http://www.sabreakingnews.co.za/2015/04/17/fish-pour-down-in-thailand/), last accessed on June 19, 2015.

7. "Respect our traditions—Ga Traditional Council tells residents." (http://www.ghanaweb.com/GhanaHomePage/NewsArchive/Respect-our-traditions-Ga-Traditional-Council-tells-residents-363346), last accessed on June 19, 2015.

8. Ray, Benjamin C. *African Religions: Symbols, Ritual, and Community, Second Edition.* (Upper Saddle River, NJ: Prentice Hall, 2000), p. 13.

9. Gbadegesin, Segun. "Eniyan: The Yoruba concept of a person." In P. H. Coetzee and A. P. J. Roux, eds., *The African Philosophy Reader, second edition* (New York: Routledge: Taylor &Francis Group, 2003), p. 179.

10. McCall, John C. "Igbo Shamanism (Nigeria)." In *Shamanism: An Encyclopedia of World Beliefs, Practices, and Culture.* Ed. by Mariko Namba Walter and Eva Neumann Fridman. (Santa Barbara, CA: ABC-CLIO, 2004), p. 925–927.

11. Christensen, James Boyd. "The Adaptive Functions of Fanti Priesthood." In William Bascom and Melville Herskovits, ed., *Continuity and Change in African Culture.* (Chicago: Univ. of Chicago Press, 1959), p. 257.

12. See Ephirim-Donkor, Anthony. "Akom: The Ultimate Mediumship Experience Among the Akan," *Journal of the American Academy of Religion* 76, 1, 2008: pp. 73–74.

13. Ibid. p. 55.

14. Ephirim-Donkor, Anthony. *African Religion Defined, a Systematic Study of ancestor Worship among the Akan, Second Edition.* (Lanham, MD: University Press of America, 2013), p. 92.

15. Ibid. p. 13.

16. Ellis, A. B. *The Tshi-speaking Peoples of the Gold Coast of West Africa: their religion, manners, customs, laws, language, etc.* (Anthropological Publications, Oosterhout N.B. The Netherlands, [1887] 1970), p. 123.

17. Appiah-Kubi, Kofi. *Man Cures, God Heals.* (New York: Friendship Press, 1981), p. 21.

18. Ibid.

19. Ephirim-Donkor, Anthony. *The Making of an African King: Patrilineal & Matrilineal Struggle Among the Effutu of Ghana, Second Edition.* (Lanham, MD: University Press of America, 2009), p. 97.

20. "Akom: The Ultimate Mediumship Experience Among the Akan," *Journal of the American Academy of Religion* 76, 1, 2008: p. 66.

21. "Twin Cult of the Akan (Ghana)." In *Shamanism: An Encyclopedia of World Beliefs, Practices, and Culture.* (Edited by Mariko Namba Walter and Eva Jane Nemann Fridman. Santa Barbara, California: ABC-CLIO, 2004). p. 944.

22. Konadu, Kwasi. *Indigenous Medicine and Knowledge in African Society,* (New York: Routledge, 2007), p. 49.

23. Davidson, Basil. *The Lost Cities of Africa: Revised Edition.* (Boston, New York, London: Little, Brown and Company, 1987), pp. 25–26.

24. Rattray, R. S. *Religion & Art in Ashanti.* (Oxford: At The Clarendon Press, 1927), p. 26.

25. Davidson, Basil. *African Civilization Revisited: From Antiquity to modern Times*. (Trenton, New Jersey: Africa World Press, Inc., 1991), p. 55.

26. Sackey, Brigid M. "Asante Shamanism (Ghana)." In *Shamanism: An Encyclopedia of World Beliefs, Practices, and Culture*. (Edited by Mariko Namba Walter and Eva Jane Nemann Fridman. Santa Barbara, California: ABC-CLIO, 2004). p. 910.

27. Appiah-Kubi, Kofi. *Man Cures, God Heals* (New York: Friendship Press, 1981), p. 27.

28. The term Ɔbrɛwo instead of the Akan Ɔkɔmfo is used by the Guan (Āwutu) speaking people of Simpa (Winneba) to refer to a diviner.

29. Ephirim-Donkor, Anthony, "Akom: The Ultimate Mediumship Experience Among the Akan," *Journal of the American Academy of Religion* 76, 1, 2008: see footnote on pp. 69–70.

30. Ibid. See footnote on p. 58.

31. Ibid. See footnote on p. 60.

32. Sackey, Brigid M. "Asante Shamanism (Ghana)." In *Shamanism: An Encyclopedia of World Beliefs, Practices, and Culture*. Edited by Mariko Namba Walter and Eva Jane Nemann Fridman. (Santa Barbara, California: ABC-CLIO, 2004). pp. 911–112.

33. Rattray, R. S. *Religion & Art in Ashanti*. (Oxford: At The Clarendon Press, 1927), p. 38.

Chapter Five

The Ethical Pathway

When examining Akan and other African cosmogonies, one thing that is clear about African creation stories relative to the physicality, appearance, and form or shape of a human being is that the human being was a created being, made and shaped specifically to reflect the form of the first goddess or goddesses that the Akan refer to as Abrewah-na-ni-mma (the Old Woman and her children), a constellation of seven led by the Abrewah (Old Woman). Thus, structurally a human being was made to stand upright like as a tree, so that the human being is actually referred to as *Nyimpa-dua* (a living or human tree). The Nyimpa-dua must stand firm, strong, tall, beautiful, and deeply rooted in the earth. For a Nyimpa-dua (a person) to be considered beautiful by the Akan, moreover, he or she must conform to certain geometric configurations best described by Kofi Antubam as:

> Looking at the body from the side or front, the shape of the head and of the neck from the top of the head to the end of the chin must appear like an egg with the wider portion uppermost. Looking at it from the side, the head must sit on the neck at an angle of about thirty-five degrees with the top part falling back. This falling back . . . has an optical effect on the viewer. For, thrown into perspective, so to say, wide, the top part of the face grows wider and gives a larger appearance from the front. This is, perhaps, what the traditional Akan Ghanaian carver is trying to express in the head of the female *Akuaba* (fertility and play doll). Again, to be beautiful, the head must fix into the neck at a point a little below the head to the bottom line of the chin.[1]

He continues:

> The neck, which should have wrinkles or rings on it, must fall into an elongated oval shape with the smaller part of it tapering towards the head. The wrinkles

> or rings here must be at odd number when counted to be a perfect beauty. The torso, starting from the shoulder line or collarbone to the waistline, must appear an oval from the larger part towards the neck. The thighs from the waistline to the bottom of the kneecap must look like an egg with the wider portion towards the waist. This requirement . . . makes . . . men . . . like substantial thighs and buttocks. And . . . ladies . . . push their buttocks out to form a concave at the back of the waist in order to appear beautiful. And, their tight western dress stresses this point. . . . Their legs, from centre of the knee cap to the ground level, must appear oval with the wider part towards the knee. The feet, when put together, must fall in a good space of an oval with its wider part towards the toes.[2]

It is precisely because a human being is a tree that the Akan begin at the very instance of birth to shape and mold a neonate into a socially acceptable tree strand. These individual tree strands, when brought together or seen from afar, constitute an Ābusua—a mother and her children; in other words, the Abrewah-na-ni-mma (Old Woman and her children) and therefore the first uterine, consanguineous linear family on earth. The tree metaphor is so important to the Akan that even their kings and queen mothers are referred to as trees. Subsequently, when a king or queen mother dies—even though they do not die—the euphemism "a tree has fallen," instead of saying a king or queen mother has died, is used, among several euphemisms and metaphors. Indeed, one of the names of God is Tweduapon (Dependable Tree), or as Kwasi Konadu defines, "the tree which when leaned upon does not break," while Danquah defines it as "Dependable God."

African creation stories further suggest spiritual realms in existence long before the corporeal world, the Wiadzie, and human existence came into being. Even after corporeal existence came into being, we still have spiritual beings descending from heaven (sky) to earth periodically to engage in certain endeavors and then ascend to heaven afterwards, as among the Yoruba, Nuer, Atuot, etc. For the Akan, for instance, the corporeal world existed in clusters of rocks (*Abo/Abu*); then the ocean arrived and engulfed most of the clusters of rocks but, she—the ocean goddess called Abena Mansa—was held in check by God in order that she does not overwhelm the world; followed by two earth goddesses: Asasi Āfua, and Asasi Yaa; then came the first earthly inhabitants of seven goddesses in human form led by the Abrewah (Old Woman). These seven goddesses collectively became known as Abrewah-na-ni-mma (the Old Woman and her children) and established the basic Akan family unit, the Ābusua: a uterine, blood-based linear group comprised of a mother and her children.

African creator gods and goddesses appear to have envisaged a human being who looked exactly the way humans beings are today, just like the first goddess in human form and after whom all subsequent humans would be shaped into being. From the physical perspective, the human physique or body is composed of blood (*Mogya*), the blood of the first female goddesses. As such, there are seven blood types or groupings that form the basis of the Akan matrilineal system of descent, the Ābusua. Most importantly, the Akan are adamant about the fact that the Ābusua originated with the Old Woman and her children who featured prominently in their creation story. Thus the all-female constellation, Abrewah-na-ni-mma (The Old woman and her children), are the mothers of the Akan. Meaning, existentially, human beings look exactly like the first women because their blood runs through all living things, as repositories of blood. Yet the Akan are quick to point out that no human being is a child of the earth (a mother). Rather, God is the progenitor of all of creation, including human beings.

Being created—or rather born—means that a human being is destined to grow up, because of an innate raw drive (*Su*) which propels us toward human potentialities. As we have seen in chapter 3, the Su is, in fact, the Ɔbosom incarnate, which manifests itself ethically in pursuance of its career blueprint, the *Nkrabea*. The drive to grow and develop begins in utero during gestation and continues through parturition and finally to old age and death. But there is more to growth existentially, and for the Akan, the very name of a living human being as *Onyimpa dasanyi* is illustrative. Etymologically, *Onyimpa* is a person who grows into an ideally ethical and intellectual person, as opposed to someone who grows up unethically and therefore becomes an empty barrel, an *Onyinpan*. Such an Onyinpan has nothing meaningful to contribute to society and as such is ignored or dismissed in public forums. As a pariah, he or she may still be allowed to attend social gatherings because he or she has a place in society, but invariably such a person is shouted down before one has the chance to spoil a function. The Onyimpa, on the contrary, is the cultured individual who turns out well because he or she is disciplined, well-mannered and behaved, courteous, and respectful of and obedient to elders and those in authority. As someone with all the right etiquette and who follows the proper protocols, he or she displays the proper disposition and temperament and is judicious in speech. As a young adult male (an Abrantsi) or female (an Akataesia), he or she would invariably find oneself in the company of elders and is sought after to accompany those in authority on important trips or during adjudicative processes. Ironically, sometimes an Onyinpan may suddenly inject himself or herself into highly charged deliberative situations in order to introduce a moment of levity to defuse a tense situation. During such moments, an Onyinpan's contribution may actually be admired, though not for too long. The point is that even an Onyinpan has his or her moment in society, if even for fleeting moments.[3]

Physically a human being is modeled after the first goddess (Ɔbosom), making a person the child of its mother within the context of the Ābusua, because the Akan insist that every child inherently belongs to his or her mother's Ābusua (blood). But while belonging to the mother physically, the Akan ascribe paternity to, first, a father, then the Abosom, and finally to God (Nyame) who is the ultimate progenitor of every human being; meaning a human is the product of—or rather invention of—God and the Abosom (Gods and Goddesses) and is therefore a spiritual being.[4] In other words, the human being is a collaborative venture between God and the Abosom, specially made for a purpose and a corporeal destination also designed by God and the Abosom.

Indeed, the Akan believe that human beings descended directly from the Abosom. Meaning, all human beings were Abosom before being born into the corporeal Wiadzie (world) as humans, explaining why every human being has an Āgya-bosom (an Ɔbosom father) who wills his children (other Abosom) into the corporeal Wiadzie (world). However, the Āgya-bosom—or one's Ɔbosom father—must be acknowledged existentially, ideally during infancy or at some point during a person's life, if one is to enjoy the Āgya-bosom's unqualified protection and guardianship. The responsibility of an Āgya-bosom, like a biological father, is to ensure not only the survivability of its human offspring, but for that offspring to successfully (ethically) navigate through life until old age and death. By acknowledging one's Āgya-bosom, a person's chances of successfully and ethically making it through life relatively unscathed are enhanced significantly, because a person places himself or herself under the aegis of one's Āgya-bosom in the same way that a biological father is supposed to protect his children. Because of difficult existential conditions exacerbated by the constant threat of witchcraft and other malign forces, the influencing role of an Āgya-bosom is seen as indispensable and the more reason for parents to divine upon giving birth to ascertain as to which Ɔbosom willed their children into the world. This is done in order that an Āgya-bosom may guide and protect its child or children against all kinds of powers, spiritual or physical.

The purpose of the joint effort in creating a human being and life in general is to create a new life-form as envisaged by the Abosom and God. Meaning, the current corporeal life-forms, including human beings, are not the final products of the collaborative venture between the Abosom and God, in the same way that the corporeal Wiadzie is not the final destination for living things. The Abosom created life-forms that were of the same essences as themselves, comprised of the blood (Mogya) or matter, and spirit (Sunsum) as an activating agency. For Rattray, it is the Sunsum/ntoro of a male that activates the blood of a female to commence with the creative process in utero. This suggests that although Mogya (blood) is also spiritual in origin, it is imbued with materialization capabilities enabling the Abosom and other spiritual agencies to put on material forms. On the contrary, the Sunsum, by its very definition, does not have materialization capabilities as it can only reveal an image. However, when Mogya and Sunsum are joined then the resultant product is the corporeal, including human beings. In fact, for the Akan, females do not possess Sunsum to the extent that they are incapable of transmitting it their offspring. What women possess and transmit to their children is blood (Mogya) and therefore that is the basis of the Akan Ābusua system, meaning one cannot divorce oneself from one's Ābusua, the mother, because a person is formed by the very blood of his or her mother. Males, on the other hand, possess Sunsum, which they transmit to their offspring, as well as Mogya, which they are incapable of transmitting, because males are incapable of gestation and parturition. Males, furthermore, have blood—although incapable of being transmitted—because males are created or born by their mothers.

Upon parturition, God provides the life essence (Ɔkra) needed for the survival of the neonate extrinsically for one to become a living being. Thus, a human being, for example, has all the essential attributes and qualities of the Abosom as well as God, as we have seen throughout this study. A human being then is an Ɔbosom (deity) in a unique human form, physique-wise, looking just like the first female Ɔbosom in the corporeal Wiadzie. The only difference between the Abosom and human beings is that the Abosom do not suffer death because they are immaterial, while a human (or a living thing) in the corporeal dies because one cannot live in the flesh forever, and hence death. Since living beings are to die, then what happens to the incorporeal agencies that constitute what it means to be a living thing, especially since originally all of the human properties are divine, as claimed by God?

To say that human beings descended directly from the Abosom is to say that humans are the children of the Abosom prior to becoming humans. That is, human beings are the Abosom who decided to become human beings as part of the creative process and return to the Abosom world upon completion of the new life-form they create in the corporeal. The new eternal life-form created by an Ɔbosom upon death seeks independent existence in a spiritual world (the Samanadzie) prepared exclusively for the new life-form that the Akan call Ɔsaman. The phenomenon whereby an Ɔbosom becomes a human being is risky for the Abosom wishing to become living things in the corporeal, because there are no guarantees that the mission to the corporeal would be successful in creating a mature adult into old age.

First, the Abosom choosing corporeal existence forfeited their knowledge of divine existence once they become human beings; and second, they would be subject to death although they depart the body just prior to death, since a spirit does not die. In that way, only the material component of a person dies.

Still, the lure of creating a human being and living in a corporeal environment is desirable, firstly, and secondly, for the Abosom to be collaborators with God to fulfill the divine mission of creating Nsamanfo in a post-corporeal world called Samanadzie is tempting enough for Abosom to scramble to be humans or any other form of corporeal beings. In itself, becoming a living being in the corporeal Wiadzie is an act of faith, to believe in the divine promises of life in the corporeal when an Ɔbosom (God or Goddess) is yet to taste existence as a human. For instance, an Ɔbosom is told that upon parturition it will be met by a mother and nurtured into adulthood by a family, an Ābusua. During the nine months that it takes for a non-corporeal being to be manifested in utero, the Ɔbosom is considered in transit and its journey monitored, still unsure of making the final leap of faith into the corporeal. In consequence, gestation is viewed with anxiety and every precaution taken to ensure a healthy pregnancy and safe delivery and, for the Akan, the survival of a neonate's first eight days. Completing the first cycle of eight days in corporeal is a clear sign of hope for a family and community of faith, in that society now views the neonate as intending to live or, as the Akan put it, stay in the corporeal Wiadzie and not return (die) to the Samanadzie. Welcoming a neonate enthusiastically, a family introduces its child to the outside world for the first time and offers a name on the eighth day as the first step towards citizenship. With its formal name on the eighth day, a neonate is now counted among humanity, Adasa.

To say that humans are offspring of Abosom suggests that living beings are offspring of agencies who themselves are not born into the corporeal Wiadzie (world). These primeval Abosom are ancient and have always been *There* with God. Like God, the primeval Abosom never choose corporeal existence although they are capable of putting on pseudo human forms in pursuance of specific objectives in the corporeal. Corporeality must be understood in the context of tangibility and intangibility, with the tangible world or Wiadzie—the abode of all things physical—being a reflection of the intangible world of the Abosom and other spirits. Even though these original Abosom are as ancient as God and were with God in the very beginning, those now in the corporeal do not occupy the same realm as God, having been sent into the corporeal in stages as custodians of the corporeal. As one Ɔbosom explained during divination, some of them were expelled later to join those already in the corporeal to help rule the corporeal until God was ready to deal with them, because they used to challenge God. The challenge to God was when the Abosom opposed to God put their collective strengths and powers together. Some of the Abosom expelled left their "parents" (Abosom) behind although they are in constant contact with them, just as they are with God.

The Abosom choosing corporeal existence as human beings have Abosom families of their own but at some point decided to depart, with the Āgya-bosom acting as the sponsoring Ɔbosom (god). Thus every human is said to have a "godfather" or Āgya-bosom. A human father then is only a representative of the Āgya-bosom on earth, with a human father acting as a custodian of children born to him. And in the same way that an Ɔbosom chooses to leave its Āgya-bosom parent for existence in the corporeal, the role of every earthly father is to protect his offspring until adulthood when the children decide to leave home in pursuance of their existential career blueprints.

If corporeal life is sustained by the constant replenishing of the Abosom choosing to relocate to the corporeal Wiadzie, then the population of the Abosom must be affected to the point of depletion. While this reasoning seems logical, it is illogical in the spiritual realm. First, one thing about all spirits is their divinity, meaning their inability to suffer death. And second, the nature of a holistic human as the amalgam of spiritual agencies is such that upon death the divine agencies depart the physical body before any death occurs. What the male Abosom contribute is spirit or Sunsum (shadow, image, and double). If the Sunsum is a shadow, image, or a person's double then does it make the Sunsum a tangible reality? The Sunsum could not be realistic because the Akan also believe that the Sunsum is intangible, and even describe God and the Abosom, for instance, as Āsunsum (spirits) and therefore unseen with the eyes. It would seem that the Akan are contradicting themselves when they maintain, on the one hand, that the Sunsum is an image to be seen, and, on the other, assert that as an intangible agency the Sunsum is incapable of being seen, like God. So while the Sunsum has been defined as that which is not seen, as well as that which is seen as a shadow, when do the two wed? The dynamism as to whether the Sunsum is materialistic or not has been argued by Kwame Gyekye.[5] Another reason is that when the intangible weds the tangible, the result is the creation of living beings and their characteristic attributes, as Gyekye notes as well.

The Sunsum, although an integral part of a holistic personality, has an independent existence sometimes seen as a person's double in dreams. The Sunsum, as a self, is very active in the dream world where we see ourselves engaging other Āsunsum (spirits), because when one wakes up from a dream state one describes him- or herself as have seen his or her Sunsum as a reality. The dream activities then give us clues as to what happens upon death. Just as the Sunsum is activated during deep sleep, the Sunsum also survives upon death and returns to its Āgya-bosom (godfather). The Ɔbosom which became a human does not die because it is a spirit and returns to whence it came—its father's house. There, it awaits another opportunity to reincarnate. Therefore, there is no decrease in the number of the Abosom; rather, they work hard to increase their numbers by creating new species, the Nsamanfo.

Similarly, the God essence which makes it at all possible for a human to become a living being, the *Ɔkra*, also departs to whence it came—God.

Sometimes a Sunsum may depart a person long before an Ɔkra's departure, because a Sunsum's departure does not always mean imminent death. However, the departure of the Ɔkra always means death because God is the one alone who decides the ultimate moment death occurs. Nonetheless, the departure of both the Sunsum and the Ɔkra leave us with that which emanates from the female and is the basis of human physicality—the *Mogya* (blood).

Ultimately, what emerges spiritually from the Sunsum, the Ɔkra, and the Mogya is a new posthumous abstract personality called the Ɔsaman. The Ɔsaman is the reason for corporeal existence, for the Abosom to become humans, and by becoming human beings in a corporeal environment for the duration of a full life term, the human being is transformed into a divine being posthumously capable of having an independent existence apart from the Abosom who became human beings in the corporeal. In this vein, the Ɔsaman does not need the original Ɔkra, which rejoined the air without upon death, because an Ɔsaman has already achieved immortality and lives eternally. Again, an Ɔsaman no longer has needs for the Sunsum that enabled it to be active and hence the Sunsum's departure upon death to join the phylogenetic Abosom for another chance of becoming a human or whatever creature it chooses in the corporeal. In spite of this, the Ɔsaman is the same as the Sunsum that it is, because an Ɔsaman is an imprint of its creator, the Ɔbosom that became a human being.

For an Ɔsaman to become an ancestor but not necessarily apotheosized ancestor, a person must have lived a good life, grow old, and upon death the resultant Ɔsaman is regarded as Ɔsaman *pa* (good Ɔsaman), as opposed to *Ɔsaman bɔn* (bad or evil Ɔsaman). This explains why human beings who die prior to old age may be allowed to reincarnate because they are not sufficiently mature enough to have lived meaningful lives as Nsamanfo (abstract personalities) in the Samanadzie. However, having matured into senior eldership and old age, many of the Nsamanfo become Abosom as apotheosized ancestors and therefore worthy of worship on earth. As such, the Nananom Nsamanfo are thought of as distinct group of apotheosized beings, the ancestors, occupying a world distinct and apart from those of the Abosom in the Samanadzie.

Concerning reincarnation of a person unable to reach full maturation as a senior elder and dying, ideally, at old age, the Ɔsaman does not travel to the Samanadzie, the ultimate destination of the Ɔsaman, but rather joins the company of similar spirits in a world different from the Samanadzie and competes with similar spirits to be born again. While the Samanadzie is aware of a death in the corporeal Wiadzie, it does not know of the Ɔsaman supposedly traveling to the Samanadzie because the Ɔsaman never arrived, meaning the Ɔsaman is not "born" in the Samanadzie. The goal of such an

Ɔsaman initially is to linger around its own relatives for an opportunity to reincarnate into the same family. This is because its own family is what an Ɔsaman knows and may be willing to take him or her, but as reincarnation becomes more and more remote, it joins other Nsamanfo (spirits) also seeking reincarnation. Sometimes, reincarnation may happen in a matter of days, weeks or months if there are pregnant women from the same household as the deceased person and provided the deceased lived a good life but died young.

The next logical question is: Is the reincarnated person the same person as the one who died? As far as the Samanadzie is concerned the answer is no, because the deceased person's Ɔsaman is not registered in the Samanadzie, meaning the Ɔsaman did not exist in that the Ɔsaman did not arrive in the Samanadzie. This is the same as when a person is born into the corporeal environment. For the Akan, the neonate must survive the eighth day, a complete cycle from the day that it is born to the next natal day. Thereupon, an extended family and the community at large gather to name the neonate as a living being and a member of the human family, Adasa. Unfortunately, some couples do not get to perform this first psychosocial rite in that fetuses are aborted or miscarried, meaning the potential babies never get to be born into the corporeal, even though society may be expecting their births, or arrivals. If they do not get to be born, then it means they do not have names as citizens of the corporeal Wiadzie. The fear of fetuses returning to the Samanadzie before they are born is one reason why throwing baby showers for expectant mothers is considered taboo, because one does not welcome a traveler—an ancestor—in transit; that is, before the safe arrival home of the traveler. Rather, the Akan wait until the eighth day after birth before a neonate is offered a name and gifts by family and society.

The same ritual scenario is also played out in the Samanadzie with regard to persons who died young. And like gestations not carried full term due to miscarriages, etc., those individuals who die prior to old age do not mature sufficiently enough to be born in the Samanadzie where they would have been welcomed in accordance with tradition. It means, such Nsamanfo do not have names to be counted among the ancestors, Nananom Nsamanfo. If, however, reincarnation is successful in the corporeal for an Ɔsaman who did not get to the Samanadzie, then the neonate may be named after the deceased because a baby may resemble a deceased person. Otherwise, a new name is offered and the reincarnated person assumes the identity of the neonate. If a reincarnated person lives a full life, then upon death its Ɔsaman enters the Samanadzie with the name bestowed on the eighth day.

Not every Ɔsaman in the spirit world gets to be reincarnated, however. One of the responsibilities of the Abosom is to prevent the Nsamanfo who lived less-than-ideal lives to reincarnate. Among these Nsamanfo are people who lived full lives but were simply bad, or those young people who were regarded simply as evil. This category of Nsamanfo, especially those who lived full lives and made it to the Samanadzie, are found to be unworthy of ancestorhood and precluded from reincarnating. Among these are those who refuse to enter the Samanadzie because of their inability to live full lives because they died young, or lived full lives but because of the evil deeds on earth are afraid to enter the Samanadzie for fear of being prevented from reincarnating. This group is made up all kinds of spirits all awaiting reincarnation. The reality, though, is that most do not get to reincarnate and yet they are unable to ascend to Samanadzie and so linger in their ancestral homes in hopes of tagging along with the Nsamanfo of dead elders on their way to the Samanadzie. Those unable to tag along become spirits in limbo, *Asasa*, because they died suddenly and violently and so their deaths are referred to as *Atɔfo wu* (violent and sudden deaths). The Asasa (agitated, angry, and vengeful spirits) are mostly negative spirits traversing the universe seeking justice, especially if they died young. They seek justice by avenging their deaths, and generally defer going to the Samanadzie, knowing very well that ultimate justice is exacted by the ancestors at the Samanadzie. While this is true, we have to remember that there is no evil in the Samanadzie requiring the ancestors (Nananom Nsamanfo) to exact needless vengeance on people who may have caused the deaths of certain people. Again, at the Samanadzie, ultimate power rests with the ancestors (Nananom Nsamanfo) as a collective body and not with an individual Ɔsaman. Therefore, rather than enter the Samanadzie and allow the esteemed Nananom Nsamanfo (Ancestors) to avenge their deaths at a time determined by the ancestors, an Ɔsaman may decide to postpone entering the Samanadzie in order to exact revenge on those thought to have caused its death. The reason is that it is easier to reincarnate from the realm of the Āsunsum (spirits) than at the Samanadzie. In fact, in some of the funeral dirges, mourners call on the dead to avenge its death if there is reason to believe that someone else might have caused a death, especially if a death is so poignant and unexpected—and there is always someone else thought to be the culprit.

Another reason why an *Ɔtɔfo* (one who suffers a violent and sudden death) postpones Samanadzie is that by its nature an Ɔtɔfo is a very possessive spirit attached to its dead body or an object that might have contributed to its demise. An Ɔtɔfo believes it is still attached to its dead body when it is not, thus creating an allusion of having a body, still in possession of the last object it held, or residing in the home in which it might have been murdered. And so it lingers on the spot or the object that caused its death. When it finally realizes the futility of not actually inheriting the body, it turns into an angry, agitated, and vengeful spirit in limbo, *Sasa* (singular of Asasa). In some cases, a Sasa would indeed assume pseudo physicality and attempt to live out the remainder of its years as a normal human being.

A distinction must be made here between a Sasa and an Ɔsaman. Normally an Ɔsaman is the posthumous spiritual personality of a deceased person that travels to the ancestral world of Samanadzie; however, because of the violent and sudden nature of a death, the spirit or abstract personality that emerges as a result of an Ɔtɔfo wu (violent and sudden death) causes the Ɔsaman to turn into a Sasa. That is, instead of being called an Ɔsaman, the Akan now refers to the spirit in limbo as Sasa (agitated and vengeful spirit).

The phenomenon whereby an Ɔsaman or Ɔtɔfo-Sasa transforms itself into a human and resides far away from relatives and friends in order to live out the remainder of its life is commonplace. The cause of this phenomenon is the lingering effect of what the Akan refer to as *Nkrabea* (existential career or professional blueprint), because an Ɔsaman or Ɔtɔfo-Sasa believes that its manner of death prevented it from fulfilling its Nkrabea, and therefore the need for it to accomplish its Nkrabea. Such pseudo individuals live cautiously, avoiding crowds and certain social functions as attending funerals and visiting cemeteries, while watching out for relatives who might discover them.

The whole purpose of corporeal existence is to achieve one's existential career or professional blueprint, the Nkrabea. However, corporeal existence is such that sometimes life is abruptly ended before a person is able to live a full life with fulfillment of an Nkrabea, ideally. The resultant Ɔtɔfo becomes a Sasa as a wandering angry spirit in limbo determined to exact revenge on whoever might have caused its death, first, and a strong desire to fulfill an incomplete Nkrabea, second. Consequently, the Ɔtɔfo (singular of *Atɔfo*) puts on a human form and moves away from areas that would make it impossible for it to be recognized or detected by relatives, friends, and acquaintances and continued living and engaging in whatever endeavor it was engaged in prior to its death. If during the pseudo human existence it is recognized by someone familiar but who does not know about its death, then the pseudo human would engage in normal conversation with the person and continue to live the remainder of his or her life. However, they are always on guard for relatives, friends or anyone who might know of their deaths, and upon spotting those relatives they vanish or simply relocate. Usually they marry their own kind, although occasionally they marry normal human beings and even may have children. When they die, again, it follows that they die just as suddenly as their first deaths. There are stories of some of these pseudo personalities actually marrying and producing offspring among the Akan. The point is that not every person walking around is actually a human being.

Another reason for the Ɔtɔfo-Sasa phenomenon which produces pseudo human beings is a Sasa's inability to find its way to the Samanadzie. The shock of a sudden and violent death confuses the dead as to where it is and what has happened, and as a consequence the posthumous abstract personality, the Ɔsaman, becomes a roaming, agitated, and vengeful spirit, or Sasa, until family members hold rites meant to bring the Ɔtɔfo-Sasa home. Otherwise, the Ɔtɔfo-Sasa phenomenon continues indefinitely for some Asasa (plural of Sasa) becoming evil spirits in the corporeal, while for some, they eventually find their way to the Samanadzie on their own or are enticed to tag along with other Nsamanfo en route to the Samanadzie.

Existentially, the only way into the corporeal world is through a woman, while spiritually the only way to the Samanadzie is through a male (ferryman) after crossing a river and climbing a ladder. These two entrances are tightly controlled and regulated, making them hard for entrants to travel through. However, to facilitate passage through these narrow entrances, entrants must be readied through a gradual process of biological, physical, and spiritual maturations in order to ensure survival. Short of this, an entrant may not survive entry into the temporal world, for example, and thus create a world for those unable to enter the corporeal and Samanadzie worlds.

The same phenomenon is true of the dead relative to an Ɔtɔfo-Sasa, as the Ɔtɔfo-Sasa might not be prepared or ready to climb the ladder to whence it originated. Convinced that it is still alive, it may put on a human form to live out the remainder of its life on earth. Actually upon death, the Ɔtɔfo-Sasa may want to travel to the Samanadzie but is unable to find its way there because it is confused as a result of the shock of its sudden and violent death. Even when convinced by other Nsamanfo on their way to the Samanadzie that it is dead, it still refuses to believe out of fear, disappointment and anger. As a wandering, agitated, and vengeful spirit in limbo, the Ɔtɔfo-Sasa is unable to enter the ladder-like wormhole to the Samanadzie due to the very nature of its death. What is fascinating—or rather tantalizing—is the notion that the two entrances (or wormholes) into the corporeal Wiadzie and the Samanadzie are just *here* with us, right next to each other, so close and yet illusively far apart. The close proximity of the two realms allow spiritual agencies to hear everything that human beings say and also see every step that a living thing takes. The key then to avoiding spiritual forces getting wind of potential plans is silence. Aware of spoken words to be used against a person's own potential plans, the Akan are very secretive about all future plans, afraid that sharing them could lead to abortive operations. However, silence is futile since the Abosom have access to the mind.

Aware of the trapped state of the Asasa, with a propensity to help them make the transition to the Samanadzie, relatives of deceased persons may employ the help of elders and traditional clergy to bring the Asasa home for "burial," because the Asasa are thought to linger where their deaths occurred. This ritual may be performed after a corpse has already been buried. The ritual entails going to where a death occurred if, say, it was caused by an automobile accident, in order to bring the dead home. After offering libations and prayers, elders collect some debris from the spot into a miniature box. Then an elder would ask the deceased to tag along home, following the party. Returning home, none of the party members looks back, because the Ɔtɔfo-Sasa would be following. At home a brief but symbolic "funeral" for the deceased would be performed, and then the box containing the deceased's debris "remains" is buried. This effectively releases the Ɔtɔfo-Sasa from its state of limbo paving the way for it to find its way to the Samanadzie. Finding familiar faces seems to have a calming effect on an Ɔtɔfo-Sasa who responds by following its family home. The point is, that it is important for living relatives of those who die as Atɔfo (away from home especially) to visit the sites that their wards died, if possible, because the dead may still be lingering around where they died. Visiting such sites offers opportunities for the dead to tag along home.

Normally, just at the point of death, an Ɔsaman (posthumous abstract personality) emerges from a physical body as a unique spiritual personality, extremely jealous and protective of the body it just vacated and it therefore stays with its body for as long as necessary. As long as a corpse remains unburied, the Ɔsaman is with its physical remains and unable to enter the Samanadzie. Meaning, an Ɔsaman is in the realm of the Āsunsum (spirits) in the corporeal, although the Samanadzie is aware of the death and awaits the arrival of the Ɔsaman, especially if the deceased is an elder. For example, the body of my queen mother and queen mother of Mprumem remained at the morgue for two years until I returned to Ghana from the United States for her interment and final obsequies as the ruler of Mprumem. During those two years, the Ɔsaman of Nana Apaaba III remained on earth, with her dead body, until she was finally buried. Prior to burial, the notion is that she visited her living relatives all over the world although each time returned to guard her corpse. The reason why an Ɔsaman stays with its corpse, as we have seen in chapter 1, is that a corpse must be hidden (buried) safely at a cemetery, a place that the Akan refer to as *Ɛsiāye* (where things are hidden or kept). A corpse then is safely kept at an Ɛsiāye until such time as the Ɔsaman owner needs it, explaining why an Ɔsaman lingers to witness where exactly its corpse is buried.

After burial, and free of its mortal remains, an Ɔsaman moves on to the next stage of rejuvenation itself in preparation for the journey to the Samanadzie. This transitional period takes place in the temporal world for a culturally defined period of at least forty days, during which time the Ɔsaman recovers from the shock of death and not having a physical body. During this stage, an Ɔsaman "heals" itself of all corporeal plights and pathogens that might have infused themselves with body and affected the Ɔsaman or even have caused its death. An Ɔsaman, after all, is a spiritual body (Sunsum)—not the physical body (Honam) already interred—and yet it is out of the physical that the Ɔsaman emerged for the first time and so an Ɔsaman must own and know the new body. Thus the forty-day transitional period is for a spiritual renaissance to undertake a final journey home to the world of the Nsamanfo, because this new world, which the Akan called the Samanadzie, has none of the suffering, pain, illnesses, or pathogens associated with the corporeal Wiadzie.

The "forty-day" waiting period is not only tied to festivities honoring the dead called Akwesidai,[6] but also the cycles or phases of the moon, although to what extent exactly is not clear. The Ɔsrɛn (moon) is the most powerful celestial symbol for the Akan because it is the emblem of God and hence referred to as Nana. As the second son of God,[7] his apparition as a crescent moon heralds rebirth and ushers in hope and faith in humanity because, as God's heraldist, the Ɔsrɛn is depicted as beating drums during the full moon, making him the consummate musician,[8] although Bosman thought that the moon was a female.

The relationship between the Akan and the Ɔsrɛn goes back to the very beginning of human existence when the Ɔsrɛn lived very closely near the earth (Asasi), the abode of humanity—or the Akan, the offspring of the Ɔsrɛn and the Old Woman. However, their close proximity proved untenable, as the earth repeatedly bumped into the moon forcing the moon to distance itself from earth and its inhabitants. Nostalgic, the Old Woman and her children built a tower of mortars to close the gap that had existed between the two worlds, but the tower collapsed, permanently separating the Ɔsrɛn from his human offspring on earth. So, the sighting of the crescent Ɔsrɛn and his wife, the nuptial star, Kyɛ-kyɛ-pɛ-awari, monthly not only renews the relationship that once existed, but bestows blessings when the moon takes away the ills and misfortunes of his offspring and dies with them at the end of the month. Most importantly, however, the appearance of the Ɔsrɛn reminds humanity that the father, the Ɔsrɛn, not only is around but that he could be reached spiritually. But by no means is the moon the Samanadzie, the abode of Nsamanfo, because it is the abode of the Ɔsrɛn and not of the dead since no one is buried there.

Prior to an Ɔsaman's departure to the Samanadzie, it makes farewell apparitions of all kinds to some living relatives all over the world, sometimes even putting on pseudo human form and visiting with those relatives or friends who may not be aware of the fact that the deceased was dead. However, during such apparitions an Ɔsaman does not speak, although its gesticulations and demeanor communicate its intentions, which the living "understands" as speech. In the same way that a fetus does not speak, a pre-

Samanadzie Ɔsaman too does not speak because a corpse does not speak as all of the senses are shut down at death. Speech—or rather speaking—in the Samanadzie follows exactly the Akan threefold welcome ritual of being offered a seat to sit on, water to drink, and then asked to offer synopses of one's travels[9] at which point the senses are opened and speech restored.

According to Ellis, at the Samanadzie "an old man becomes young, a young man a boy, and a boy an infant. They grow and become old. But age does not carry with it any diminution of strength, or wasting of the body. When they reach the prime of life they remain so, and never change more."[10] Following Ellis' logic, what becomes of an infant boy after death in the Samanadzie? While Ellis is right about lack of diminution, there are, however, no such dramatic transformations or growth at the Samanadzie. If that were the case, then there would be no point in being a human in the corporeal or belief in reincarnation, because the belief in reincarnation is predicated on the assumption that one did not maturate fully into old age and therefore was unable to achieve or fulfill one's Nkrabea. An Ɔsaman, who as a human, was unable to fulfill its Nkrabea because it died young and was a good person, is afforded another chance on earth to grow to old age in the hopes that he or she would live ethically and achieve one's Nkrabea. So what Ellis interpreted as "growth" is actually transformation of the posthumous abstract personality, the Ɔsaman, after emancipating itself of all physical atrophies and diseases associated with the corporeal, which give the appearance of growth or youthfulness. An old person with wrinkles upon death does not have the wrinkles anymore; someone unable to walk due to old age, walks normally at the Samanadzie. So while the Nsamanfo may appear "young" during apparitions, in actuality nothing changes about them, because they exist in ethereal form; that is, the Nsamanfo do not have physical form or flesh. For example, the late queen mother of Mprumem, Nana Adjoa Apaaba, was very fair in complexion, but at old age she dimmed perhaps due to her ill health. About one month or so after her burial she revealed herself to me one early morning in my bedroom, and the "person" I saw was a very beautiful, fair woman, dressed in white calico cloth tied around her chest like a traditional priestess or diviner. She was the same queen mother that I knew and buried, with no sign of diminution, although she was not the same old and feeble woman who had difficulty walking sometimes. Instead she had regained all of her glory as a refined agency; her complexion was just like when she was a young adult—with no trace of the maladies that afflicted her during her elderly years. The apparition must be seen in the context of traditional forty-day posthumous apparition in preparation for the journey to the Samanadzie. In other words, it was her farewell address to me, her king, son, and "husband."

However, Ellis redeemed himself by offering another "commonly held" viewpoint—the correct one—that "each srahman [Ɔsaman] is of the age at which the living man had arrived" at the Samanadzie. Arriving at the Samanadzie exactly as one was in the Wiadzie is needed for the ancestors to render judgment as to whether or not an Ɔsaman before them lived a life worthy of emulation by the living. Such a judgment could not be rendered against an Ɔsaman who died young and unable to fulfill its Nkrabea. This is one reason why some of those who die young, and as Atɔfo especially, postpone entering the Samanadzie to be judged. Rather, they stay in the realm of the Āsunsum (spirits) in order to reincarnate before finally arriving at the Samanadzie, because once an Ɔsaman is found guilty in the Samanadzie there is no chance of it reincarnating. The Nsamanfo (plural of Ɔsaman), especially elders found to be worthy, are apotheosized as ancestors (Nananom Nsamanfo) and full speech is restored. When invoked during divinations, for example, the Nananom Nsamanfo speak clearly as Abosom because they lived worthy lives for which they have full use of their tongues. The ordinary non-ancestral Nsamanfo do not speak as clearly as the Nananom Nsamanfo (Ancestors) or speak from their nasals because their tongues are not restored due to not living good lives.

The Ɔsaman emerges from a physical body just at the point of death as a unique agency as a result of a collaborative venture between the Abosom—with male Abosom contributing Sunsum (spirit), and female Abosom providing Mogya (blood)—and God, who blesses the human being with an Ɔkra, to occupy a realm specially designed for them, the Samanadzie. Contrary to some popular notion, the Samanadzie then is not for the dead, *Āwufo*, but rather for resurrected abstract personalities called Nsamanfo (or Asaman) and hence the Samanadzie. The dead or Āwufo, as we have seen, are actually hidden on earth at the Ɛsiāye (cemetery), insofar as dead bodies are concerned. Therefore, while the corporeal Wiadzie is the final destination for dead bodies, the living human being is absolutely convinced that it has a home other than the corporeal. As it happened, an Ɔsaman too is privy to the belief that the corporeal is not its final destination because an Ɔsaman is the same as the living being who died. The teleological certainty of a journey is undertaken by an Ɔsaman, who, unlike the human being, finds its way to the ultimate destination, the Samanadzie, because an Ɔsaman is a spiritual being. In the larger sociological context, the intrinsic notion of not belonging to the corporeal Wiadzie is a phenomenon shared by Africans and African-descended peoples worldwide. In other words, Africans and African-descended peoples firmly believe that they originated from a place other than the corporeal and therefore the innate desire to return to some place other than this world. For example, during slavery the African slaves were absolutely convinced that upon death their souls would return to Africa. This then is the basis of black spirituality; the innate feeling that one misses home, and therefore the intrinsic desire, the longing to return home. What then is the basis of this phenomenon? How did we get here as human beings and therefore the need, desire to return home? What is home like, to cause us to want to return?

As already expatiated on in previous chapters, becoming a corporeal being begins when an Ɔbosom (God or Goddess) takes leave of God within a phenomenon called *Ɔkra* or *Kra*. Etymologically, Ɔkra/Kra means "to take leave of" or bid farewell to; that is, to Kra is to take leave of somebody of importance, like parents, while *Ɔrekra* is the process of taking leave of God and other Abosom related to the Ɔbosom about to undertake earthbound residency. This process is an absolute necessity for all spiritual agencies wishing to relocate, whether they desire corporeal existence as humans or even as Abosom (Gods and Goddesses) wishing to relocate to realms other than where they currently reside.

One such common story among Akan involves the Abosom Kɔbena Ayɛnsu and his younger brother Yaw Dɛnsu who entered the corporeal world with Yaw Dɛnsu chasing after Kɔbena Ayɛnsu after both left their father in their spiritual abode and after Kɔbena Ayɛnsu outwitted his brother of gold that their father intended to give to Yaw Dɛnsu.[11] What the entry of the two Abosom into the corporeal world teach is that prior to their departure, they were given final tests. Meaning, nothing in life is free, whether spiritually or existentially. In the case of Kɔbena Ayɛnsu and Yaw Dɛnsu, the task was for Yaw Dɛnsu to prepare a meal for their blind father and receive the gift of gold for his earthbound relocation. His father could have given the gold to his son right away, without having to ask him to work for it, because by all accounts Yaw Dɛnsu was a dutiful son.

Hearing what their father just told Yaw Dɛnsu, Kɔbena Ayɛnsu "quickly and secretly prepared a meal and then tricked their blind father into eating it" by disguising himself as his hairy younger brother, Yaw Dɛnsu. When asked during a divination rite as to the kind of animal he used to prepare his meal, Kɔbena Ayɛnsu revealed that he used fish instead. Afterwards, their father, perhaps knowing all along that it was Ayɛnsu, still offered Ayɛnsu the gold that he was to have given to Dɛnsu, because Ayɛnsu passed the test set by their father. "Outwitted and incandescent with rage, Yaw Dɛnsu set out in pursuit of Kɔbena Ayɛnsu to claim what he thought was his. However, Ayɛnsu ran quickly into the ocean and gave the gold to the sea-goddess, Abena Mansa, for safekeeping, ending any chance of Dɛnsu ever getting the gold,"[12] although Ayɛnsu maintains that he has given his younger brother, Dɛnsu, his share of the gold.

Didactically, the divine drama involving Kɔbena Ayɛnsu and his brother Yaw Dɛnsu, which occurred long before human beings were ever created, serves as a guide to corporeal existence and ethical choices that future habitations of earth would make in pursuance of life's objectives. Living on earth involves a series of moral and ethical choices, decisions and tests embarked on during adulthood with the aim of gaining the ultimate prize, discovering one's Nkrabea and living a meaningful life. Following Kɔbena Ayɛnsu, we know that living is a competitive act, even among siblings, and sometimes the path to achieving one's goals and objectives might not necessarily be ethical, but as long as a prize is won fairly after surmounting every obstacle, then the end justifies the means. In achieving an Nkrabea, there is an obligation to help others, in the same way that Kɔbena Ayɛnsu gave Yaw Dɛnsu a share of his money.

As evidenced by Kɔbena Ayɛnsu and Yaw Dɛnsu (and their sister Birim) taking leave of their father, any human being does the same thing. After all, prior to becoming human beings, the future human was an Ɔbosom. Subsequently, an Ɔbosom wishing to become a human being informs the head of its helm about its intention to depart. The process of taking leave is a spiritual phenomenon, as a way of accounting for all spiritual agencies and their eventual return into the fold at a point dictated by the content of an *Nkra* (message) during the taking of leave ritual.

Originally, corporeal existence for human beings was supposed to be permanent, like those of the Abosom. In fact, in the beginning people just lived almost in perpetuity until evil became the norm. Furthermore, the propensity to depart and explore new horizons is also spiritual, highly desirable, and very individualistic. Individualism then is innately personal because of the privacy of taking leave, prompting the Akan to say that *Obi rekra ni Nyame no, nna obi ngyina hɔ* (when one was taking leave of God, no one else was around). Since the taking of leave is subsumed under Ɔkra (soul), it also means that an Ɔkra is uniquely individualistic. If no one else was privy to the existential career or professional blueprint (Nkrabea) of another during the interaction between a godhead and an Ɔbosom about to undertake corporeal existence, then no one else can take away anyone else's Nkrabea. This then is the basis of individuality and pursuance of one's divinely ordained existential career or professional blueprint. Therefore the notion that Africans are communistic is only to a point, because during adulthood when the quest for Nkrabea commences, Africans—at least the Akan—are very individualistic in pursuance of Nkrabea. Guess what happened to the Ɔbosom Yaw Dɛnsu when his brother, Kɔbena Ayɛnsu, overheard their father's instructions to Yaw Dɛnsu about what to do before obtaining gold for his journey into the corporeal Wiadzie: Kɔbena Ayɛnsu quickly and cleverly obtained the gold instead by doing for their father exactly what Yaw Dɛnsu was supposed to have done. In other words, when an opportunity presents itself, one must seize the moment and do everything ethically and legally possible to take advantage of the opportunity. As such, the Akan are very secretive people, because they believe that if others know or hear of one's secret plans, then chances of the plans being thwarted are highly probable. Therefore, the notion that Africans—or at least the Akan—are communistic peoples may partially be true, occurring before adulthood.

Yet another very important reason why an Ɔbosom wishing human existence must take leave of God is that only God gives life to all living things and so it is imperative for an Ɔbosom to inform the author of life, God, about its intention to relocate to earth. The ensuing conversation between God and an Ɔbosom during the taking-leave ritual becomes a secret, exclusively codified information called *Nkrabea* (information/message for a journey or destination), which becomes a part of the overall phenomenon called an Ɔkra. The Ɔkra, then, is the bearer of Nkrabea into the mundane, just as the Nkrabea is also the bearer of death. This is essentially what Danquah postulated when he argued that it is the "*e-su*" or the Su that breaks away from the collective and presents itself before God for an Nkrabea and an Ɔkra.[13] Clearly, for the Akan, a dialogue ensues with God and the godhead of a family of Abosom and any Ɔbosom wishing to depart to a realm other than its original abode. The content of the discussion (Nkra) may be about what an Ɔbosom was already engaged in occupationally and its desire to continue with the same or similar endeavor in the corporeal. Such undertakings are always risky propositions since there are no guarantees of success once the Abosom become human beings in the corporeal Wiadzie. Still, it is a risk that the Abosom take, however.

The relationship between God and a godhead of an Abosom Kuu (a colony of gods and goddesses) vis-à-vis an Ɔbosom wishing to relocate as a human to the corporeal is that a godhead knows about the Nkrabea of every Ɔbosom departing from the Kuu (colony). Actually, the conversation may not take place between God and an Ɔbosom at all, but rather between a godhead and the Ɔbosom wishing to depart, like what transpired between Yaw Dɛnsu and his father. This is tantamount to an Ɔbosom having a conversation with God directly. During divination, for example, an Āgya-bosom may reveal the Nkrabea of its human child. Among the Yoruba, for instance, a neonate's destiny or "head"[14] could be revealed to parents as early as three days after birth. The point is that what is told to God is not different from what is told to an Āgya-bosom—they are all the same.

The Nkrabea then is an individually crafted existential occupational or career blueprint, the ultimate existential endeavor that a person would engage in during adulthood. Most importantly, the Nkrabea also includes the enigma of and manner of death. However, the belief in Nkrabea has more to do with crafting an ideal ethical path, Ɔbra, in pursuance of Nkrabea in a universe that is sometimes chaotic and unforgiving. As such, every Nkrabea is unique with regard to a person's distinct achievements since an Ɔbosom's audience with God was a private one. The challenge, existentially, is the ability to decipher the precise nature or contents of an Nkrabea in order to know if one has achieved one's career or professional goals and objectives, because once in the mundane a person is incapable of recalling what his or her initial Nkrabea before God was all about. Consequently, the realization of an Nkrabea is an arduous task, prompting some people to question their initial audience with God when life's career opportunities become painfully elusive. Frustrated, one may be heard saying: *Mankra yae koraa* (I did not take leave of God properly), wondering if the lack of progress professionally is due to having missed his or her Nkrabea. But while natural to question God, God is not culpable in that God could not be responsible for any existential delinquency due to free will. Therefore, an individual may not blame God at all; rather, one questions oneself as to why such freely made choices end up so badly. Far from blaming God, individuals rather blame witchcraft and other family members for being responsible for their wrong career choices.

ƆBRA BƆ AND NKRABEA

It is a commonly held notion in the West that Africans are communistic, lacking individualistic personalities or even consciences outside of the collective or communities that brought them up.[15] While this study is not concerned with the purported communistic nature of the African life, it has everything to do with the notion and praxis of an individualistically pursued existential career or professional blueprint (Nkrabea), sometimes also defined as destiny,[16] although Nkrabea is more than destiny. Contextually, the pursuance of individuality is ethical, a period when an individual becomes morally and ethical responsible for one's own actions socially. Developmentally, the Akan refer to this state as the Ɔbra bɔ (ethical existence and generativity) stage. Of course, the individuation process began at the previous education stage, where a family—with some support from an extended family—prepare a boy or girl for a highly competitive individualistic existence in the larger arena of the world.

The concept of Ɔbra bɔ as ethical existence and generativity must be explored very carefully. As seen previously, Ɔbra bɔ was utilize within the context of Erikson's use of *generativity* in three ways, namely, procreation, production, and creativity to specifically describe the concept and praxis of "bɔ," which Konadu, for example, defines as "living, physical existence."[17] But, as will be expatiated upon, bɔ is more than encompassing praxis, as ethic, Ɔbra, must be put into action. Conceptually, bɔ means to create, shape, or fashion something into whatever form, image, or symbol an individual so chooses. In a practical sense therefore, bɔ is an indispensable component of Ɔbra (ethic) and must be understood as positioning oneself professionally or career-wise due to the individualistic nature of Ɔbra bɔ during adulthood. Ideally, bɔ has to do with planning, shaping, and creating one's own career endeavors in the hope that it would lead to the achievement or discovery of one's Nkrabea.

However, practically bɔ has another meaning that receives no mention at all when discussing an existential career or professional pathway to achieving Nkrabea, and that is, bɔ can lead to isolation and stagnation during young and mature adulthood, as Erikson puts it.[18] The reality is that bɔ can be bad or evil, unethical, and self-destructive in that one can destroy that which one has worked so hard to create or establish. The simple fact is that Ɔbra bɔ may be led creatively and productively, or delinquently and destructively leading to "despair" and regrets during old age. In response, a family may recall their ward who may be having difficulty fitting in socially in order to offer him a fresh start. Invariably such invitations back home are turned down as acceptance is tantamount to failure, and so young adults fruitlessly tough things out. This is especially so for many Africans who travel to large cities for greener pastures and end up sick, in jails, homeless, or have a difficult time making ends meet. In its social context, bɔ is how an individual crafts one's own life as an adult. The good news ethically is that most people transit well into young adulthood as good citizens, but there are always a few who become delinquents because they are unable to transit well, and unfortunately end up in jails or even die before reaching mature adulthood.

Conceptually, Ɔbra bɔ is intrinsically dualistic, although it is not so much a contradictory or diametrically opposing thought as it is an *either/or* phenomenon. In practice, Ɔbra bɔ has to do with making the right or even wrong choices in life; meaning there is no neutrality in life, because one is either in favor of something or not in favor. As evidence, Ɔbra bɔ is led ideally (*pa*) or destructively (*bɔn*) with the results resting solely on an individual adult, although its rippling effects may be social in scope. It does not mean rejecting something as being good or bad or evil; rather, it means making choices and knowing that choices have consequences.

The disposition manifested by an individual is determined by an individual's essential nature, the *Su*, which, although neutral, can develop into a good or bad character disposition. However, young adults may alter their *Abra bɔ* (plural of Ɔbra bɔ) if the Abra bɔ are found to be incongruously disruptive to societal ethos and polity. The generative individual during adulthood is the person who marries and produces children, gives back altruistically in supportive of society, and at old age inculcates in the younger generation the wisdom of ethical living; hence Ɔbra bɔ as ethical existence and generativity. For Danquah, "obara," which he defined as "ethical existence," has to do with immortality[19] and the sum total of life's activities computed meritoriously until the highest good is attained.

Next, the belief in Nkrabea is divine because it originates with God, making it a teleological quest and its ultimate attainment spiritual. However, a human being must utilize the ethical principles as the means to achieving Nkrabea, the discovery of which is tantamount to attaining spirituality (immortality), because anyone who realizes his or her Nkrabea is a generative person. Ethics and spirituality encompass every aspect of existence beginning in adulthood. So whether referred to as spirituality, immortality, or eternal life, the end result is the same ethically or spiritually, because they are ultimately eschatological. Spirituality, then, is the quest by an individual to aspire to the original, ideal epoch of immortality and eternity now superseded by the finitude and impermanence of the corporeal Wiadzie. Defining spirituality this way presupposes certain fundamental notions, the most important of which is that a human being is a spiritual being, a pre-potentiated sojourner in the corporeal Wiadzie, and therefore destined to return to its source of origination as a new spiritual being now called Ɔsaman. In other words, a human being must round itself up during the course of its complete existence[20] as a spiritual being, then a corporeal being, and finally, a transformed spiritual being now called Ɔsaman. This, of course, is after the Sunsum and the Ɔkra have joined their respective collective phylogenetic sources. We have already explored the Sunsum and the Ɔkra, and so we will concern ourselves with the ethical path (Ɔbra bɔ) leading to the achievement of Nkrabea (existential career or professional blueprint) here.

Existentially, the human being is a pre-potentiated sojourner on earth who embarks on a lifelong ethical quest, charting an ethical course (Ɔbra bɔ) in order to actuate one's career blueprint (Nkrabea) during adulthood. The concept and praxis of Ɔbra bɔ then is the test designed for human beings, the successful completion of which leads to the discovery of one's Nkrabea. One must therefore set out with clear objectives to achieving spirituality existentially, and also with the ultimate goal and focus of achieving immortality as ancestor (Nana Saman). This is where Danquah's rendition of Ɔbra bɔ as having to do with immortality comes into play, because it is not enough to simply become an Ɔsaman—as that could mean unfulfilled Nkrabea due to living an unethical life or one's life being cut short prior to adulthood—but instead concerned enough to live an altruistic life in the hopes of bequeathing to succeeding generations a legacy worthy of emulation. The praxis of Ɔbra bɔ has a definite period of commencement at adulthood, when for the first time as a young adult an Abrantsi (male) or Akataesia (female) embarks on an ethical path in order to actualize his or her Nkrabea.

The inherent dualistic nature of Ɔbra serves as the basis for moral and ethical choices, as well as being an idealistic concept, especially for young adults because it is aspirational in spite of not knowing the full practical ramifications of Ɔbra bɔ in the larger societal context. Ɔbra bɔ has to do with choices made and opportunities missed because of indecisions, all actions and deeds and thoughts as an adult, although thoughts not acted out are not held against anyone. Neutrality does not apply here, because, as the Akan say, only a fool would say a situation does not apply to oneself because it may be happening to neighbor. Everybody is affected by decisions and choices made by others and society as a whole. The point is that Ɔbra envisions an end point during which time one gives account of oneself before those who entrusted the living with certain endeavors, the Nana Nsamanfo (Ancestors). There is an expectation—indeed an obligation—to act, to engage, endeavor, speak up, therefore to not apply oneself as an adult is one of the most serious crimes there is, engendering condemnation even before death.

While Ɔbra (ethic) is idealistic, it is the praxis of bɔ (procreativity, productivity, and creativity) that makes Ɔbra bɔ very difficult, because it takes into account every activity an adult does. It entails the moral principles governing behavior and the way one interacts socially. The absence of neutrality means that Ɔbra must be put into action in order to actualize and achieve concrete results that society judges one by. It means taking one's life into one's own hands and following the ethical path (Ɔbra) as laid down a long time ago by the esteemed ancestors as a guide to eternal life. Furthermore, it means becoming morally and ethically responsible for one's actions and deeds, because whether responsible personally or not, society is the ultimate arbiter of one's actions and their repercussions. Consequently, Ɔbra is not only an ethical principle to right living, but rather a way of living—bɔ—entailing the creativity of judiciously meandering one's way through life, the world, or inability to cope with life's vicissitudes and ending up a failure. It is precisely because of the built-in mechanism for failures or successes that makes Ɔbra bɔ tantalizingly difficult, yet also the reason why society rewards individuals who attain a certain degree of altruistic living after realizing their Nkrabea. Comprehensively, *Abra bɔ* (plural of Ɔbra bɔ) are the creative (and destructive) praxes and principles of proper living. Therefore, when musicians sing songs about Ɔbra bɔ (or Abra bɔ), they are simply acknowledging the harsh socio-economic and political realities of life and the ethical imperatives surmounted prior to the attainment of eldership. And contrary to the notion of African life being communistic, Ɔbra bɔ by its very nature is inherently individualistic and lived thus; practically, it must be followed and lived in concert with the socially ascribed path no matter how difficult one's ethic (Ɔbra) might be. Life, then, goes on, irrespective of what the future may hold. Ultimately, it must be recalled that Ɔbra bɔ has to do with actuating one's own career or professional blueprint, the Nkrabea, as one told it first to God.

During young adulthood an individual is prepared for an ethic (Ɔbra) meant to help him or her discover one's role in society without losing sight of one's ultimate prize, Nkrabea. The pursuance of Nkrabea is not something that any society or even a so-called communistic group can achieve for anyone, because the very nature of Nkrabea makes it individualistic. Unlike the Abosom who are "born" fully conscious and therefore ready to engage in any task before embarking on existence other than their original existence, human beings, on the other hand, are born as the most helpless creatures on earth and must therefore be nurtured and inculcated in societal norms of what it means to survive as a part of a group in the corporeal Wiadzie. Consequently, tests about what it means to belong to a group and survive as a member of a much larger world body are deferred until young adulthood during the stage of Ɔbra bɔ (ethical existence and generativity) when one becomes morally and ethically responsible for one's own actions relationally. This is to say, that tests for human beings to determine whether or not one passes the moral and ethical test leading to discovery of one's Nkrabea are delayed until adulthood or the commencement of the ethical stage of Ɔbra bɔ when one is mature enough to make personal decisions and stand by them. Meaning, the Ɔbra bɔ period is when the Nkra (message) that an Ɔbosom made before God prior to corporeal existence is put into action or practice insofar as its pursuance is concerned. Therefore, there is a delay in the pursuance of life's existential career blueprint (Nkrabea) until adulthood because children do not exercise independence of thought and judgment. Children are not held responsible for their actions behaviorally because they are not morally and ethically mature enough to be held responsible for their actions. Instead, their parents are. Developmentally, then, the role of family and society is to equip children ethically before adulthood knowing full well that they, as a society, cannot guarantee any individual a successful ethic, except to point to the path leading to ideal living (*Ɔbra pa*). Consequently, society's role becomes indispensable to the development of a person toward the realization of an Nkrabea by inculcating in the youth through traditional education the ethical principles for ideal citizenship. These goals include respecting the elders and those in positions of authority, supporting the community that nurtured an individual, and exhibiting a readiness to carry out traditions of the ancestors. The moral responsibility, duty, and obligation then is to preserve, protect, and defend the same cultural traditions for posterity that first nurtured an individual into adulthood. The goal is to sustain the cornerstone of Akan society and culture as was handed over to the present generation.

The praxis of Nkrabea is such that its contents are voluminous (*Nkrabea musɛm dɔɔso*) in that the affairs of human beings are incalculable and inexhaustible. As such, one's own affairs may be lost in the maze of competing interests. Nonetheless, there is the expectation that one's affairs and voice would be heard, uniquely, in the cacophony of voices and activities from sunrise to sunset. However, the voluminous nature of Nkrabea is deliberate and not meant to be exhausted in a lifetime. Hence, it is said that: *Onyimpa bɛyɛbe, na woanbɛyɛ ni nyinaa* (a person only endeavors a portion, not the whole). That, no matter what we do as humans, there will always remain something else to be done: We cannot exhaust everything that there is to do in a life's time. What is implied here is the recognition of human finitude and how a person will never, really, complete everything that one is destined to.

The source of this is traceable to the taking-of-leave (Nkra) conversation with God. While it may appear to be a simple ritual spiritually, it is actually a long ritual conversation when transmitted corporeally about everything that one would want to accomplish. Based on my experiences in divinations, intra-Abosom conversations are ultra-fast. For instance, what takes minutes or even hours for a human being to explain or say, an Ɔbosom will say in nanoseconds. This is because they are spiritual agencies existing in non-corporeal realms. The reality is that what is communicated in nanoseconds spiritually between God and an Ɔbosom, when the Ɔbosom becomes a human being it takes a lifetime or so to achieve, if at all. In the corporeal sense, the contents of Nkrabea are simply inexhaustible, making it very difficult for one to know everything that was said in heaven during a lifetime in the corporeal. For one thing, as human beings we are incapable of remembering or knowing what exactly transpired in heaven let alone trying to fulfill every detail on earth of what was said in heaven. What appears to be enigmatic about Nkrabea is trying to discover and fulfilling an Nkrabea, because an Ɔbra bɔ is not meant to be easy as one encounters others with the same purpose. However, all may not be lost due to the belief that an individual may be reincarnated in order to achieve whatever was first decreed in the presence of God. Unlike conceptions of reincarnation in some non-African religions where an individual may be reincarnated into, say, an animal until such time as he or she is finally reincarnated a human being, an Akan is always reincarnated a human being in order for one to continue from where one left off previously. In this vein, there is a built-in soteriology in Akan religious and cultural beliefs due to reincarnation which enables a person to have several chances at salvation as one works his or her way up to the Samanadzie.

The reason why the Nkrabea originates with God even though an Nkrabea is a personalized existential career blueprint told to God by an earthbound human is that Nkrabea always accompanies the Ɔkra (soul), meaning without an Ɔkra there is no Nkrabea, which, in turn, means that one cannot live since it has no Ɔkra (soul), which originates with God. The Ɔkra then is the bearer of the distinctly personalized Nkrabea, because one has to live by inhaling its first breath at birth. It is only after one becomes a living being that a person thinks about Ɔbra bɔ and what one would accomplish existentially. Since the Ɔkra originates with God as a life agency, it also means that God knows about everyone's Nkrabea. In other words, God has foreknowledge of what sort of life an individual would lead existentially even before one is born. God does not, however, intervene or control one's Nkrabea, because every person is endowed with the freedom to determine and shape one's own ethic so as to be responsible for one's own actions. After all, an Nkrabea is what an Ɔbosom willed in the presence of God prior to becoming a human being. For this reason an Nkrabea cannot be altered. God's role is to codify what is willed by an Ɔbosom as a part of what God himself contributes as an Ɔkra.

The Akan, like other African groups, are thought to be communistic socially, but when it comes to ethical existence and generativity (Ɔbra bɔ) they are very individualistic, because everyone assiduously tries to discover one's own niche in a highly competitive world. While one reason may be purely selfish, the other is the pressure to be successful in order to ameliorate one's life and community for socio-political and spiritual affirmation resulting in the conferral of eldership title on a person. Far from being communistic, it is rather individualism in community. The very nature of Ɔbra bɔ is such that the youth must be psychologically, emotionally, and socially ready in community before embarking on a path of individualism. Independent living is not the same as the individualistic pursuance of Nkrabea through Ɔbra bɔ, because Ɔbra bɔ entails the ethic of owning up to decisions and choices made as a consequence of one's acts and deeds. The individuation process must be deliberately inculcated to enable a young adult—the Abrantsi (male) or Akataesia (female)—to withstand the shocks and sometimes disappointments of Ɔbra bɔ. Even where careful consideration is given to ensuring a successful Ɔbra bɔ for a young adult, sometimes families find themselves disappointed in how their wards turn out. Some parents may take responsibility for the failure of their children when in reality they did everything humanly possible to prepare their wards. What they fail to take into consideration is the fact that every person is born with a unique and unchanging *Su*. While parents certainly influence their children, they are incapable of changing the essential, raw nature (Su) of their children. Once an Ɔbra bɔ is embarked upon, then it is out of the hands of parents, such parents having completed their task of preparing children for Ɔbra bɔ at adulthood, the beginning of an individualistic quest to discover one's own place in the universe. People then may say of a person who is not so successful in life: "Ethical existence is an individual creation or invention" (*Ɔbra nye woara abɔ*). For good or ill, life is how one crafts it. Sometimes *Ɔbra nye woara abɔ* is said within the context of a warning for a person to reexamine one's life ethically.

In adulthood, for instance, we find that the *Suban*—character, disposition, temperament—once again determines the kind of ethic that an individual leads as either *Ɔbra pa* (ideal or good) or *Ɔbra bɔn* (bad, unethical) life. If during young adulthood an individual has been well trained and cultured at the previous education stage and inculcated in what it means to cultivate an ideal life—the requisite for leading *Ɔbra pa* (ideal or good)—then chances are that an individual would invariably master the art of living as an elder. After all, the goal of educating children is to mold them into developing good character attributes in the hope that children become model citizens as adults. And by education, I am referring to both Western education, and above all, traditional teachings as to what it means to be a person within the larger social context ethically. A person well grounded in one's cultural traditions would invariably surmount most of the challenges that Ɔbra bɔ has to offer. However, the uneducated young adult, the Abrantsi (male) or Akataesia (female), might not be able to make the transition into adulthood properly and end up delinquent and stagnated because one lives by the whims of others and normally engages in unethical activities (*Suban bɔn*). To avoid unethical behavior, we find that a neonate is pre-endowed with a Su (essential raw nature) as the basis of ethics, and parents work hard preparing and equipping children in the ethical principles that young adults must embrace during Ɔbra bɔ. Having done all that they could as parents, the hope is that children would lead good and altruistic lives that lead to eldership.

Another cause for ethical failure may be attributed to premature engagement of Ɔbra bɔ; that is, for some youths to think that they are ready to engage the world as individuals when they are not. A song by a musician says, that when he was a boy, he used to envy his father's meals because the meals were always sumptuous and he wished that he was old enough to enjoy the benefits of marriage and adulthood. However, now that he is an adult, he realizes that the sumptuous meals that he thought his father enjoyed came with hosts of social and economic issues and problems. That, what he thought were enjoyable meals were actually meals of Abra bɔ, as he now faces the same voluminous socio-economic issues that his father faced. Indeed, children who rush to become adults end up failing because they did not allow their parents to prepare them adequately. Many of these children or young adults become isolated from their loved ones and turn out incorrigible, petulant, and vagabonds. In frustration, parents of such children sometimes hand over the Abra bɔ (plural of Ɔbra bɔ) of their children to them, having nothing to do with the ethical responsibilities of the children. A parent may say in anger and frustration to his or her incorrigible youth: *Medzie wo bra ahyɛ* wo *nsa* (I have handed over your life into your own hands). This may be a death sentence to the children because invariably many of the children end up as failures, although such youths may not fully see the ramifications of their acts until perhaps years later. What this premature surrendering of Abra bɔ to youths also shows is that parents and guardians are the custodians of ethical principles, which they must teach children until such time as parents are ready to send away young adults into the world with their blessings. Therefore any premature handing over of Ɔbra bɔ is a course for concern because it is tantamount to rejection of a youth, which may carry with it the potential for failure due to the fact that a youth may not be fully prepared to adequately and successfully meet the challenges of the wider world. Another danger for young adults is that they cut off the societal fulcrum needed for regeneration should they end up isolated and in despair. In situations like these, other family members may intervene and force petulant and impatient youths to change course and ask parents to retract their pronouncements of doom when they handed over to their wards their Abra bɔ prematurely in anger.

To say that parents or society is the custodian of the ethical principle governing life (Ɔbra bɔ) is to admit that elders have been entrusted with traditions that they inherited from their predecessors. The mandate being that the ancestors have handed over to them traditions that they must preserve, protect, and pass on to succeeding generations. Subsequently, parents and elders learn the principles governing life as children themselves, and now as adults they see it as their duty to ensure transmission to their children the same teachings that they received from their parents and elders. Aware that culture is dynamic, parents and elders try to ensure that their wards are solidly inculcated and grounded in values and mores of their cultures in a rapidly changing world. Therefore, when an anxiously impatient youth is dismissed by parents or society prematurely, there is a genuine fear that such a youth might not be sufficiently educated to survive the harsh realities of city life. Some youths actually turn out as delinquents or criminals, and may end up in jail or even die.

While there are no qualms about the individualistically dynamic nature of Ɔbra bɔ, there is also the notion that Ɔbra bɔ may not be endeavored without assistance; that is, it may not be engaged in alone. The implication is that there is room for help, casting doubt on the notion of a "self-made man or woman." At some point during the maturational processes one must have received help along the way. After all, human beings are social beings; meaning, we interact with people every step of our social, economic, political, religious, and professional lives. Someone must have laid down the structures that all societies are built on to enable societies to use them, to achieve success as no one can claim to have made it on his or her own when the avenues for productive living have already been made available. In light of this, the Akan would admit that it is because of fanning each other's eyes that two animals walk together as opposite partners. This saying is in reference to marriage as an institution that serves to sustain societies. In a long continuum of socio-cultural traditions, young adults, while liberating themselves from their parents during the individuation process of leaving home, turn around and embrace the institution of marriage when they choose suitable spouses. So people enter into marriages in order to establish a new family unit as extensions of families and societies.

When Erikson uses the term *generativity* as the instinctual power behind various forms of selfless caring,[21] he has in mind procreativity. That the young adult—the Abrantsi (male) or Akataesia (female)—is expected to marry and have children. Thus the first of his tripartite meaning of generativity is procreation, timed to coincide with adulthood for a reason. Similarly for the Akan, Ɔbra bɔ is timed to coincide with marriage in order that one may not undertake the ethical path alone. Ethically then marriage has its place in Akan society because it ensures survival and continuity of society. The practice now is that Ɔbra bɔ is initiated singularly, first before marriage is contracted, later due to the need to adequately care for the other. Nowadays, due to harsh economic realities marriage may be postponed, but in the past as soon as one became an adult, one was expected to marry so the couple could start life (Ɔbra bɔ) together. Therefore the Akan speak of their spouses as those that they are engaging Ɔbra bɔ with, or those that they are enacting Ɔbra with, together. The praxis of Ɔbra bɔ then is a paradox. On the one hand, the Akan are adamant that Ɔbra bɔ is an individually engaged phenomenon because one is held to account for one's Ɔbra bɔ existentially. But on the other, they also insist that one needs a helper in the opposite spouse to serve as a guide during Ɔbra bɔ so as to keep a pathfinder spouse in a straight and narrow path ethically. Opposite marriage partners see things differently and therefore each is able to offer unique criticisms during the ethical journey together.

The need for marriage during Ɔbra bɔ has to do with the fact that prior to marriage, a youth is free of ethical improprieties, as one is still be under the tutelage of one's parents who assume responsibilities for all youthful mistakes. Even in adulthood, society still believes one needs a "parent" in the form of the opposite sex to serve as a corrective partner in the absence of the parents, since an adult is encountering a much bigger arena of men and women. But with marriage also comes responsibilities as a couple assumes full control of their lives within the socially acceptable norms. The individualized ethic (Ɔbra bɔ) is what leads to discovering the precise nature of an Nkrabea depending on whether or not a particular undertaking is unethical (*Ɔbra bɔn*) or ideal (*Ɔbra pa*). Though a couple, each spouse is still held to account individually for one's deeds as unethical or ethical, because Nkrabea is acquired privately in conversation with God thus making Nkrabea uniquely individualistic. Therefore the need for companionship during Abra bɔ for a couple is meant to ease some of the difficulties associated with the pursuance of Nkrabea. In other words, Ɔbra bɔ is such that one needs a life's partner in marriage for support during each other's ethical journey.

The reason for this seemingly contradictory statement that Ɔbra bɔ is an individualistically pursued praxis in search of Nkrabea, and yet a phenomenon needing a spouse to help in its pursuance, makes Ɔbra bɔ difficult to untangle. The answer to the conundrum may be found in what the Akan say of Ɔbra bɔ itself: *Ɔbra* yɛ *bɔna* or *Ɔbra ni bɔ* yɛ *bɔna* (the ethical life is a conundrum, difficult, wanting and therefore a tease). Consequently, one may be told that if *Ɔbra nnyɛ bɔna a nkyɛr* . . . to say that if ethical living was not so difficult, wanting, elusive, everyone would have been, say, successful or not, to be in such a miserable situation. Or, it may be said: Even those tackling Ɔbra bɔ straightforwardly find it so difficult—with pitfalls everywhere—that those engaging it backwardly are definitely doomed to failure. This is meant as a warning to those leading reckless lives to mend their ways or else end up worse or even die. Ultimately, there is an acknowledgement that Ɔbra bɔ is a difficult (*Ɔbra nibɔ yɛdzin*) activity, explaining why most people do not discover their existential career blueprints. The point is that Ɔbra bɔ is a path, an ethical path applied to attempt to discover one's existential career blueprint. Teleologically, Ɔbra bɔ is a spiritual journey, a journey traveled with the aim of taking into account everything that a person does and the consequences thereof. Conceptually, it is an eschatological phenomenon that must be taken seriously. So young adults who postpone marriage are constantly being pressured to marry because society believes marriage brings along stability, which may propel a person, perhaps, to the discovery of one's Nkrabea. This may be the reason behind the saying: Behind every successful man is a good woman or vice versa.

How then does the Nkrabea feature in this divine and existential drama? The Nkrabea and its role in human activity leading to its discovery may be said to be a matter of trial and error, because if one were clearly aware of one's Nkrabea from the very beginning as a child, then realization of an Nkrabea would be achieved easily. But, as is the case most times, one has no clue as to what one's own Nkrabea is all about, thus a person may go through life not knowing what one really wants. Subsequently, if an individual enjoys a considerable degree of prosperity, then it is interpreted as having discovered one's Nkrabea. Likewise, if a person finds oneself in a perpetual cycle of failures, then the culprit is almost always the Nkrabea.

Some Abosom take leave of God with the aim of acquiring wealth, to be poor, sick, healthy, happy, sad, childless, etc.[22] Every existential condition imaginable has its spiritual antecedents, with the difference between spiritual and corporeal conditions being that spiritual conditions are permanent minus the pain and hassle experienced in the mundane, while existential conditions are difficult, stressful, and painful. This does not mean, however, that an individual is resigned to a permanent state of existence, because only death, the eschatological component of Nkrabea, puts an end to life's goals and existence as a whole. Yet, even this is decreed by an individual's Nkrabea as willed before God. An existential condition then is not fixed permanently, because the nature of Ɔbra bɔ is such that it could be changed if a particular ethic proves untenable. The idea is to keep on improving on an existential situation until a situation or condition is ameliorated.

The inherently good thing about Nkrabea is its universal message of salvation for adherents, because an individual may have many chances of starting over again and again until such time as one attains his or her existential career goals, ultimately. Soteriology, however, is contingent on living a life free of evil in order to make it the first time around. Ideally, one need not resign oneself to any single unproductive state of Ɔbra bɔ, but must be dynamic and work indefatigably hard to improve on any unhealthy and unproductive situation in which one finds himself or herself. After all, a reason for wishing to locate as a human is to try new possibilities and adventures in the corporeal, and the degree to which one succeeds in the corporeal leads to far greater reward in heaven (Samanadzie) upon death.

God has foreknowledge of everyone's Nkrabea since every Ɔbosom appears before God to discuss its reasons for wanting corporeal existence. For this reason, God is not responsible for existential failures when trying to discover an Nkrabea, because knowing about an Nkrabea or someone else's plans, and whether or not those plans are executed according to plan by an owner, are not the same. The only role God plays is one of an enabler, because God is the author of life, the Ɔkra (soul). Indeed, there is a symbiotic relationship between the Ɔkra and the Nkrabea making both the Ɔkra and the Nkrabea divine in origin. As such, both agencies have everything to do with life's conditions although an Nkrabea is the personalized coded career or professional blueprint for life's journey. The presence of Ɔkra and Nkrabea make life meaningful and worth living. However, life can also be a living hell when all possibilities seem to elude an individual in search of a meaningful life due to the lingering nature of Nkrabea. So, rather than live as a generative person dexterously and ensure an ideal life (Ɔbra pa), one may become a delinquent living a life of isolation, despair, and regrets due to unethical life (Ɔbra bɔn).

Developmentally, ethical existence and generativity (Ɔbra bɔ), as we have seen, begin when an individual becomes morally and ethically concerned with existential and spiritual issues, their paradoxes, ramifications, and repercussions. This period ordinarily coincides with a culturally defined age of adulthood when a person is confronted and presented with the full spectrum of being a spiritual person. Furthermore, it means being ethically and morally responsible for one's own actions as well as the actions of the collective. Most importantly, it means finding one's own ethical and spiritual niche professionally within the matrix of a socio-culturally constructed norm. Consequently, a person must maintain a delicate balance between the demands of his or her spiritual, physical, emotional, and psychological needs and societal demands and obligations, which are emblematic of a generative personality leading to discovery of an Nkrabea. In praxis, Ɔbra bɔ is every activity and action engaged in by an adult from the moment one awakes to when one goes to bed. In response, every action or activity generates a reaction—ethical or unethical—in ways that serve as basis for accountability and judgment. There is no neutrality when it comes to Ɔbra bɔ, as Ɔbra bɔ entails and demands action and reaction.

The term Nkrabea, as we have seen, means a message or messages[23] (*nkra*), and journey or destination (*bea*), suggesting that all living things sojourn in the corporeal Wiadzie with definite divine "messages" or blueprints. This unique message or life's blueprint is what one may or may not accomplish. Not accomplishing an Nkrabea does not mean that an Nkrabea is nonexistent, rather it suggests that one is unable to access it at all or aspects of Nkrabea were realized but not the full scope. What it suggests, furthermore, is that Nkrabea could not be destiny, because to destine something is to guarantee its occurrence or accomplishment. However, as expatiated already, Nkrabea is more than destiny—it is all of existence beginning at adulthood when one is culturally equipped to stand on one's own two feet ethically as an individual apart from others. More than destiny, Nkrabea has room for failure or an unaccomplished career blueprint, something that destiny does not allow because destiny is fixed, like death. Above all, destiny alone is too fatalistic and eschatological, which Nkrabea is not because the realization of Nkrabea is the attainment of satisfaction, pleasure and happiness, patience, and peace and wisdom. Another reason why the Nkrabea could not be defined as destiny has to do with the belief in reincarnation (*Bɛbra*). If a person has several chances of refining the quality of his or her existential status until such time as one attained what one willed before God in a series of births and rebirths, then Nkrabea could not be destiny. The only inescapable guarantee that Nkrabea offers, as we have seen in chapter 1, is death. Ultimately, Nkrabea encompasses destiny, although destiny does not determine a person's deeds, otherwise God would be the culprit of all unfulfilled career blueprints and evil deeds of people.

Starting as a spiritual being, an Ɔbosom has a clear mandate, a uniquely coded blueprint for its earthbound existence. It has to do with what it is that an earthbound Ɔbosom would accomplish prior to its return to the spiritual world; first, as the original Ɔbosom that took on corporeal existence, and second, creating a spiritual agency now called Ɔsaman for the Samanadzie. Again, the reason why the Abosom, together with God, chose corporeal existence was to create their own kind to populate a world that is unique from theirs. Having achieved that, an Ɔbosom returns triumphantly to the collective Abosom Kuu (colony of gods), while the Ɔsaman that it created departs to the Samanadzie. However, the triumphant return of an Ɔbosom is contingent on the person that it became leading a successful life (Ɔbra pa), achieving or discovering one's Nkrabea, attaining eldership, and dying at old age. Apotheosized upon death, the Nana Saman (Ancestor) joins the esteemed collective deities, the Nananom Nsamanfo (Ancestors), who are constantly worshipped privately by individuals and publicly by the collective Ābusua Kuu during situational and annual festivities honoring the ancestors and Abosom. However, if a person failed in the aforesaid achievements, then the Ɔbosom, upon its return to the collective Abosom Kuu, would be given a chance to reincarnate, provided as a human being one lived a good life but died before having the chance to fulfill an Nkrabea. The goal of this corporeal experiment was to create good or ideal Nsamanfo, and so evil individuals are prevented from reincarnating.

In the end, Nkrabea is a conundrum. Yet an Nkrabea, insofar as the revelatory nature of a career blueprint is concerned, is close and right here with us especially during childhood, because children show signs of their Nkrabea during the innocence of the young when children are at play. Therefore, the only thing insightful parents need to do is identify those unique gifts and talents of their children and nurture them into adulthood. Unfortunately, the difficult realities of African societies often preclude parents from identifying those gifts and instead misdirect the Nkrabea of their children for life, coercing children into living the failed Nkrabea of parents instead when children choose occupations that have absolutely nothing to do with their innate desires. Thus, children miss out professionally as astronomers, philosophers, mathematicians, musicians, engineers, dieticians, etc., because parents force them into professions that children have absolutely no interest in. The salient point about the Nkrabea, as we have seen, is that it is a privately willed phenomenon before God, meaning every person is responsible for one's own actions.

On a visit to Ghana in 2013, one of my brothers-in-law, Nɛānyi, offered an insightful exposition on Nkrabea that I had not thought of before. Speaking about the unhealthy competition among Ghanaians, Nɛānyi said that there is no reason for the Akan to jealously compete with one another when it comes to career or professional choices and opportunities relative to Nkrabea, because to compete for and be jealous of another for having a good job is futile since no one knows what one willed professionally before God. Since, he explained, many are called to specific professions, to be jealous of someone who has found his or her calling professionally and go as far as to compete with such a person will lead to total failure. His reasoning is that since Nkrabea is unique, one should rather spend time finding one's own profession and aspire to the highest pinnacle. The fact is that Nkrabea is achieved differently for everyone, so that while a person may find fulfillment early on in his or her life, another may discover his or hers later on in life, because Nkrabea is a highly secretive conversation with God during unique times. As long as one is on the right ethical course (Ɔbra bɔ), a person would ultimately find his or her Nkrabea. So, to compete with a person who has found fulfillment professionally is symptomatic of a misplaced Nkrabea.

While the appearance of a healthy competition—insofar as inspirations are concerned—is good, one can only aspire to what one willed before God in the search for one's Nkrabea unless that person too willed the same career blueprint. But even here they may not occur at the same time, because each person appears before God separately, privately, and on their own time. We are speaking about timing, and divine time is not the same as human time. Hence the Akan would say, insofar as time is concerned, that: *Wodzie wɔmu a, wo nsa bɛka* (what is meant for one, will be received in due time)—that is to say that Ɔbra bɔ cannot be rushed. After all, each person enters the corporeal environment at a time selected by God, and for this reason, we cannot all discover our Nkrabea at the same time. Inherently, though, the notion of Nkrabea has less to do with competition, rivalry, jealousy, or envy, than the ability to creatively and relentlessly pursue one's objectives among throngs of humanity all pursuing unique objectives. In the context of Ɔbra bɔ, then, Nkrabea is the ultimate reward of life.

Finally, Nkrabea may not be unique at all in the realm of the spiritual, in that Nkrabea exists as the normal way deities undertake their distinct tasks as agents of God. The mystery of Nkrabea is attempting to replicate one's spiritual occupation on earth when one does not have any memory on earth of what one did divinely. So when the decision is made to enter corporeal existence and an appearance before God is made to bid farewell, career-wise nothing changes from what the Ɔbosom was already engaged in as a spiritual entity. This original profession becomes the Nkrabea for the potential corporeal being. In the corporeal, the human being undertakes Ɔbra bɔ as an adult in hopes of capturing his or her previous non-corporeal existence and what it used to do career-wise, relying instead on parents and society to steer one into culturally defined professions. If, for instance, an Ɔbosom was a "priest" and informed God about its intentions to enter corporeal existence and God blessed the Ɔbosom, then it means the deity's Nkrabea as a human would still remain to be a priest or have a career related to the clerical profession. Therefore, the very moment that ordination is achieved, it means the Nkrabea has been achieved. It does not, however, mean that one is successful, but rather the beginning of the path to a successful living as someone in the service of God. If during the course of one's clerical profession, a priest aspires to the highest ecclesiastical office of his or her religion, then that may be considered as a reward accompanying the office of priest.

Corporeally and spiritually, existence is in the form of families. These families, whether humans or Abosom, may all engage in similar duties or professions as, say, priests. Subsequently, an Ɔbosom may "emigrate" the spiritual world with an entire priestly "family" to the corporeal world at varying periods, so that generations later certain households of priestly descendants are established. In this case, anyone in that household may be "called" into the clerical vocation. This may be one of those few cases where parents may be right in allowing their children to enter the clerical vocation as viable careers. So Nkrabea has to do with continuation on earth of careers and duties that the Abosom performed in the spiritual world. This explains why the spiritual world takes precedence over the corporeal because the corporeal is only a reflection of the spiritual realm, suggesting that life on earth may not be perfect.

The praxis of Ɔbra bɔ is the way, road, path of life traveled by all. The path of Ɔbra bɔ could lead to infamy, depravation, and shame when Nkrabea is unattained due to insurmountable obstacles that one may face, or glory and vindication which makes life meaningful and worth living upon discovery of one's existential profession or career, endeavor, mission, or duty as willed divinely. But whichever ethical existence is led—whether Nkrabea is achieved or not—in the end, Ɔbra is unto death (*Ɔbra twir owu*).

NOTES

1. Antubam, Kofi. *Ghana's Heritage of Culture*. (Leipzig: Koehler & Amelang, 1963), pp. 90–93.
2. Ibid.
3. For further discussion on the Akan conception of personhood, see Kwame Gyekye, *Tradition and Modernity: Philosophical Reflection on the African Experience*. (New York: Oxford University Press, 1997), pp. 48–52.

4. Konadu, Kwasi. *Indigenous Medicine and Knowledge in African Society.* (New York: Routledge, 2007), p. 38.

5. Gyekye, Kwame. *An Essay on African Philosophical Thought: The Akan Conceptual Scheme.* (Cambridge: Cambridge Univ. Press, 1987), pp. 85–128.

6. For detailed account of Akan funerals see J. H. Nketia. *Funeral Dirges of the Akan People.* (Achimota, 1955), pp. 5–18.

7. Rattray, R. S. Capt. *Akan-Ashanti Folk-Tales.* (Oxford: At The Clarendon Press, 1930), p. 73.

8. Bosman, William. *A New and Accurate Description of the Coast of Guinea: Divided into The Gold, The Slave, and The Ivory Coasts.* (New York: Barnes & Noble, 1967 [1704]), 147.

9. Ephirim-Donkor, Anthony. *African Religion Defined, a Systematic Study of ancestor Worship among the Akan, Second Edition,* (Lanham, MD: University Press of America, 2013), p. 169.

10. Ellis, A. B. *The Tshi-speaking Peoples of the Gold Coast of West Africa: their religion, manners, customs, laws, language, etc.* (Anthropological Publications, Oosterhout N.B.: The Netherlands, [1887] 1970), p. 157.

11. Ephirim-Donkor, Anthony. *African Religion Defined, a Systematic Study of ancestor Worship among the Akan, Second Edition,* (Lanham, MD: University Press of America, 2013), p. 9.

12. Ibid.

13. Danquah, J. B. *The Akan Doctrine of God* (London: Frank Cass & Co., Ltd., 1968), p. 111.

14. Gbadegesin, Segun. "Eniyan: The Yoruba concept of a person." In P. H. Coetzee and A. P. J. Roux, eds., *The African Philosophy Reader, second edition* (New York: Routledge: Taylor &Francis Group, 2003), pp. 180–181.

15. See Paul Riesman. "The Person and the Life Cycle in African Social life and Thought." *African Studies Review,* Vol. 29, 2, 1986.

16. Konadu, Kwasi. *Indigenous Medicine and Knowledge in African Society.* (New York: Routledge, 2007), p. 44.

17. Ibid.

18. Erikson, Erik. *A way of Looking at Things: Selected Papers from 1930–1980.* Ed. Stephen Schlein (New York: W. W. Norton & Company, 1987), p. 606–607.

19. Danquah, J. B. *The Akan Doctrine of God* (London: Frank Cass & Co., Ltd., 1968), p. 162.

20. Erikson, Erik. *A way of Looking at Things: Selected Papers from 1930–1980.* Ed. Stephen Schlein (New York: W. W. Norton & Company, 1987), pp. 597–598.

21. Erikson, Erik. *Insight and Responsibility: Lectures on the Ethical Implications of Psychoanalytic Insight.* (New York: W. W. Norton & Company, 1964), p. 131.

22. Appiah-Kubi, Kofi. *Man Cures, God Heals.* (New York: Friendship Press, 1981), pp. 10–11.

23. Danquah, J. B. *The Akan Doctrine of God* (London: Frank Cass & Co., Ltd., 1968), p. 82.

Glossary

Abofra: Child.
Abosom (singular *Ɔbosom*): Primeval Gods and Goddesses.
Abosom Kuu: The Gods and Goddesses as a collective body.
Abosom'ma: Divine or Abosom children born after barren women sought the intervention of the Abosom.
Abrewah-na-ni-mma (the Old Woman and her children): A constellation (of seven stars) that corresponds to the seven *ābusua* divisions of the Akan people.
Ābusua: A uterine, consanguineous linear descent group—an Akan mother and her children.
Afibɔɔr: Infinity, everlasting, forever.
Āgya-bosom: An Ɔbosom-father who wills Abosom into the corporeal world as his children; father or patron deity, spiritual protector.
Ahom: Breath.
Ahontɔ: Contented life or living.
Akɔmfo (singular *Ɔkɔmfo*): Diviners; clerics specifically called by Abosom.
Asasi: The earth.
Asasi Āfua and *Asasi Yaa*: Earth goddesses.
Asomdwe: Peace.
Āsunsum: Plural of Sunsum.
Atsenayae: Satisfactory, prosperous living or life.
Bɛbra: Reincarnation.
Dzin: Name; *Dzin-to*: Naming rite.
Ɛguradzie: Funerary or neonatal cosmetics used on babies and the dead.
Ɛsiāye: Cemetery; where things are hidden or kept.
Fuun: Corpse.
Honam: Physical body, skin, flesh.

Kuu: Group or pack.

Kyɛkyɛ-pɛr-awari: A star (North Star), and wife of the moon.

Mframa: Wind or air from which all life-forms depend.

Mogya (*bogya*): Blood. Also, the basis of the *ābusua* descent system as composed of a mother and her children.

Nana: Title for God, a god or goddess, ancestor, king or queen mother, elder, grandparent, and grandchild.

Nana Nyame: God.

Nana Saman: Ancestor.

Nananom Ahenfo: Living ancestors (kings and queen mothers), ancestors in human form.

Nananom Mpānyinfo: An assemblage of elders.

Nananom Nsamanfo: The collective body of ancestors in the Samanadzie.

NaSaman: Primordial woman and mother of all living beings; ruler of the Samanadzie.

Nkrabea: A unique occupational or career blueprint, including life's ultimate end, to be achieved existentially beginning in adulthood.

Nkwa: Life.

Nsamanfo (*Asaman*): Posthumous abstract personalities residing in the Samanadzie or spirit world.

Ntoro/Huaba: Semen.

Ɔbosom: A god or goddess.

Ɔbra bɔ (plural *Abra bɔ*): Ethical existence and generativity, starting in adulthood when one is ethically and morally responsible for one's own actions.

Ɔdomankoma Nyame: Eternal God.

Ɔkratseasifo: The soul as an eternally innate (seated) phenomenon.

Ɔkɔmfo ba: A diviner-in-training after a call by an Ɔbosom.

Ɔsaman: Posthumous abstract or spiritual personality that resides in the Samanadzie or spirit world.

Ɔsrɛn: The Moon.

Ɔtɔ: A sacred meal of yam (and plantain), one white and the other red.

Ɔtɔfo: One who suffers a sudden and violent death.

Onyimpa: A human being.

Onyimpa dasanyi: A finite human being.

Owu: Death.

Samanadzie (also *Nsamankyir/Asamando*): The abode and world for resurrected Nsamanfo (posthumous abstract personalities) headed by the NaSaman.

Sasa: An angry, agitated, and vengeful spirit in limbo (plural *Asasa*).

Su: Raw nature or essence of the potential human; basis for ethics during adulthood.

Suban: Character, disposition, temperament.

Sunsum (plural *Āsunsum*): Spirit, image, shadow; it originates with the Abosom as genetic characteristic attributes or disposition transmitted via a father's semen to his offspring.

Wiadzie: The tangible corporeal world occupied by human beings and other living things seen and unseen; under the sun.

Bibliography

Antubam, Kofi. *Ghana's Heritage of Culture*. Leipzig: Koehler & Amelang, 1963.

Appiah-Kubi, Kofi. *Man Cures, God Heals*. New York: Friendship Press, 1981.

Baines, John. "Society, Morality, and Religious Practice." In *Religion in Ancient Egypt: Gods, Myths, and Personal Practice*. Ed. Byron E. Shafer, 123–203. Ithaca, NY: Cornell University Press, 1991.

Bartle, Philip I. W. "Forty Days: The Akan Calendar." *Africa* 48, 1 (1978): 80–84.

Boahen, Adu. *Topics in West Africa, Schools Edition*. London: Longman Group, 1966.

Bosman, William. *A New and Accurate Description of the Coast of Guinea: Divided into The Gold, The Slave, and The Ivory Coasts*. New York: Barnes & Noble [1705] 1967.

Budge, Wallis E. A. *From Fetish to God in Ancient Egypt*. New York: Benjamin Blom, 1972.

———. *The Egyptian Book of the Dead: The Papyrus of Ani*. New York: Dover [1895] 1967.

Christensen, James Boyd. "The Adaptive Functions of Fanti Priesthood." In *Continuity and Change in African Culture*. Ed. William Bascom and Melville Herskovits, 257–278. Chicago: University of Chicago Press, 1959.

Danquah, J. B. *The Akan Doctrine of God*. London: Frank Cass, 1968.

Davidson, Basil. *The Lost Cities of Africa, Revised Edition*. Boston, New York, London: Little, Brown, 1987.

———. *African Civilization Revisited: From Antiquity to Modern Times*. Trenton, NJ: Africa World Press, 1991.

Debrunner, H. *Witchcraft in Ghana: A Study on the Belief in Destructive Witches and Its Effect on the Akan Tribes*. Kumasi: Presbyterian Book Depot, 1959.

Ellis, A. B. *The Tshi-Speaking Peoples of the Gold Coast of West Africa: Their Religion, Manners, Customs, Laws, Language, etc.* Oosterhout N.B. The Netherlands: Anthropological Publications, [1887] 1970.

Emeagwali, Gloria, and Mariko Namba Walter . "Ancient Egyptian Shamanism." In *Shamanism: An Encyclopedia of World Beliefs, Practices, and Culture*. Ed. Mariko Namba Walter and Eva Jane Neumann Fridman, 906–910. Santa Barbara, CA: ABC-CLIO, 2004.

Ephirim-Donkor, Anthony. *African Personality and Spirituality: The Akanfo Quest for Perfection and Immortality*. Ann Arbor, MI: UMI Dissertation Services, 1994.

———. *African Spirituality: On Becoming Ancestors*. Trenton, NJ: Africa World Press, 1997.

———. *African Spirituality: On Becoming Ancestors, Revised Edition*. Lanham, MD: University Press of America, 2011.

———. "Akom: The Ultimate Mediumship Experience among the Akan." *Journal of the American Academy of Religion* 76, 1 (2008): 54–81.

———. *African Religion Defined: A Systematic Study of Ancestor Worship among the Akan, Second Edition*. Lanham, MD: University Press of America, 2013.

———. *The Making of an African King: Patrilineal and Matrilineal Struggle among the Effutu of Ghana, Second Edition*. Lanham, MD: University Press of America, 2009.

———. "Twin Cult of the Akan (Ghana)." In *Shamanism: An Encyclopedia of World Beliefs, Practices, and Culture*. Ed. Mariko Namba Walter and Eva Jane Neumann Fridman, 942–946. Santa Barbara, CA: ABC-CLIO, 2004.

Erikson, Erik. *A Way of Looking at Things: Selected Papers from 1930–1980*. Ed. Stephen Schlein. New York: W. W. Norton, 1987.

———. *Insight and Responsibility: Lectures on the Ethical Implications of Psychoanalytic Insight*. New York: W. W. Norton, 1964.

Fowler, James. *Stages of Faith: The Psychology of Human Development and the Quest for Meaning*. San Francisco: Harper & Row, 1981.

Gbadegesin, Segun. "Eniyan: The Yoruba Concept of a Person." In *The African Philosophy Reader, Second Edition*. Ed. P. H. Coetzee and A. P. J. Roux, 175–191. New York: Routledge: Taylor & Francis Group, 2003.

Gyekye, Kwame. *An Essay on African Philosophical Thought: The Akan Conceptual Scheme*. Cambridge: Cambridge University Press, 1987.

———. *Tradition and Modernity: Philosophical Reflection on the African Experience*. New York: Oxford University Press, 1997.

Idowu, E. Bolaji. *Olodumare: God in Yoruba Belief*. London: Longmans, 1962.

———. *African Traditional Religion: A Definition*. New York: Orbis Books, 1973.

Konadu, Kwasi. *Indigenous Medicine and Knowledge in African Society*. New York: Routledge, 2007.

Lipinski, Jed. *A Visit from the Devil: Feared Traditional Priest from Ghana Spends a Year in the Bronx*. http://www.nytimes.com/2013/07/21/nyregion/feared-traditional-priest-from-ghana-spends-a-year-in-the-bronx.html. Last accessed on April 12, 2015.

McCall, John C. "Igbo Shamanism (Nigeria)." In *Shamanism: An Encyclopedia of World Beliefs, Practices, and Culture*. Ed. Mariko Namba Walter and Eva Jane Neumann Fridman, 925–928. Santa Barbara, CA: ABC-CLIO, 2004.

Nketia, J. H. *Funeral Dirges of the Akan People*. Achimota, 1955.

Rattray, R. S. *Ashanti.* Oxford: Clarendon Press, 1923.

———. *Religion & Art in Ashanti.* Oxford: Clarendon Press, 1927.

———. *Akan-Ashanti Folk-Tales.* Oxford: Clarendon Press, 1930.

Ray, Benjamin C. *African Religions: Symbols, Ritual, and Community, Second Edition.* Upper Saddle River, NJ: Prentice Hall, 2000.

Riesman, Paul. "The Person and the Life Cycle in African Social Life and Thought." *African Studies Review* 29, 2 (1986): 71–138.

Sackey, Brigid M. "Asante Shamanism (Ghana)." In *Shamanism: An Encyclopedia of World Beliefs, Practices, and Culture.* Ed. Mariko Namba Walter and Eva Jane Neumann Fridman, 910–914. Santa Barbara, CA: ABC-CLIO, 2004.

Tishken, Joel E., Toyin Falola, and Akintude Akinyemi. *Sango in Africa and the African Diaspora.* Bloomington: Indiana University Press, 2009.

Turner, Victor W. "Ndembu Divination and Its Symbolism." In *Culture, Disease, and Healing: Studies in Medical Anthropology.* Ed. David Landy, 175–183. New York: Macmillan, 1977.

Walter, Mariko Namba, and Eva Jane Neumann Fridman, eds. *Shamanism: An Encyclopedia of World Beliefs, Practices, and Culture.* Santa Barbara, CA: ABC-CLIO, 2004.

Wiredu, Kwasi. "On Decolonizing African Religions." In *The African Philosophy Reader, Second Edition.* Ed. P. H. Coetzee and A. P. J. Roux, 20–34. New York: Routledge: Taylor & Francis Group, 2003.

Index

About the Author

Anthony Ephirim-Donkor is associate professor of religion and Africana studies and chair of the Department of Africana Studies at Binghamton University, State University of New York. He is also known as Nana Ɔbrafo Ɔwom X, the traditional king of Mprumem, Ghana.